The Sexualization of Childhood

The Sexualization of Childhood

EDITED BY SHARNA OLFMAN

Childhood in America

Westport, Connecticut
London

Library of Congress Cataloging-in-Publication Data

The sexualization of childhood / edited by Sharna Olfman.
    p. cm. — (Childhood in America)
 Includes bibliographical references and index.
 ISBN 978–0–275–99985–8 (alk. paper)
 1. Girls in popular culture—United States. 2. Sexually abused teenagers—United States.
3. Children—United States—Social conditions—21st century. 4. Children—Health and
hygiene—United States. 5. Body, Human. 6. Exploitation. I. Olfman, Sharna.
 HQ777.S435 2009
 305.23082'0973—dc22   2008028205

British Library Cataloguing in Publication Data is available.

Library of Congress Catalog Card Number: 2008028205
ISBN: 978–0–275–99985–8

First published in 2009

Praeger Publishers, 88 Post Road West, Westport, CT 06881
An imprint of Greenwood Publishing Group, Inc.
www.praeger.com

Printed in the United States of America

The paper used in this book complies with the
Permanent Paper Standard issued by the National
Information Standards Organization (Z39.48–1984).

10 9 8 7 6 5 4 3 2 1

For Lisa and Bess Olfman:
May the circle be unbroken

Contents

Acknowledgments

I would like to express my appreciation to each of the contributors, whose research and advocacy is helping to ensure a healthier future for tomorrow's children. I am particularly indebted to Gail Dines for her many thoughtful suggestions and generous support. Debbie Carvalko continues to shepherd this book series magnificently. As always, my husband Dan, and children Adam and Gavriela were a constant source of loving support throughout this endeavor.

1

The Sexualization of Childhood: Growing Older Younger/ Growing Younger Older

SHARNA OLFMAN

A few decades ago in the United States, childhood was understood to be a unique and vulnerable stage of development; a time for play and protection from adult preoccupations and responsibilities. In recent decades, however, we appear to have jettisoned these norms, and the lines that separate the lifestyles of even very young children from adults are blurring. In today's world, children dress like miniature adults, and creative outdoor play is being replaced by media entertainment that is saturated with sex, violence, and gender stereotyping. Internet pornography is easily and routinely accessed by preteen boys, and pornographic depictions of women and girls have been glamorized, mainstreamed, and marketed to children through dolls, clothing lines, video games, comic books, music, magazines, television, and movies.

A sexualized society places all children at risk for internalizing impoverished models of gender and human relationships. Girls are vulnerable to sexual harassment and abuse in a culture that depicts females as objects for male pleasure. According to the landmark 2007 report by the American Psychological Association (APA) task force on the sexualization of girls, girls who are sexualized are more prone to eating disorders, depression, low self-esteem, impaired concentration, risky sexual behaviors, and unsatisfying sexual relations when they are older. Boys are also victims; they risk losing a piece of their humanity when they are flooded with images—through video games, film, television, and online pornography—of sexually brutalized women whose sole function is to pleasure men. But the children who are most harmed by a sexualized culture are those who are already at risk because they are growing up with poverty or abuse. When our culture desensitizes us to the idea that having sex with children is a violent, immoral act, child sexual abuse through prostitution and pornography rises and children who are already living marginalized lives are most likely to be targeted.

Another way that girls are being sexualized is that they are entering puberty at increasingly younger ages, partly as a result of exposure to endocrine-disrupting toxins that are flooding our environment because of lax environmental protection laws. It is no longer rare for girls as young as 8 and 9 years of age to have begun breast development, and their physical precociousness makes them even more vulnerable to intense societal pressures to "grow older younger."

PSYCHOSEXUAL DEVELOPMENT BEGINS AT BIRTH

Throughout this volume, the phrase "sexualization of childhood" will refer to *derailed* psychosexual and gender development as a consequence of cultural values, beliefs, norms, and practices that

- teach girls that their primary worth is in their ability to be sexual objects for male pleasure
- teach boys that sex and violence are conjoined and that girls and women should be valued primarily for their ability to give them sexual pleasure
- isolate sexuality from personhood and the capacity for emotionally intimate and committed relationships
- treat children as if they are sexually mature because of the outward trappings of wardrobe, makeup, or precocious puberty
- allow corporations to use materials or methods of production that release endocrine-disrupting chemicals into the environment, contributing to early puberty

Although sexualization is by definition an unhealthy process, children nonetheless begin the journey toward sexual maturity at the very beginning of life. Healthy psychosexual development should be acknowledged, supported, and clearly demarcated from sexualization. When we deny children access to meaningful education about their burgeoning sexual development, we give them no choice but to glean what they can through a highly sexualized media.

Psychosexual development begins from the moment that the newborn experiences the sensual pleasure and feeling of "rightness" when she is held in her parents' arms. During infancy, through the repeated experience of her parents' timely and tender responsiveness to her myriad needs, she will acquire the capacity to love and be loved, a process which the famed British psychiatrist John Bowlby termed "attachment." Attachment between infant and caregiver teaches children about the power and pleasure of committed and loving relationships. When a child travels through toddlerhood, early childhood, middle childhood, and adolescence enveloped by a supportive family, community, and culture, she will develop autonomy, creativity, industry, and a sense of identity, and she will mature intellectually, socially, emotionally, and morally. She will then have the capacity to enter into an intimate relationship with another person who is drawn to her intellect, personality, values, interests, and passions, and sexual intimacy becomes part of the tapestry that they weave together.

When I observe a young child who is being treated abusively by a parent—who only seems to know how to communicate by barking commands, finding fault, and asserting control by threatening violence—I see fear in the child's eyes that is almost too painful to bare witness to, and at the same time, a yearning, a holding out of hope for a gesture of tenderness and a sign of love from her abuser. If this child does not find escape from her abusive parent or an alternative source of affirmation, she may very well grow up—her heart hardened against love—to be similarly abusive to her own children. Likewise, when I witness a little girl who is sexualized—dressed in a belly shirt with a provocative phrase written across the backside of her shorts, her lips glossed and her hair streaked—her playful, curious nature is palpable just beneath the surface. But when a girl or boy is not rescued from these soul-destroying scripts, in 15 years they may become, either a young woman with damaged self-esteem and an eating disorder or a young man who cannot experience sexual pleasure with a woman whose body has not been surgically altered to reflect the pornographic images that he has been compulsively downloading since he was 10 years old.

The APA report on the sexualization of girls noted a glaring absence of research on the impact of our sexualized culture on children. *The Sexualization of Childhood* brings together the expertise of leading authorities on gender and sexual development and on the subjects of sexual abuse, pornography, and child prostitution in order to investigate the impact on children's health and welfare of growing up in a sexualized culture. It also details ways that parents, mental health professionals, educators, and policy makers can intervene effectively.

This book addresses

- how boys' and girls' gender and sexual development is affected by our sexualized culture

- the exploitation of black adolescent girls through rap music and hip-hop culture
- the dramatic rise in the production and consumption of child pornography
- sexual exploitation of children through Internet crimes and prostitution
- the falling age of puberty in girls as a result of toxic chemical exposures
- how parents, academics, professionals, and policy makers can make a difference

I

Growing Up in a Sexualized Culture

Pornography, Lad Mags, Video Games, and Boys: Reviving the Canary in the Cultural Coal Mine

Matthew B. Ezzell

If you have sex with her when she's passed out, you're taking advantage of the situation.
  If she wakes up, then you're taking advantage of her.

—male college student

A man made the above comment to me during a college antirape presentation that I was leading in the year 2000. The program was for incoming pledges to the fraternities and sororities on campus. I had just read a scenario in which a woman drinks until passing out, at which point the man she is with "has sex" with her. Such scenarios are played out in real life on college campuses every week across the United States. They are, in fact, clear cases of date-rape. I asked the group of men if this was the case. No one said anything. After a moment, the man in question raised his hand and made the above statement with a sense of certainty and authority. The other men in the group nodded thoughtfully as he spoke. There were no women in the room.

I was stunned. Disturbing and victim-blaming comments are quite common in rape crisis education programming, but such bald statements of misogyny and rape-prone ideology are not often uttered. I waited to see if any of the participants would challenge this comment and, when they did not, I pointed out that a woman who has passed out is clearly unable to give consent. By any definition of sexual assault, this is rape. At that point, six women entered the room, arriving 10 minutes late for the program, and the men stopped talking. I was granted only 15 minutes with the group in total, and the remaining 5 minutes were quickly up.

This experience stayed with me. As I look back, I wonder about how many men in the room did not fully agree with the man who spoke but remained silent. In the all-male setting, and in the larger context of the hypermasculine fraternity system in the United States, no one stood up to the display of open rapist ideology. Rather than rock the boat and potentially cast doubt on their status as "real men," the other men simply nodded. Regardless of whether the entire group endorsed the view of women as only bodies designed for male pleasure or if it was only one man's view, this event raises a disturbing question: what has to happen to boys and men—as others teach them how to be boys and men—to get them to the point that their empathy for women is apparently nonexistent?

The cost to women in such an environment is clear: men systematically target women for acts of sexual objectification, degradation, and abuse. Women bear the brunt of our sexist society. But there is also a cost to men in maintaining male dominance; we pay for it with the forfeiture of our humanity.

How do we make sense of a society in which such comments could go unchallenged? There are many aspects of our culture that undergird dominant social systems and the status quo. One of the most powerful agents of socialization in our culture, though, is the pervasive media system. The state of mass media today may well be the canary in our cultural coal mine. And the canary isn't looking well.

MASS MEDIA AND RAPE CULTURE

Any discussion of media must be grounded within a larger analysis of the social order in which those media are produced and consumed. Media products, after all, do not fall from the sky. Media can be viewed then as both a reflection and a shaper of social reality. In other words, media can both tell us something about where we are as a society and at the same time influence our society. What is the social context in which media is being produced and consumed today?

In a word, we are living in a patriarchy. Sociologist Allan Johnson notes that a society is patriarchal to the extent that it is male-dominated, male-identified, and male-centered.[1] This doesn't mean that all men have power over all women or that all men feel powerful in their daily lives. What it means is that men tend to be in positions of power and authority, that what is considered normal and valuable within the culture tends to be associated with men and masculinity, and that the cultural focus of attention tends to be on men and the things that men do. One facet of a patriarchal society, as Johnson notes, is the oppression of women. And one facet of that oppression is men's violence against women. In other words, we live in a rape culture. What does this mean?

In brief, to say we live in a rape culture means that we live in a culture in which rape is pervasive, prevalent, and normalized through societal attitudes about gender, sex, and sexuality. There is a great deal of research to support this claim.[2] For example, in the United States, researchers predict that one in four women will be raped by a man in her lifetime.[3] Leaving statistics aside though, most women understand what it means to live in a rape culture because of their lived reality of doing so. When I ask men what they do in their day-to-day lives to protect themselves from being sexually violated, most just stare silently. Although many men know what it is like to be afraid and many do things to promote their safety, this is generally because of the threat of physical violence. In our daily lives, most of us do not think about rape at all. However, women do. When I ask women what they do in their daily lives because of the threat of sexual violence, they offer a long list of actions and thought processes—everything from paying attention to where they park their cars to having a man's voice on their answering machine to holding their keys as a weapon when walking across a parking lot. Every action of women within a rape culture is tainted by that culture. Going to get their mail, driving to work, going out with friends—none of these actions are "free." One way of thinking about this is to realize regardless of how many women experience a rape or attempted rape within their lifetime 100 percent of women experience the *threat* of rape within a rape culture. This means that *all* women's lives are impacted.

What role does mass media play? Some would say, none. But if media played no role in affecting attitudes and behavior, would colleges across the United States offer journalism and mass communication majors? Would elementary-school children be watching, on average, 21 hours of television a week?[4] Money talks. If media had no impact on us, would our advertising industry in 2005 have a total estimated market of $267 billion in the United States alone?[5] No.

Media matters. And it reflects and reinforces the rape culture. It may not *cause* anyone to do anything—not every person who watches a violent movie will engage in an act of violence—but media is implicated in real social interaction. Many argue that the connection is profound. In the year 2000 the American Academy of Pediatrics, the American Academy of Child and Adolescent Psychiatry, the American Psychological Association, the American Medical Association, the American Academy of Family Physicians, and the American Psychiatric

Association issued a joint statement noting over 1,000 studies that point to connections between media violence and aggressive behavior. The statement notes that media is not the sole factor to take into consideration but observes that, "The conclusion of the public health community, based on over 30 years of research, is that viewing entertainment violence can lead to increases in aggressive attitudes, values, and behavior, particularly in children."[6] Psychologists attribute this connection to media-based repetition and modeling of aggressive behavior, positive reinforcement of violence, teaching social scripts that serve as guides for behavior, cuing aggressive schemas that affect perception, and desensitizing the emotions.[7]

Sociologists view media violence and sexist media as enabling conditions for men's violence against women.[8] In other words, in a society in which media images of women disproportionately portray women as sexual objects that are degraded and less than men, and in which images of men are disproportionately tied to aggression, competition, sexual conquest, and control, it is more likely that women will be systematically targeted for acts of men's violence. You can see such images and messages about men and women across our cultural landscape. As the American Psychological Association (APA) noted in their 2007 report on the sexualization of girls:

> In study after study, findings have indicated that women more often than men are portrayed in a sexual manner (e.g., dressed in revealing clothing, with bodily postures or facial expressions that imply sexual readiness) and are objectified (e.g., used as a decorative object, or as body parts rather than a whole person). In addition, a narrow (and unrealistic) standard of physical beauty is heavily emphasized. These are the models of femininity presented for young girls to study and emulate.[9]

This is particularly disturbing considering that, in the absence of comprehensive sex and sexuality education in the schools and in the absence of comprehensive and timely discussions about sex between children and their parents,[10] adolescents are largely getting their sex education and socialization through media—and the higher their "sexual media diet," the earlier their sexual experimentation begins.[11] Experimentation in and of itself is not a bad thing. In fact, it can be healthy and positive. However, when the content of media, and thus the content of children's dominant sex and sexuality education, promulgates gender-stereotypical and sexualized images of girls and women, the consequences for girls can be far-reaching and quite harmful.[12]

Boys grow up in this environment as well. And although boys and men as a class receive social privileges and benefits from the sexual objectification and oppression of girls and women, there is a cost to boys and men as well. Men are not systematically targeted for acts of sexual aggression by a group of non-men, they are not paid less than women on the dollar for the same work, they are not encouraged to base our value primarily on our physical appearance, and others' sexual pleasure is not tied to men's degradation and pain. But, at a basic level, patriarchy is bad for our health. In fact, in a 2005 study of global sex inequality and health, British researchers found that patriarchal societies are associated with a shorter life span for men.[13] And the harm to boys and men goes deeper—to the very core of what it means to be human. In being socialized into the narrow box of what it means to be a "real man" in this culture, men have to give up aspects of their humanity, their ability to connect intimately with others, and their ability to connect intimately with themselves. Violence prevention educator Paul Kivel summarizes the dominant and impossible masculinity taught to boys in our culture: "Be tough, be aggressive, don't back down, don't make mistakes, be in control, take charge, have lots of sex, have money, be responsible, don't show any feelings, and don't cry."[14] And boys know all too well the names, taunts, and threats of violence that follow any deviation from this prescription. Boys receive the lessons of dominant masculinity from many sources but, as noted, one of the most consistent and pervasive is the media industry. In the remainder of this chapter, I will outline three specific types of media that play a significant role in many boys' lives: pornography, "lad mags," and sexualized and violent video games. I will close the chapter by discussing the potential implications of these media for boys.

Pornography

A new pornographic video is produced every 39 minutes in the United States. Worldwide, pornography is a $97 billion industry, 10 times the size of Hollywood box office revenues. The industry is larger than the combined revenues of Microsoft, Google, Amazon, eBay, Yahoo!, Apple, Netflix, and EarthLink.[15] But it's strictly an adult thing, right? Wrong.

The impact of the pornography industry on children occurs in three direct ways: the explicit sexualization of children and childhood, child sexual abuse, and children's exposure to and consumption of pornography. Child pornography (pornography featuring depictions of actual people under the age of 18) is illegal in the United States; but, a common feature of the pornography industry is the use of computer-generated images of children and, more commonly, the sexualization of adult women who appear much younger—what Gail

Dines[16] calls "childifying" women in pseudo child pornography. The use of children in the production of pornography is clearly child sexual abuse in and of itself. As such, child pornography is not just the representation of abuse but its documentation. The connection between the sexual abuse of children and pornography, however, goes beyond that. Interviews with convicted child sex offenders and consumers of child pornography make clear that *some* men use pornography to choreograph abuse, to groom or "disinhibit" their victims, and to desensitize themselves to the harm done to children through abuse and victimization.[17]

The third and most far-reaching avenue of impact for the industry on children is children's exposure to and consumption of pornography. This occurs in both deliberate and inadvertent ways. In 2006 34 percent of U.S. children aged 10 to 17 reported experiencing *unwanted* exposure to pornography while on the Internet.[18] In another study, 90 percent of boys and 70 percent of girls aged 13 and 14 reported accessing sexually explicit media in the previous year at least once, and 35 percent of the boys reported viewing pornographic Internet content "too many times to count."[19] Boys' high consumption rates continue into early adulthood. In a 2008 study researchers reported that 87 percent of college-aged men, compared to 31 percent of women, consume pornography, with over a quarter of the men doing so once or twice a week and 5 percent consuming it every day.[20] This is our reality check: the overwhelming majority of boys are exposed to pornography, and most of them will become active consumers. Pornography is a core component of boys' sex and sexuality education, a rite of passage in masculine socialization. We should ask: what are they learning?

The modern pornography industry overwhelmingly produces artifacts for a heterosexual male audience. These products largely consist of still images in magazines and on Web sites, in addition to videos and movies available on the Internet or on DVDs. Still images are produced across a wide continuum: glossy and "pretty" pictures of women by themselves with varying amounts of clothing; images of women by themselves masturbating or penetrating themselves with everything from their fingers to vegetables to household products; images of women in bondage; and images of women with other people, male and female, engaged in a range of sex acts. Two types of pornographic films dominate the market. "Features" follow at a basic level the style of mainstream Hollywood movies. They have a minimal plot structure and dialogue designed to introduce and present explicit sex. "Gonzo" films, on the other hand, feature sex acts from start to finish with no pretense of plot or narrative structure. As Robert

Jensen argues, regardless of what type of pornography you're looking at, a few basic themes predominate:

- All women at all times want sex from all men.
- Women like all the sexual acts that men perform or demand.
- Any woman who does not at first realize this desire can be easily turned with a little force. Such force is rarely necessary, however, for most of the women in pornography are the "nymphomaniacs" that men fantasize about.[21]

In both features and gonzo films, oral, vaginal, and anal sex are common. Scenes typically end in a "money shot" of the man (or men) ejaculating into a woman's mouth or onto her face or body. Gonzo films tend to be rougher than features, and they more often involve multiple men.

Over the last few decades, pornography has become more mainstreamed than ever. At the same time, it has become more explicitly degrading and dehumanizing. Women are frequently referred to as bitches, sluts, cum-dumpsters, whores, and worse. The dehumanizing aspects of the pornography industry go beyond language. Jensen identifies the following five sex acts as "commonplace" in gonzo pornography since the early 2000s, with increasing occurrence in features as well:

- double penetration, known as "DP" in the industry, in which a woman is penetrated vaginally and anally at the same time
- double anal, in which a woman is penetrated anally by two men at the same time
- double vag, in which a woman is penetrated vaginally by two men at the same time
- ass-to-mouth, known as "ATM" in the industry, in which a man removes his penis from a woman's anus and, without cleaning it, places it in her mouth or the mouth of another woman[22]

Again, these practices are not fringe or marginal, but *mainstream* within the industry.

Industry insiders don't try to hide this rising trend for harsher and more degrading material. In a 2004 interview with "pornography gossip columnist" Luke Ford,[23] pornography director and president of Acid Rain Productions[24] Mitch Spinelli, himself the son of a pornography director, discussed the changing industry:

I started [pornography production company] Rain in 1997. At that time, it was cutting edge. But when things started changing two years ago,

Rain became antiquated. For a long time, if you put a pretty girl on the cover, you got a winner. Before the Internet, people didn't pay much attention to what was inside. I had good-looking covers with girls such as Tera Patrick, Brianna Banks, Mary Carey. . . . That was good enough. But about two to three years ago, I saw my numbers start to fall. . . . I got panicky. I took a trip around the country and talked to distributors. . . . I took my name off the box and tried to reinvent myself as Acid Rain which is aggressive, hardcore, in your face, ass-to-mouth take no prisoners.[25]

And it's not just the types of sex acts that have changed; the women—"girls" in the industry—have changed as well. From the same interview:

How are the girls different today? They're younger. They do nastier stuff at a younger age. They're a little harder. Back in the old days, 25 was young. Anal was taboo. My father never did anal in his shows. Ever. . . . [What consumers want today is] in your face. That's what today's gonzo is. And that's what the girls are. They're younger and totally nasty, but in a good way.[26]

Controversial porn star and producer Max Hardcore says this more bluntly. Speaking of the changes in the industry, he noted:

Look at what's happened since 1992. That's when women routinely showed up with a full bush on their pussies. Back then, a hot cumshot was on the tits. Nowadays, almost every woman is completely shaved . . . and they're all into getting throat-fucked and ass-gaped. . . . Women are much more understanding and aware of their true purpose in life than ever before. That purpose, of course, is to be receptacles of love; in other words, fuck dolls.[27]

In the United States, the average age for a boy to first download pornography is 11.[28] How does an 11-year-old make sense of "ass-to-mouth?" When he knows that he is "supposed" to get sexual pleasure from viewing girls and women "getting throat-fucked and ass-gaped," what does it do his gender and sexual development? How does this affect the way he views and treats girls? How does it affect the way he views and treats himself? When this is his sex education, what does sex and sexuality mean to him?

"Lad Mags"

The boundaries of the pornography industry are not firm. Images of women as sexual objects and the patriarchal ideology of women as good for sex and always ready can be found across our cultural landscape. The "seepage" of the pornographic mind-set has reached the point that mainstream culture is, as Pamela Paul puts it, "pornified":

> The all-pornography, all-the-time mentality is everywhere in today's pornified culture—not just in cybersex and *Playboy* magazine. It's on the *Maxim* magazine covers where even women who ostensibly want to be taken seriously as actresses pose like *Penthouse* pinups. It's in women's magazines where readers are urged to model themselves on strippers, articles explain how to work your sex moves after those displayed in pornos, and columnists counsel bored or dissatisfied young women to rent pornographic films with their lovers in order to "enliven" their sex lives. It's on VH-1 shows like *The 100 Hottest Hotties* where the female "experts"—arbiters in judging the world's sexiest people—are *Playboy* centerfolds (the male experts are pop stars and journalists), and on Victoria's Secret prime-time TV specials, which attracted a record 9 million viewers in 2003. Soft-core pornography has now become part and parcel of the mainstream media.[29]

"Lad mags" are perhaps the most direct and obvious example of this mainstream soft-core pornography—magazines such as the afore-mentioned *Maxim, Stuff,* and the now online-only *FHM (For Him Magazine)* and *Monkey.* Unlike explicitly pornographic titles, these magazines and Web sites are not age-restricted and can be purchased in most grocery stores, supermarkets, and bookstores across the United States.

"Lad mags" are lifestyle magazines aimed at a young and specifi-cally male audience. They emerged in their modern form in the mid-1990s. The term "lad" is a UK reference to stereotypical and youthful masculinity.[30] Although magazines aimed at male audiences have existed for centuries, the first "lad magazine" was published in the UK in 1935. It was a pocket-sized journal called *Men Only* that included articles about "male topics." Its editorial motto was, "We don't want women readers, we don't have women readers." This magazine faded from publication in the mid-1950s, only to be revived in 1971 by Paul Raymond, a London nightclub owner, as the start of a "top-shelf" (pornographic) publishing career.[31]

By the early 1980s, many in the publishing world did not believe that a general interest magazine for men would succeed. Magazines were split between specific-interest magazines (for example, sports) and pornographic publications. The early 1990s, however, saw the emergence of the modern lad mag in the UK with the first issue of *Loaded* magazine in May 1994.[32] This magazine was explicitly aimed at "laddish" culture, and the editors consciously worked at constructing what it meant to be a young man. James Brown, founding editor, opened the magazine as follows:

> What fresh lunacy is this? *Loaded* is a new magazine dedicated to life, liberty, and the pursuit of sex, drink, football, and less serious matters. *Loaded* is music, film, relationships, humour, travel, sport, hard news, and popular culture. *Loaded* is clubbing, drinking, eating, and playing. Loaded is for the man who believes he can do anything, if only he wasn't hungover.[33]

The first edition sold 59,400 copies. By the ninth edition, over 100,000 magazines had sold. More magazines emerged on the scene competing for the lad market, and the magazines jumped to the United States by the late 1990s.

Today *Maxim* dominates the U.S. and UK lad mag markets. At a time when magazine sales are dropping across the board, *Maxim's* sales have risen. In early 2008 Maxim, with a circulation of 2.55 million, was the twenty-third top-selling magazine in the United States. It reaches more readers than *O, the Oprah Winfrey Magazine*; *Glamour*; *Rolling Stone*; or *Vanity Fair*.[34] *Maxim* also dominates the online market, increasingly the method of access for young consumers. In fact, in the UK *Maxim* alone had 479,000 unique online viewers in the first month of 2007.[35] Although the target audience for lad mags is men in their twenties, the breadth of reach through print and online editions, coupled with the lack of age restrictions for purchase and accessibility, place the magazines firmly within those media sources constructing the sex and sexuality education for adolescents and young men.[36]

The question emerges again: what are young men learning? In a content analysis of *Maxim* magazines from the year 2007, Laura Morrison[37] identified the core components of the "Maxim Man": aggressive and predatory sexuality, the consumption and enactment of violence through entertainment and sport, the shaping of the body into a weapon, and an emphasis on consumerism and economic competition. Laramie Taylor's[38] work supports Morrison's findings. His analysis of representative articles from a range of lad magazines found the dominant construction of masculine sexuality to be narrowly defined, gender stereotypical, and aggressive, emphasizing both multiple sexual partners and multiple sexual practices.

Lad mag insiders, like the pornography industry insiders discussed above, do not disagree. Consider these words from Sean Thomas, a founding member of *Maxim* magazine:

> magazines like *Maxim* are not in the business of news reporting—there are papers and TV stations for that. No, the purpose of the lad mag is

to tell guys that it is OK to be guys—to drink beer, play darts, and look at girls. When we started *Maxim* we consciously felt that we were leading a fight-back against the excesses of sneering feminism. I believe we succeeded.[39]

Here the story of the lad mag is laid bare: Producers are purposefully constructing a masculinity equated with sports, drinking, and sexual conquest, constructing a femininity equated with being a sexual object, and deliberately fighting against the gains of feminist movement(s). Thomas's words state this explicitly, but the content of the magazine itself is no less clear. In November 2003, *Maxim* ran an article called "How to Cure a Feminist: Turn an Unshaven, Militant, Protesting Vegan into an Actual Girl."[40] The images accompanying the text included four pictures of the same woman "transforming" from being a feminist with hairy armpits into being an "actual girl" who is shaved, smooth, sexualized, and in lingerie. In addition to suggesting that "actual girl(s)" are not feminists, the article offered men a step-by-step guide to manipulate a woman who speaks out for women's rights into thinking they [the men] support feminism. "Pretend to share her beliefs," the article advises, and then slowly push the woman to change with the goal of having sex with her: "To preserve any chance of getting your chin buttered, you'll have to reshizzle [reshape] her feminist-tinged interests so you can actually spend time with her."[41]

Other articles and features of these magazines extend the theme of woman as sexual object and prey. The UK *Maxim*, for example, ran a 2005 and 2006 feature called "Fresh Off of the Boat." In this series the magazine displayed pictures of supposedly immigrant women stripping their clothes off in a photo booth. The following (geographically confused) text ran alongside photos of a woman called "Dagmara":

The statuesque Dagmara has come all the way from Poland to study French—and she loves British men. MAXIM LOVES IMMIGRATION! It's the only way we get to see lovely foreign women without having to go to other countries, which is too much effort! Just imagine if we had to go all the way to Poland, in Russia, to see a girl like the lovely Dagmara! She's Poland-ese and she's saved you a trip by coming over here! Quick, woo her before she's deported![42]

The text continued:

The Home Office wants to take some of the sexiest girls away from us. But you can help stop this by joining our Asylum Programme—just send your picture and reasons why you'd like to marry a hot economic migrant to fotb@maximmobile.com.[43]

Here we see the *Maxim* editors encouraging men to exploit women who are made vulnerable by poverty and immigrant status, a common aspect of many women's entrance into pornography and prostitution.[44]

Another UK *Maxim* series that ran from 2004 through 2006 was called "You Are the Voyeur." This series positioned the reader as a variety of objects or animals that provided views of women disrobing. For example, the reader's gaze is positioned from the view of a slug, a spider, a baby, a pigeon, and an alarm clock, among other things.[45] Each pictorial includes a series of images that show a woman unaware that she is being watched while disrobing, only to be surprised when she discovers that she is not alone. Many of the final images show the woman scared. For example, a woman naked in her bed is scared to discover the moth from whose vantage point we, as the reader, can see her. One of the pictorials positions the reader as a baby whose babysitter arrives and promptly disrobes. The final image in this scene has the baby (the reader) urinating on the woman's exposed breasts as she screams. The text with this pictorial reads, "You spend all day in your playpen playing with your toys and dribbling. . . . And then along comes the babysitter. . . . Wait a minute, what's this? Her clothes seem to be falling off. Hmmm, dribble, nipples, dribble."[46] Still another pictorial in this series shows a woman sunbathing topless. The reader is positioned as a pigeon, and the final image is of the woman covered in bird droppings.

The ideology of the lad mags, which constructs masculinity as being sexually aggressive, competitive, and consumerist, is virtually indistinguishable from that of the mainstream pornography industry. The biggest difference between the two media is the more ready accessibility of lad mags—although the Internet has essentially made accessibility to pornography ubiquitous, even for people not trying to access it. What are the consequences for boys and young men whose "entertainment" and sex education consists of lad mags? What impact might these images and articles have in a boy's life? How might they alter how a boy views the real women in his life: his babysitter, immigrant women, or feminists?

Sexualized *and* Violent Video Games

Video games are often excused and celebrated as entertainment. We grant that they are indeed designed for entertainment, but video games have other purposes as well. For one, they are big business. U.S. revenues for the video game industry in 2007 topped $18 billion[47] and global revenues topped $26.5 billon[48]—nearly equaling the box office earnings of the global film industry. *Grand Theft Auto IV (GTA IV)*, repeating the record-setting sales of previous versions of the game, sold a record 2.5 million units on its first day of release in North America.[49] Industry analysts predict that lifetime sales of the game will reach 16 to 19 million units.[50] So much profit and interest has been generated around this one game, published by Take-Two Interactive, that industry giant Electronic Arts offered $2 billion to seize control of Take-Two, a price rejected as insufficient.[51] More than just big sellers for the industry, though, video games are widely played and wildly popular. The average U.S. child aged 2 to 17 plays video games for 7 hours a week, and the average adolescent boy plays for 13 hours.[52]

A wide variety of games are available for purchase and play. Some focus on memory, spatial arrangement, and even physical movement (for example, *Brain Age, Tetris,* and *Dance Dance Revolution*). Other games, such as *GTA IV,* center on violence, sexism, racism, and sexualized and racialized violence. These games are consistently the top selling titles in the industry.[53] Video games are rated and monitored by the Entertainment Software Rating Board (ESRB).[54] Ratings run from EC (early child) to AO (adult only). Many explicitly violent or sexualized games receive an M (mature) rating, which in theory prohibits sales to minors. When Mothers Against Drunk Driving (MADD) criticized *GTA IV* for including drunk driving in the game, Rockstar Games, the development company issued a statement on that very point: "We have a great deal of respect for MADD's mission, but we believe the mature audience for *Grand Theft Auto IV* is more than sophisticated enough to understand the game's content."[55]

In practice, however, the ratings system does not do much to deter underage play. In one study of fourth through twelfth graders, fewer than half said that their parents understood the rating system, and only 25 percent said that a parent had stopped them from getting a game because of the rating.[56] In another study of 9- to 16-year-olds, 70 percent reported playing M-rated games, close to half had bought M-rated games themselves despite being underage, and almost half of those children had made the purchases without a parent or adult present.[57] As with pornography, "adult" content is not confined to adult audiences.

The *Grand Theft Auto* series is known for its explicitly sexual and violent play. The basic plot of all of the games surrounds a protagonist who navigates and rises through a criminal underground. Carjackings, murder, and prostitution are common features of the games. When the health of the protagonist drops, there are many ways that the game player can replenish it. One way is to hire (exploit) a prostitute. In most editions of the game, the protagonist approaches a prostitute, she gets into his car, and the protagonist drives to a secluded area. The car rocks back and forth and the protagonist's health measure goes up while his money goes down. As the prostitute gets out of the car, the protagonist can beat up or murder her to get the money back.[58]

The series has been controversial for years because of its sexually violent content, but it attained the most notoriety (as of the writing of this chapter) with the release of *Grand Theft Auto: San Andreas* in 2004.[59] Specifically the controversy erupted over the "Hot Coffee" mini-game.[60] In the game, the protagonist can date up to six girlfriends across the city. The protagonist dates these girlfriends with the goal of acquiring new items or perks in the game. After a successful date, the girlfriend asks the protagonist into her house for "coffee." The game player then sees the exterior of the house and hears the muffled noises of the protagonist and the girlfriend having sex. The "Hot Coffee" mini-game, however, accessible by downloading a free "mod" (modification), allows the game player to view and control the protagonist as he enters the house and has sex with the girlfriend. This feature of the game was included in the original programming but was disabled (although not removed) by the developers prior to release. When news of the "Hot Coffee" mod came out, a firestorm of criticism erupted. The ESRB changed the rating of the game from M to AO, and the publisher and developer of the game were charged with violating the Federal Trade Commission Act by misrepresenting the content of the game. The FTC settled this case in 2006, requiring the publisher and developer to "clearly and prominently disclose on product packaging and in any promotion or advertisement for electronic games, content relevant to the rating, unless that content had been disclosed sufficiently in prior submissions to the rating authority."[61]

The newest version of the *GTA* series, *GTA IV*, may prove just as controversial. Technology journalist Seth Schiesel, in a positive review of the game, characterized it as "a violent, intelligent, profane, endearing, obnoxious, sly, richly textured, and thoroughly compelling work of cultural satire disguised as fun."[62] The game is set in a fictionalized version of New York City known as Liberty City. The protagonist is Niko Bellic. Schiesel describes him as

> one of the most fully realized characters video games have yet produced. A veteran of the Balkan wars and a former human trafficker in the Adriatic, he arrives in Liberty City's rendition of Brighton Beach at the start of the game to move in with his affable if naïve cousin Roman. Niko expects to find fortune and, just maybe, track down someone who betrayed him long ago. Over the course of the story line he discovers that revenge is not always what one expects.[63]

In the first week of the game's release, IGN Entertainment,[64] a Fox Interactive Media Internet services provider, released a series of video montages highlighting different aspects of the game. One of them was called "The Ladies of Liberty City: Very Bad Things."[65] With a nod to the previous controversy with *GTA: San Andreas*, the subtitle read "Grab a cup of hot coffee and enjoy the working girls of the city." Although decontextualized from the larger game, the video featured real game clips exclusively focused on the protagonist's relationships with women.

"The Ladies of Liberty City" opened with graphic images of women stripping, pole dancing, and giving the protagonist a lap dance. The next scene showed Niko shooting a woman in the middle of the street. It went on to show Niko picking up prostitutes. In a change from previous editions in the series, the sex in the car is shown clearly although there is no nudity. A verbal exchange between Niko and the women is also included in the video. He approaches one woman who says, "I'll suck your cock real nice." "Get in," he replies before driving her to a baseball field. Once parked, he says, "You get what you pay for, right?" The woman sits on his lap. As they bounce up and down, the woman squeals, "Fuck the shit out if it! Yeah, you nasty fucker!" They finish, and Niko says, "Life is strange, don't you think?" The woman gets out of the car and walks away. As she does, Niko pulls out a gun and shoots her several times. You can hear her scream as Niko says, "Stay down or I will finish you off!" She does not get up.

After seeing the video, Florida lawyer Jack Thompson wrote to the U.S. Attorney for the Southern District of Florida demanding that legal action be taken against publisher Take-Two Interactive. He wrote that *GTA* is the "gravest assault upon children in this country since polio."[66] Following this, IGN pulled the video from its site, saying "IGN's goal is to show our users all aspects of popular games on the market. In this case, we crossed a line in how we portrayed some aspects of the game and we've taken the video down."[67] Killing prostitutes and frequenting strip clubs is not all that goes on in the game. In fact, the game can be played without doing these things. However, it is telling that the buying and selling of women's bodies and the murder of already exploited women is tied to the "health" of the protagonist of the game. It may be up to the individual game player exactly how he or she will play the game; but the publishers and developers did not have to include the sexual exploitation and murder of women in the first place.

GTA represents one series. However, with repeated record-breaking sales, it is one of the most popular series in video game history. It also has a wide reach. Craig Anderson and Douglas Gentile report that 75 percent of 12- to 16-year-old boys have played the game.[68] Still it is only one series. Many other games, though, feature sexist portrayals of women and sexualized violence as core components of game play. Some titles include *Dead or Alive Xtreme Beach Volleyball 2, BMX XXX, Saint's Row, Resident Evil, Gears of War, Leisure Suit Larry,* and *Lara Croft: Tomb Raider.* Other violent games use sexist and sexually violent imagery in advertising. An ad campaign for the game *Hitman: Blood Money,* for example, had the text "Beautifully Executed" over an image of a splayed young woman wearing lingerie and high heels with a bullet hole in her head. Another, titled "Shockingly Executed," featured a young nude woman electrocuted in a bathtub.[69]

Beyond sexist imagery and sexualized violence, there is also a direct connection between the pornography and video game industries. In 2005, Playboy Enterprises released the video game *Playboy: The Mansion.* The player is positioned as *Playboy* founder Hugh Hefner, "Hef," in the game. The goal is to build the *Playboy* empire from the ground up, although, as IGN reviewer Ed Lewis noted, there are other aspects of the game as well. He opened his prerelease game review by saying:

> In the past hour I've had sex with four different women on every piece of soft furniture available. It's not too hard to do it either as long as you master the art of conversation and give plenty of compliments. That's the main lesson that I've learned so far in *Playboy: The Mansion,* the game that lets you inhabit Hef's clothes and screw everything on two legs as you build up a publishing empire. It's good to be the king.[70]

Other explicitly pornographic games include *Dream Stripper 3D* ("Your own personal virtual 3D stripper and strip club on your own computer!"[71]), Jenna Jameson's *Virtually Jenna* ("a stunning unique 3D world filled with incredibly realistic interactive erotic experiences"[72]), and *Virtual Hottie 2* ("includes threesomes, lesbians, toys, realistic environments, lingerie, sexy outfits, and much more!"[73]). *Playboy* is also included in the Internet virtual world *Second Life,*[74] and a *Second Life* pornography magazine called *Slustler,* created and distributed within the virtual world, is available for purchase. In a further extension of the video game world into the pornography industry, the real-world *Playboy* magazine has a running pictorial series called "Women of Video Games" that features nude images of popular pixilated female game characters,[75] and, at the time this chapter was written, the top selling pornographic movie at Adult Video Universe was called "Grand Theft Orgy."[76]

Knowing that the ratings system is not keeping minors from accessing "mature" games, the state of the video game industry, and its explicit connections to the pornography industry, should give us pause. Many have commented on the potential impact on children, notably boys, of playing explicitly violent games.[77] But what are the potential impacts on boys' sexual development in playing explicitly sexualized and sexually violent games?

IMPLICATIONS

You may read the depictions of mainstream pornography, lad mags, and video games and think, as people have said to me, "Well, that sounds bad, but so what? This is just entertainment, a good way to blow off steam. Boys will be boys, after all." But media is more than simply entertainment. And these media are teaching boys to be boys in particular ways. Further, although the research isn't conclusive or without limitations, existing studies of the implications of media—specifically pornography, lad mags, and video games—on thoughts, beliefs, and actions provide cause for concern.

Supporters of pornography, lad mags, and video games often frame the question of implications in simplistic terms of causation: do pornography, lad mags, and video games cause boys and men to sexually assault women? The answer to that question is clearly, "No." Not every boy who downloads pornography, reads a lad mag, or plays a video game will assault a girl or woman, and not every boy who assaults girls and women consumes these media. Said another way, if we eradicated sexist media today, the rape culture would not be eradicated tomorrow. However, there is another way for us to approach an understanding of implications that is related to our discussion of sexist media as an *enabling condition* for men's violence against women. To quote Robert Jensen:

> The discussion should be about the ways in which pornography [and other forms of sexist media] might be implicated in sexual violence in this culture. Pornography alone doesn't make men do it, but pornography is part of a world in which men do it, and therefore the production, content, and use of pornography are important to understand in the quest to eliminate sexual violence.[78]

What have researchers found? Definitive conclusions about the correlations between media consumption and behavior are difficult, if not impossible, to ascertain. However, a number of studies point us toward greater understanding of the ways that the consumption of pornography, lad mags, and video games may impact boys' lives. For example, researchers conducting a thorough review of the existing experimental literature about adults' pornography consumption and violent attitudes and behaviors found that men who are already sexually aggressive or predisposed to violence (i.e., men who are impulsive, hostile to women, and promiscuous) may seek out violent pornography, which may increase their likelihood of engaging in sexually aggressive and controlling behavior.[79]

Research on children's and adolescents' exposure to and consumption of pornography points in a similar direction. In a review of such research, Patricia Greenfield found that pornography "can influence sexual violence, sexual attitudes, moral values, and sexual activity of children and youth."[80] Specifically she reports that most children's experiences of early pornography exposure are negative (embarrassment, fear, guilt, and confusion were the most common emotions experienced by children aged 12 or younger), and notes that frequent pornography consumption by "high-risk males" may produce an increase in sexual aggression.[81] Research from other countries, although undertaken within different cultural contexts, is also illustrative. Two Dutch studies by Jochen Peter and Patti Valkenburg found (1) that young people's exposure to and consumption of online pornographic material was associated with recreational attitudes about sex,[82] and (2) that exposure to sexually explicit online movies was related to adolescents' views of women as sexual objects.[83] A Swedish study found that boys who were heavy consumers of pornography were more likely to drink alcohol, suffer from depression, sexually abuse others, and buy or sell sex.[84] And, finally, a Taiwanese study found that adolescent exposure to Internet pornography was associated with sexually permissive attitudes and behavior.[85] Pornography, particularly in the Internet age, demands our attention because Peter and Valkenburg conclude that it may play "a crucial role in the sexual socialization of adolescents."[86]

Boys' and young men's exposure to lad magazines has not been studied as much as their exposure to pornography. However, as we noted in our overview of lad mag content, Laramie Taylor's work is instructive. Similar to research on young men's exposure to pornography, Taylor found that reading lad mags was "associated with more permissive attitudes towards sex, as well as the belief that a wider variety of sexual behaviors is an expected part of a sexual relationship and the possession of a more aggressive sexual self-schema."[87] Interestingly, he found that consuming lad mags was more directly tied to a young man's "aggressive sexual self-schema" than consuming pornography. He offers a potential explanation by noting that young men may perceive lad mags as having been made *for them* and thus speaking directly to them. In another study coming out of the UK, David Giles and Jessica Close[88] found that young men's exposure to lad magazines increased their body dissatisfaction. Nondating men who consumed lad mags were particularly more likely to internalize a muscular and hypermasculine body norm, some even considering or turning to excessive exercise and steroid use to alter their physiques. In other words, there is some evidence to suggest that lad mags may be associated both with boys' negative beliefs about women and their negative beliefs about themselves.

Many studies have analyzed the impact of violent video games. A review of the existing literature shows that while conclusions should be approached with caution, a "preponderance of the evidence from the higher quality experimental studies suggests that short-term exposure to video-game and virtual reality violence engenders increases in aggressive behavior, affect, and cognitions and decreases in prosocial behavior."[89] Fewer studies, however, have addressed sexually violent games. Three notable exceptions are found in the works of Karen Dill[90] (both as a solo researcher and in conjunction with others), Tracy Dietz,[91] and the research team of Mike Yao, Chad Mahood, and Daniel Linz.[92]

Dietz first addressed gender roles within video games in 1998. She found that female characters were largely absent from games, and they tended to be presented in stereotypical and sexist ways when they did make an appearance. Specifically, female characters were most likely to appear as victims (damsels in distress) or as sex objects. Male characters, although often presented as heroes within the context of the game, were most often presented as violent perpetrators. Seventy-nine percent of the top-selling games in her study included violence and aggression, and 21 percent specifically featured violence against women. Video games, particularly given their popularity among U.S. children, are powerful agents of socialization.

Yao, Mahood, and Linz extended Dietz's work by addressing the impact of playing sexually explicit games, such as the *GTA* series, on participants' reported likelihood to engage in sexual harassment. They focused on male participants who played either a sexually explicit or nonsexual game in an experimental setting. Following game play, participants went through a series of word games and completed the Likelihood to Sexual Harass (LSH) survey. The researchers' concluded that their study "provides strong evidence that a sexually explicit video game with themes of female 'objectification' may prime thoughts related to sex, encourage men to view women as sex objects, and increase the likelihood of self-reported tendencies to behave inappropriately toward women in social situations."[93]

Dill's research on the impact of video games is arguably the most extensive and far-reaching. She has found that those who play violent video games are more likely to endorse rape myths[94] and to hold sexist attitudes toward women.[95] In another study conducted with Kathryn Thill,[96] Dill found that top-selling video games construct a vision of masculinity tied to power, dominance, and aggression and a vision of femininity tied to inferiority, sexual objectification, physical beauty, and, increasingly, sexualized aggression. Importantly, because of the wide popularity of video games and video game characters, Dill found that children did not need to be active game players to have been affected. She concludes: "video game characters and their common, stereotypical portrayals of gender are part of general popular culture for youth and thus are important to understand."[97] Virtual game play then can have real consequences for real people.

Experimental research, such as the studies just referenced, can give us hints about how children (and adults) interact with media. But such research has limitations. Answers to questions about attitudes toward women, for example, do not necessarily speak to the enactment of any particular behavior. Experiments also do not replicate the conditions of playing games or consuming pornography as part of a daily or weekly practice over the course of years. Also, particularly for studies on lad mags and pornography, experimental studies do not replicate the ways that boys and men are consuming these media. In other words, experiments miss the fact that boys and men are often consuming lad mags and pornography to facilitate masturbation. This research then should be approached with caution. However, the findings outlined here speak in concert with another form of investigation that may yield deeper understanding: interviews with consumers and with girls and women in relationships with those consumers.

Taking a multipronged approach, Robert Jensen notes the following:

> The public testimony of women, my interviews with pornography users and sex offenders, and various other researchers' work, have led me to conclude that pornography can:
>
> - be an important factor in shaping a male-dominant view of sexuality;
> - be used to initiate victims and break down their resistance to sexual activity;
> - contribute to a user's difficulty in separating sexual fantasy and reality; and
> - provide a training manual for abusers.[98]

As one example, consider the following report of a street prostitute who was beaten by a john. As he beat her, the john said:

> I know all about you bitches, you're no different; you're like all of them. I seen it in all the movies. You love being beaten. [He then began punching the victim violently.] I just seen it again in that flick. He beat the shit out of her while he raped her and she told him she loved it; you know you love it; tell me you love it.[99]

That report is clearly an extreme example of one man's use of pornography to excuse and choreograph his own violent treatment of women (including the buying of women in prostitution). But interviews with "normal" men reveal similar—if not as severe—stories of impact.

Pamela Paul[100] interviewed over 100 people about their consumption of and feelings about pornography in addition to conducting the first nationally representative pornography-focused poll. The men she interviewed, who began consuming pornography as preteens or teens, spoke of a range of personal effects. Although they sometimes mentioned positive effects, often the impact of pornography on their lives, and on the lives of the women with whom they interacted, was negative. Some representative themes she uncovered include:

- objectifying women in and outside of pornography ("I find that when I'm out at a party or a bar, I catch myself sizing up women."[101])
- habituation and desensitization ("At first, I was happy just to see a naked woman. I was like 'Wow!' each time I saw a really hot girl. But as time has gone on, I've grown more accustomed to things. I look for more and more extreme stuff."[102])
- pushing sexual partners to try positions/practices seen in pornography ("I like sex the way it's shown in porno."[103])
- seeing sex with partners as "boring" ("My heart would race less and less. Sex just seemed so ordinary; it was no longer thrilling or magical the way it had been before [internet] porn."[104])
- dependence on pornography to facilitate masturbation ("When I don't have those images in front of me, I just can't get that aroused."[105])
- dependence on mental images of pornography to maintain erections during sex with a partner ("I think my erections have been affected because I'm not as hyperstimulated by sex as I am by porno. I've gotten used to a certain heightened level of stimulation, and when compared with porn, real sex just isn't that exciting."[106])
- pressuring women to have sex ("I would never have pushed women to have sex the way I did back then had it not been for the amount of sex I could look right in the eye through porn. I became this asshole I didn't want to be because I didn't care about women."[107])

- feelings of depression/lack of control ("I began to feel really gross. It would be a gorgeous sunny day outside and here I was sitting inside, looking at porn on the computer."[108])

The consequences for boys growing up in today's Internet culture may be particularly powerful given the breadth of boys' exposure to harder material at younger and younger ages. Paul quotes clinical psychologist Judith Coché:

> Pornography is so often tied into video game culture and insinuates itself even into nonpornographic areas of the Web. It's very hard for a twelve-year-old boy to avoid. . . . This is where they're learning what turns them on. And what are they supposed to do about that? Whereas once boys would kiss a girl they had a crush on behind the school, we don't know how boys who become trained to cue sexually to computer-generated porn stars are going to behave, especially as they get older.[109]

Some examples of real boys enacting pornography in their lives are troubling indeed. In 2004, teenagers in Scarsdale, New York, filmed two drunk 14-year-old girls in a sexual encounter at a party. Although one of the girls repeatedly said no and resisted the other girl's attempts to grope her, off-camera male onlookers egged them on, shouting, "Come on, do it!"[110] In 2005, a 19-year-old boy in Florida taped himself "having sex" with an unconscious 15-year-old girl while three other boys watched. Seeing nothing wrong with his behavior, the following morning he told his victim, who remembered nothing from the night before, "You know, I had sex with you and I videotaped it."[111] In 2007 in Lincoln, Nebraska, two 13-year-old boys videotaped themselves sexually assaulting a 5-year-old girl with an object, going on to film further sexual contact between their victim and another 5-year-old girl and a 3-year-old boy.[112] And, as Paul reports, in 2004 three teenage boys in Orange County, California, videotaped themselves assaulting an apparently unconscious 16-year-old girl with a pool cue, a juice bottle, a juice can, and a lit cigarette. The boys took turns putting their penises into her mouth and vagina while the others filmed. This occurred in front of a crowd at a party. During the trial that followed, the girl, although she was seemingly unconscious during the assault, was called a "tease," a "porn star," and "out of control."[113]

Obviously the cases just described are just that—individual cases. Thankfully we can't generalize these few boys' actions to all boys growing up in today's pornography-saturated culture. However, it is telling that when these boys sexually assaulted others, they videotaped it, in the process both replicating and making their own pornography.

If not through pornography, where would teenage boys learn to assault girls with objects and record everything for viewing later? Where would they learn that this is how to view and treat women? Where would they learn that this is what it means to be a man in this culture?

Popular pornography, lad mags, and video games promote a sexist, domineering, and aggressive vision of masculinity and an objectified, submissive, and inferior vision of femininity. Boys engage with lad mags and pornography similarly, often using the images to facilitate masturbation. A central feature of boys' use of these media is the concept of control. There are three ways this emerges: (1) through depictions of men controlling women (physically, sexually, financially, or otherwise); (2) by commodifying female sexuality such that it can bought, sold, and consumed at will; and (3) through the use of technology that allows the consumer to fast-forward, pause, or zoom closer to the visual or video image, furthering control of the consumer's sexual experience.[114] Video games are consumed and used differently, but the issue of control is even more central—gamers are not simply consuming created media but controlling the action made possible within the parameters of the game. A boy playing *GTA IV*, for example, is not simply watching the protagonist visit strip clubs and murder prostitutes; he is controlling those actions himself. He is taking on the role of the protagonist, virtually engaging in the acts of violence directly.[115] The text promoting the explicitly pornographic video game *Virtually Jenna* positions the aspect of control as the central draw of the game:

> Choose the actors, the scenes, rooms and sets. Decide what your models will wear and perform in. Choose what they do and how they act selecting different poses. Direct your characters to play naughty or nice. Make them suck and fuck hard and wild. Select the sex toys Jenna and friends will use with each other; dildos, vibrators, whips and chains. Insert them into her pussy, asses or wherever.[116]

With these violent and sexist games, the consumer does more than simply consume. He (or she) becomes the virtual agent of violence, choreographing abuse, murder, objectification, and exploitation.

To repeat a phrase I used earlier, media matters. As a final example of this, consider the fact that the U.S. military is banking on it. In 2002 the U.S. Army launched *America's Army*,[117] a "T for Teen"-rated, free, multiplayer, first-person shooter game. It was developed specifically as a form of propaganda and recruitment for the military at a cost of $7 million to taxpayers.[118] On its Web site the "Game Leadership Team" notes the following:

> The game has exceeded all expectations by placing Soldiering front and center within popular culture and showcasing the roles training, team-work and technology play in the Army. Over the past few years, in more than twenty updates and new game versions, we have opened the world of Soldiering to players and provided them with a soup to nuts virtual experience within which to explore entry level and advanced training as well as Soldiering in small units. We have virtually taken our players through boot camp, Ranger and Airborne training, and even introduced them to the Army's "Quiet Professionals," the elite Special Forces.[119]

The U.S. government, in a time of war and (at the time of game development) suffering in its recruitment efforts for the military overall, has been pouring millions of dollars every year into video game propaganda efforts. They have not been doing this to provide a form of entertainment to the masses. They are making use of the role of video games as an agent of socialization that can work, along with other such agents, to affect thoughts and behavior. This helps us to make sense of our militarized culture, and the popularity and success of the pornography, lad mag, and video game industries helps us to make sense of our rape culture.

CONCLUSION

In 2006 I took part in a discussion for men who were attempting to address issues of men's violence against women. Toward the end of the event, men began sharing why they had been moved to get involved. One young man spoke emotionally of dealing with the rape of his female partner by a mutual friend. Her body and rights, and their trust in a friend, had been savagely violated. He wanted to make sense of the assault without re-creating the cycle of violence. He wanted to support his partner and find support for himself. He wanted, much more broadly, to eradicate the rape culture. He began reading widely and thinking deeply as part of these efforts, and he began to realize his own role in perpetuating the problem. He said:

> I've never raped a woman, and I've never even been in a fight. I strive to treat women with dignity and respect. But I've realized that rape is in me. It's in the way I look at women walking down the street. It's in the music I listen to and the movies I watch. It's in the games that I play. It's in me. And I don't want it there.

What this man had realized is that although individual cases of rape are perpetrated by individuals or groups of individuals, the systematic targeting of women and girls for sexual assault is supported by the imagery and belief systems of our wider culture. That culture is the water we're swimming in, and he was starting to realize that it was toxic. It was in him. Despite his desire to live differently, it had an impact on how he viewed women in his life. His ability to empathize with other human beings was diminished, and he wanted that ability back.

Rape is in me. That's a powerful realization. It speaks to the damage that can be done to boys and men growing up in a culture in which our sex education and socialization is largely derived from and through sexist media such as pornography, lad magazines, and video games—media that teach us that we should be tough, aggressive, emotionally disengaged, and sexually competitive. Some boys, like the ones discussed above, may be emboldened to act out violently. Others, like the young men interviewed by Pamela Paul, may become dependent on pornography to experience and express their own sexuality. Still others may not be damaged to that extent, but they are damaged all the same. Like the thoughtful man who attended the antiviolence discussion, they may realize that they do not exist separately from the culture in which they live. *Rape is in me.* Even if this man and other men like him never commit a direct act of violence against another human being, they have been harmed. When our sexual pleasure is conditioned to come from women's pain, exploitation, and objectification, when our "entertainment" consists of murder, war, and prostituting women, we forfeit a bit of our humanity, our ability to empathize. The pornography, lad mag, and video game industries are cashing in, but all of us are paying the price. Rape—viewed as both an act and an ideology that denies the full humanity of women— is in us, and I don't want it there.

These industries are multi-billion-dollar powerhouses, but they are neither natural nor inevitable. The ideologies they promote and reproduce can be challenged and changed, and the canary in our cultural coal mine can be revived. It will take a lot of work, organized resistance, and collective action at both grassroots and structural levels to change things. The task feels daunting. It is daunting. But as Marian Wright Edelman, the founder and president of the Children's Defense Fund, has said, "We must not, in trying to think about how we can make a big difference, ignore the small daily differences we can make which, over time, add up to big differences that we often cannot foresee."[120] Change is possible. As a basic start, it will require honest, open, and comprehensive communication about sex and sexuality in the home *and* the schools. It will require role models who refuse to participate in systems of domination and exploitation for profit. It will require looking squarely in the mirror and dealing with ourselves, and it will require looking squarely at the increasingly denigrating and abusive aspects of mainstream culture without flinching. It will require engaged, mindful, and conscientious consumerism. It will require empathic connection and action. It will require us. It will require me. It will require you.

A Royal Juggernaut: The Disney Princesses and Other Commercialized Threats to Creative Play and the Path to Self-Realization for Young Girls

Susan Linn

I am a psychologist whose work involves engaging children in play therapy, primarily using puppets. I'm also the director of a national advocacy coalition, the Campaign for a Commercial-Free Childhood (CCFC), which works for the rights of children to grow up—and the freedom for parents to raise them—without being undermined by commercial interests. In recent years I've found that these two passions—promoting creative, therapeutic play, and stopping the commercial exploitation of children—often intersect. The children with whom I play seem increasingly entrenched in rather rigid, stultified fantasies, rooted in their immersion in commercialized culture.

For twenty-first-century little girls, commercialized play manifests in repetitive, media-driven scripts in which female characters are characterized by entitlement, helplessness, and dependence—the same rigid roles that triggered rebellion in the women's movement of the 1960s. It is both sad and ironic to find that the granddaughters of mid-twentieth-century feminists are locked into the same stereotyped roles from which their grandmothers struggled so hard to break free. One reason for what seems like significant backsliding is that commercialized media, with its accoutrements and the constricted role of women that it promotes, has never been so omnipresent in children's lives. The unfortunate combination of ubiquitous, sophisticated technology and unfettered capitalism translates into an unprecedented immersion in media culture that tends to overshadow and crowd out other influences. With the press of a button, children can repeatedly conjure up screen versions of beloved stories and characters and—depending on media viewing rules at home—at will.

COMMERCIALIZING GIRLHOOD: UBIQUITOUS MEDIA AND UNFETTERED COMMERCIALISM

Children's attraction to commercial media is certainly nothing new. As a child, my exposure to television and movies triggered a devotion to the glamorous space hero Flash Gordon and that fountain of youth, Peter Pan. What *was* different was availability. I was able to see Flash Gordon movies only once a year when they were serialized on television. I have a treasured memory of seeing Walt Disney's *Peter Pan* at a movie theater just once with my family. I got a second dose of Neverland when an adaptation of the Broadway play was broadcast annually for a few years. Unlike children today, who have essentially unlimited access to the media programs they love, the children of my generation had unlimited access only to our own imperfect memories of the stories and characters we saw on the screen. The only way I could satisfy my desire to immerse myself in the world created by screen versions of *Peter Pan*, for instance, was to construct it myself, relying on my own resources and imagination. The reality is that were I growing up today and able to watch a *Peter Pan* video every day, I'm quite sure that I would do so. I'm glad it wasn't an option: there is no need to imagine anything about a story whose script and characters are indelibly imprinted in your memory.

I'm not arguing that children's lives would be better if only we could bring back programs from the 1950s. These shows were vehicles for all kinds of cultural stereotyping and sneaky marketing techniques. The portrayal of Indians as inept stooges in *Peter Pan*, in both the Disney film and the televised stage play, is racist. Wendy is a simpering wimp. I recently spent a nostalgic few hours laughing at the primitive special effects and melodrama in *Flash Gordon's Trip to Mars*, which was in movie houses in the 1930s and which I saw on television 20 years later. But it isn't funny that the only black character is a bumbling servant and the main female character, Dale Arden, who blasts off in a suit and heels, spends an inordinate amount of time in a dead faint, shrieking or breathlessly cooing, "Flash! Oh, Flash!" at the hero's every move. So it's not that the content of screen media was better when I was a kid. In some ways it was worse, but there was so much less of it. These days, children's exposure to screen media extends way beyond television or film. MP3 players, cell phones, and personalized DVD players all display media content targeted at children. Children are subjected to screens at home, in restaurants, at school, in their pediatrician's waiting room, in the back seats of mini-vans, in airplanes, and even on supermarket shopping carts. Explaining that screen media programming is now targeted at children in the interstitial moments of their lives—when they're between places—an executive at the children's cable station Nickelodeon quipped, "Nickelodeon is everywhere kids are."[1]

When J. Paul Marcum, the head of Sesame Workshop's interactive group, commented on his company's contract with Verizon for downloading television content onto cell phones, he denied that the venerated children's media company advocated selling cell phones to young children. Then he added, "But you can't ignore the convenience factor when people are in motion. A parent can pass back a telephone to the kids in the back of the car. And it's a device that families are going to carry with them everywhere."[2] According to the *New York Times*, cell phones are the new rattle.[3]

To understand the extent to which many of today's children are immersed in commercialized media culture, think about the children you know. How much time do they spend engaged with electronic media—most of which is commercially based? On average, children ages 2 to 18 are "tuned in" about 40 hours a week after school.[4] In addition, the plethora of media-linked toys—including video and online games based on movies and TV shows—that dominate the market is another commercial phenomenon inhibiting creative play and locking children into rigidly prescribed versions of how women and men behave.[5]

I believe that the commercialization of childhood, including its promotion of unhealthy, sexualized roles for girls, is a societal issue and needs to be addressed as such. That's why my colleagues and I founded Campaign for a Commercial-Free Childhood. Societal change takes time, however, and like so many other parents, grandparents, caretakers, educators, and health care professionals, I find myself grappling with how to respond to the little girls I encounter today whose imagination and play are so molded by their immersion in commercial culture.

THE DISNEY PRINCESSES: EXACERBATING THE PROBLEMS AND UNDERMINING THE BENEFITS OF FAIRY TALES

"Let's play princess," 4-year-old Abigail suggests. We are playing in the dress-up corner of her preschool, furnished with a battered old wooden sink and stove, a paint splattered table, and a treasure trove of discarded adult finery. "Okay," I reply. "Which princess are you?" she asks. I am puzzled. Her question implies a set of particular princesses and was a less open-ended query than, "What's your name?" I glom onto the first name that pops into my head. "Umm . . . I'm Princess Anna," I said. In a tone of amused exasperation, she responds instantly and authoritatively. *That's* not a princess." "Really?" I ask, bewildered. She reels off a list including Belle from *Beauty and the Beast*; Ariel from *The Little Mermaid*; Aurora from *Sleeping Beauty*; and the eponymous Cinderella—the main properties in the Walt Disney Company's stable of princess characters culled from animated movies based primarily on fairy tales.

When they are not being used as marketing tools, I have to admit that I love fairy tales. Populated with fantastical beings and abounding with wonder, they are terrific springboards for make-believe. From the safety of "Once upon a time . . ." fairy tales allow children enough distance to grapple safely with the most passionate of human emotions—grief, envy, fear, rage, and joy. With plots simple enough for even young children to follow and with enough twists and turns to stand up to retelling, fairy tales explore the trials of family strife and the human capacity for greed, loneliness, and courageous fortitude in the face of overwhelming odds.[6]

Fairy-tale plots tap into primordial themes: good triumphs over evil, the weak outwit the strong, cleverness outwits brawn, and— against seemingly impossible barriers and long struggle—virtue is rewarded. A happy ending is assured—except, of course, in the stories made up by Hans Christian Andersen, such as *The Little Match Girl*, which I find almost too painful to bear.

Most of the stories we know as fairy tales are hundreds of years old and have their origin as folk tales passed on through generations for amusement and education. All cultures have such stories and many of them have similar themes. The roots of many of the most well-known fairy tales lie in Eastern and Middle Eastern folklore that made its way West during the Middle Ages.[7] It's ironic that Cinderella, currently imprinted by Disney in the national—and international—psyche as blonde and blue-eyed, is thought to have her origin in a ninth-century Chinese story called *Shen Teh*. Walt Disney based his animated film on a seventeenth-century version told by Charles Perrault, a Parisian intellectual who was spinning his stories for the French court.[8]

In Germany a century later, Jacob and Wilhelm Grimm also collected and retold old stories. The Grimm fairy tales are thought to be truer to the originals than Perrault's versions—and they can be quite gory. Because they describe explicit acts of violence, some people balk at reading the Brothers Grimm versions to young children. In *Cinderella*, the eldest stepsister obeys her mother's order to cut off her toe in order to fit the lost slipper. The youngest sister cuts off her heel. As retribution, their eyes are pecked out by doves.[9] In *Snow White*, the Wicked Queen sends a hunter out into the forest with our heroine to kill her. Instead, he lets her go and slaughters a deer, bringing back its heart and liver as proof that Snow White is dead. The Queen promptly cooks them up and eats them. In the end, as punishment for her misdeeds, she is forced to don red hot iron shoes in which she dances "until she dropped down dead."[10]

Fairy tale violence shared with children in books or stories may certainly be hard for some of them, but it is not equivalent to screen violence in its potential to terrify. When reading or listening to stories, children aren't assaulted with precreated graphic visual imagery. They don't have to see close-ups of a knife slicing through flesh or of feet sizzling in an iron shoe, or the agony of pain in the queen's eyes as she dances to her death. Children have more control over how vividly they envision the violence.

I'm not, however, above skipping the torture scenes when I read these stories to kids. This is a personal predilection and not a philosophical stance. The specifics aren't really essential to the plot, and they always leave me queasy. Sword fights, an occasional giant slaying, or the rapid demise of wicked ogres don't bother me—but I tend to be haunted even by truncated descriptions of slow, painful death. Some people, including children, have a higher tolerance for that sort of thing. For some, the violence is just scary enough to serve as a springboard for playing about and safely exploring their own feelings of fear and anger.

"My four-year-old granddaughter loves the gruesome parts of Snow White," a grandmother tells me. "She likes me to put on my red bedroom slippers, dance wildly, and then fall down dead. We do that over and over." With older children, the violent punishments concocted in fairy tales can even lead to conversations about social issues such as justice, retribution, and torture.

Even aside from the violence, I suppose that my love of fairy tales rests uneasily on my social conscience. Although their emotional content in the stories runs deep, the characters do not—and therein lies their biggest problem. There's no getting around, for instance, the fact that they originated at a time when the roles of woman and men were severely constricted or that they often promise young girls a happily-ever-after in the form of marriage to a handsome prince.

I admit that I've tried on occasion to retell the stories from a more feminist slant—and have seen similar attempts in plays and puppet performances—but they often fall flat and end up seeming like political tracts. One of the best retellings of a fairy tale from a more feminist perspective is the book *Ella Enchanted*, by Gail Carson Levine, but it's really more of a riff. Levine uses the plot structure and characters from *Cinderella* to tell a more complex story, in much the same way that Tom Stoppard elevates and expands the minor characters of *Hamlet* in the play *Rosencrantz and Guildenstern Are Dead* or the way Gregory Maguire humanizes the Wicked Witch of the West in his novel, *Wicked*.

Speaking of wicked witches, the villains in fairy tales are especially one-dimensional. Bad characters are thoroughly bad, and with a few exceptions such as the Wicked Queen in *Snow White*, thoroughly ugly. When children repeatedly receive the unchallenged message that physical traits reflect character flaws, we are training them to embrace societal stereotypes that are both wrong and deeply hurtful.

This came home most painfully to me when I was working with an 8-year-old girl who had Aperts Syndrome—a rare congenital disorder that results in facial deformities. Somehow the subject of play-acting came up. "I don't like it when kids want me to be in plays," she said passionately. "They always make me be the witch, or the monster." She paused for a moment. "How would *you* like to always be the witch?"

In complement to the misshapen hags and dwarves, the heroines in fairy tales are as beautiful as they are good. As a child I remember them often described as "fair of face," which can be read simultaneously as "nice to look at" and "light complexioned." That beauty and a fair complexion are equated in these stories is not particularly surprising. Eighteenth- and nineteenth-century Europe was hardly a diverse or equitable society. Discrimination against the darker Semitic populations who were cordoned off in ghettos was common, as was the enslavement of Africans. That the stereotypes are explainable, however, does not eliminate the challenges fairy tales pose for those of us struggling to build a society that embraces similarities between people and celebrates the differences.

Because the stories are so rich, and because they lend themselves so well as springboards for make-believe, I think that it's worth wrestling with fairy tales to allow them a place in children's lives. It's possible to find fairy tales that do feature strong women. Various versions of the same fairy tale portray women differently. Cinderella as characterized by the Brothers Grimm is significantly more resourceful than the Cinderella portrayed by Perrault.[11]

Race and gender are the most common stereotypes perpetuated in fairy tales, but there are others as well. As a child I was particularly delighted that younger siblings were not only invariably good, but usually triumphant—often over their more powerful older siblings. (I am, of course, a youngest sister.) As an adult, I'm continually bothered by the ubiquitous characterization of stepmothers as wicked. "Not all stepmothers are bad," a 5-year-old informs me. I'm glad someone thought to tell him—although "most stepmothers are good" might have pleased me more. (As you've probably guessed, I am a stepmother.)

If, as I do, you believe in the value of traditional fairy tales despite their flaws, then it's essential to share them thoughtfully with children, in the context of lots and lots of other stories featuring a whole range of cultures and characters. Since fairy tales originate in oral tradition and evolved to reflect particular cultures, I don't have a problem with editing a bit as I read or tell them to children. Giving heroines coal-black hair and beautiful brown skin doesn't alter the plot or diminish the themes. There's no reason for Cinderella to be either blonde or white. The argument that we need to be true to the historical roots of these stories just doesn't make sense. If we were being really true to the historical roots of Cinderella, she would be Chinese.

When fairy tales become commercial mega-brands, their depth and malleability diminish, and so does their value as springboards for creative play. Once fairy tales become visual versions of someone else's values—viewed over and over and sold to us in combination with tiaras, jewels, ball gowns, and castles, and plastered with images of specific princesses with specific physiognomies—they lock children into a set script for playing from which it is very hard to deviate. Immersion in the Disney Princess brand—with its focus on glitter and acquisition—precludes playing out the more psychologically meaningful aspects of the stories that take place before the heroine becomes a princess—themes of loss, sibling rivalry, and parent–child conflicts.

A few minutes into playing with Abigail, the little girl who wanted me to be a Disney princess, she assigns me the task of scrubbing the floor. Looking up from my hands and knees I say brightly, "I must be Cinderella." "'No!" she responds authoritatively, "You're Anastasia," I remember that in the Disney version of *Cinderella* Anastasia is the tall, skinny stepsister. "Anastasia never scrubbed a floor in her life!" I retort rather scornfully. "She does in *Cinderella III*," Abigail replies sweetly. I stop scrubbing. "There's a *Cinderella III*?" I ask in amazement. "Of course," she said, "after Cinderella is married."

Disney Princess retail sales reached $3.4 billion in 2006,[12] with over 40,000 licensed items for sale.[13] I found 235 items on the ToysRUs Web site alone, including *Disney Princess Monopoly, A Disney Princess Magical Talking Kitchen* with 11 phrases and 18 accessories, *Leapster Educational Disney Princess Enchanted Learning Set*, and *Disney Princess Uno*. In addition to *Cinderella I, II,* and *III* on DVD, there's also *Disney Princess Stories* and *Disney Princess Sing Along Songs, Volumes One, Two,* and *Three*; Disney Game World: *The Disney Princess Edition; Disney Princess Party, Volumes 1* and 2; *Little Mermaid I* and *II*; *Aladdin I, II,* and *II*; *Beauty and the Beast* and *Beauty and the Beast*: *The Enchanted Christmas.*

The negative impact that Disney's presentation of women has on little girls' conception of themselves and what it means to be female have been discussed in detail elsewhere.[14] Their ultrathin body types, their clothing, and the stories they tell embody a commercialized, stereotypic image of beauty and womanhood. More than ever before, Disney is having a profound effect on make-believe. Like the super-hero/action figure phenomenon, the Disney Princess films and their accoutrements trap children—little girls this time—in an endless, intensifying loop of commercially constructed fantasies. Instead of pointing them toward violence, commercialized make-believe for girls steers them toward a view of femininity based on stereotypes of beauty, race, class, and behavior. "I was shocked," a friend said, "when I saw my 3-year-old niece reject a doll saying, 'She can't be a princess, she's too fat!'"

"What's a princess?" I ask Abigail. "A rich girl," she answers promptly, "with a kingdom." She is a bit fuzzy on exactly what a king-dom is, however. "It's got lots of rooms," she explains tentatively. Then her eyes grow big and round, sparkling with excitement. "And now there's no food in it!" "Oh, no!" I groan. "Yes!" she says with joyful urgency. "The servants have run out of ingredients!"

Once the royal trappings are removed from Abigail's play, it's hard to miss the values promulgated by the Disney brand, even aside from body image. The female ideal is a rich white girl who lives in a big house with servants who do the work. A friend of mine relates this story: "I was in the kitchen getting Thanksgiving dinner ready and I heard my granddaughter say, 'Grandpa let's play princess. I'll be the princess, you be the king and grandma can be the servant because she's cooking!'"

Unless we make a special effort, Disney's animated version of fairy tales like *Cinderella* and the values they promote may be the only ones to which children are exposed. Disney is one of three multinational corporations controlling most of children's commercial culture.[15] Its dominance—reinforced by an endless loop of toys, clothing, food, accessories, and media—is used to ensure that little girls buy into a lifestyle rooted in all the things that Disney sells.

Newborn baby girls can come home from the hospital to be ensconced in a room decked out with princess furniture and paraphernalia. Videos, toys, accessories, and a longing to visit a Disney theme park will see them through childhood. Disney began selling wedding dresses in 2007,[16] but the company was hyping weddings long before that. A 2003 commercial for the Princess Dolls features wedding dresses for Belle, Aurora, and Cinderella.[17] Brand-loyal preschoolers can grow up to have their Disney fairy-tale dreams come true by getting married in a Disney wedding gown at a Disney resort, which have long been advertised as a haven for honeymooners. The Disney bride can look forward to having her own little princess and starting the cycle all over again.

BEYOND SEXUALIZATION: RACISM AND OTHER STEREOTYPES IN COMMERCIALIZED BRANDS

"But what about the Bratz Dolls?" I'm asked during a presentation to parents, "At least they're clearly ethnically diverse. Aren't they better?" The Bratz Dolls—"The Girlz with a Passion for Fashion"—were introduced in 2001[18] and are now a huge hit all over the world.[19] Chloe, Sasha, Jade, and Yasmin—the Bratz pack—are certainly a more ethnically diverse quartet than Belle, Cinderella, Ariel, and Aurora.

The problem with extolling the Bratz brand for its cultural diversity is that the lessons children learn from toys are not compartmentalized. When children play with a multiracial collection of dolls or action figures with bodies that appear to be anorexic or enhanced by steroids, they can't be expected to get one cultural message and ignore the other. As with the Disney Princesses, The Bratz brand, replete with videos, films, cars, accessories, clothing and so on, locks girls into preset scripts rife with stereotypes about women and materialistic values. In addition to their anorexic bodies, they feature heavily made-up faces and an in-your-face sexuality that's a slightly watered down version of the pervasive trappings of "raunch culture," often described as pornography gone mainstream.[20]

The Bratz brand doesn't promote dreams of acquiring the accoutrements of royalty. Instead, it promotes dreams of acquiring the trappings of rich teenage sluts. There's even a Bratz Limousine—complete with a bar,[21] and the Bratz Forever Diamondz Convertible. In the

United Kingdom, the Bratz Remote Control Car is sold with the following pitch: "Hit the streets in style with the Bratz Itsy Bitzy Remote Control Vehicle. Remember, it's not how well you drive, but how good you look while you're doing it."[22] The Bratz are all about conspicuous consumption. Although they aren't royalty and don't reside in fabulous castles in make-believe lands, they have more in common with the Disney Princesses than not. Both brands are competing with Barbie for the hearts, minds, and playtime of little girls.

If we want children to embrace diversity as a value, then providing them with multicultural toys, books, and media that counter prevailing stereotypes is essential. Diversity in toys and media doesn't replace the value of enabling children to live and play in ethnically diverse environments, but it's important for two reasons. One is that minority populations of children have a right to see themselves in the stories that permeate popular culture—inclusion in popular culture is a powerful form of societal validation. The other is that all children benefit from experiencing the similarities and differences among cultures.

At this point, the Disney Princesses are hardly ethnically diverse. Although Disney has rolled Mulan, an Asian character, and Pocahontas, a Native American, into the Princess brand, they take a back seat to the white princesses—mainly Belle, Cinderella, and Ariel. Jasmine, the Arabian princess from *Aladdin*, is also included, but when Disney released the *Aladdin* movie, there was outcry from Arabs and Arab Americans that both the hero and heroine were lighter skinned, with more Caucasian looking features than other characters, while the villains were drawn with stereotypically Semitic features.[23]

Unless you're the target population, it's hard to understand the depth of anger and pain brought on by living in societies whose cultural and commercial icons perpetuate racism, either directly by perpetuating stereotypes, or indirectly by exclusion. Although the presence of stereotypes in literature, music, and art is particularly hurtful to the people reduced to caricature, stereotypic fantasy characters are problematic for everyone because they limit our understanding of the complexities of being human and can even incite us to do harm. The notion that we are how we look feeds racism and prejudice. In the extreme, linking physical characteristics to character traits can be dangerous enough to result in genocide. Unless a conscious effort is made to counter them, societal stereotypes may be absorbed by children as young as two.[24]

In 2009 Disney will add a black Princess to the brand, but it remains to be seen how integral to the princess line she will be.[25] The African American parents I've talked to see this as a mixed blessing.

On the one hand, a black Disney Princess eliminates the terrible pain experienced by black girls who get the message every day that being a princess is desirable and that only white girls can be princesses. On the other hand, for parents who have chosen to opt out of Disney Princess culture, partly because there is no black princess, opting in means allowing their daughters to immerse themselves in a commercial culture that places disproportionate importance on being rich and beautiful and finding a prince to marry. When I asked Enola Aird, a colleague and noted advocate for mothers and children, about the new doll, she urged black parents to be cautious: "We have to ask what values a 'black' princess will teach our children. Will she reinforce white standards of beauty? To what extent will she contribute to what is already an intense over-commercialization of our children's lives? Any benefits will probably be outweighed by the costs."

I have colleagues who have worked for years to push the media industry to make diversity a priority. Although there have been some successes, it's an uphill battle. Think about the race and ethnicity of the heroes and villains in popular media and television programs today. How are Arabs portrayed? How many Asian characters are present? Who is considered to be beautiful? Who are the villains? How are African Americans and Latinos characterized?

Psychologist Kenyon Chan, chancellor of the University of Washington Bothell, remembers being brought in to consult on a popular animated cartoon series from the 1980s that featured the Smurfs—diminutive creatures with large noses and blue skin tones—and was set in medieval Europe. "I suggested that to make the setting more multicultural, they should integrate the walled city where the action takes place—that they could include people of color in the population, like a sage from Asia or a traveler from Africa," he said. "The writers objected, explaining patiently that people of color didn't really live in medieval Europe." "That's true," Dr. Chan responded. "But neither did the Smurfs!"

SHIFTING THE PARADIGM: INTRODUCING NEW IDEAS WHEN CHILDREN PLAY

Aside from the fact that it's fun, one of the benefits of playing with children is that we can use our shared make-believe as an opportunity to introduce new ideas—including those that counter prevailing stereotypes. Mostly I try to follow children's lead whenever I play with them. But there are times—whether I'm playing with children for therapy or just for fun—when I do try to interject alternative points of view.

I once worked with a 4-year-old boy who fell in love with my puppet, Audrey Duck. He pretended that they got married and had a baby. "When the baby is born you have to say 'Oh what a beautiful baby,'" he told me. "I'm the father!" he added proudly. Later he invited Audrey and the baby to come watch him play basketball. "You have to cheer for me," he said. After several minutes of sitting on the sidelines, I couldn't resist making Audrey wonder when it would be her turn to play. "This doesn't seem fair," she said to him. "Can't you watch the baby while I play basketball?" At first he resisted, but Audrey kept pointing out the inequity. "Can't we take turns?" she asked. Finally, he agreed and tenderly, if reluctantly, relinquished the basketball for the baby—at least for a short time.

One of the problems with children being immersed in brands that span media and toys is that when left to their own devices—which, ideally, is how children should be playing much of the time—the content of their play is dictated by the brands. Immersion in commercial culture, reinforced by multiple viewings and branded toys, means that children's "own devices" are no longer really their own. Just as the Spiderman or Power Ranger brands lock little boys into violent play, little girls immersed in the Disney brand can be locked into playing at being helpless females waiting to be rescued.

The same grandmother who put on her bedroom slippers and danced to her demise also takes requests from her Disney-enamored granddaughter to tell princess stories. She uses this as an opportunity to provide alternative views of gender roles. "I invented a prince who visits the princess and washes the dishes," she says.

In another episode of playing princess, 4-year-old Abigail was in the process of simultaneously sorting through princess movies and the story of Passover, the Jewish holiday celebrating the exodus from Egypt. "Let's pretend that I'm a princess drowning in the Red Sea," she said. "And you're the prince coming to rescue me." Plopping herself on the ground she began calling out, "Help me! Help me! I'm drowning!" I stood on the edge of the Red Sea debating my next move. Abigail stopped drowning for a moment to remind me that I was the Prince. "Come on!" she said urgently. "Oh dear," I said. "The princess is drowning and I don't even know how to swim. I guess I'll have to try to rescue her." Curious to see what Abigail would do with her helpless princess persona when rescue was not forthcoming, I leaped into the Red Sea calling out, "Help! Help!" a few times. Suddenly the story changed. "I remember how to swim!" she announced, and promptly came to the rescue, saving herself and the prince.

If our contributions to children's play deviate too far off course or if particular plot points or themes are important to children, they have no hesitation about digging in their heels. When Abigail pretended to be a princess walking through a field of beautiful birds, she closed her eyes and began to wish aloud that her fairy godmother would send her a beautiful bird as a pet. She opened one eye and explained, "You're my fairy godmother." I thought for a minute. "I hear the princess wishing for a bird." I said. "But these are wild birds, and they don't like to be pets. I don't think I can send her a bird." Abigail opened both her eyes disapprovingly. "No! No! No!" she said severely. "These are the kind of birds that *like* to be pets." "Oh," I said meekly. And—as Abigail's designated fairy godmother in her very own creation—I sent her one of the imaginary birds in answer to her prayers.

We can do our best to challenge the stereotyped gender roles, unrealistic body types, and materialistic values promoted by brands like the Disney Princesses, Bratz, and Barbie, but even aside from the negative effects I've described, their domination of the toy market for preschool girls is troubling. They contribute to what is primarily a commercially constructed phenomenon that is depriving children of middle childhood, which for the purposes of this book I'll define as between the ages of 5 or 6 to 10 or 11.

THE LOSS OF MIDDLE CHILDHOOD

"Kids are getting older younger," is a common plaint in the toy industry, clothing, and marketing industries and is used as an excuse to market to 6-year-olds everything from cell phones to thong underpants. The market has usurped the years between 6 and 12 and transformed them into "tweens," a monolithic consumer demographic of teenage wannabes. Now these industries are working at usurping the preschool years as well. Referring to 4- to 6-year-olds as "pre-tweens," companies like Bonne Bell are targeting little girls with what might be called "pre-makeup," in the form of lip gloss spiked with M&Ms, Dr. Pepper, and other flavors.[26]

Sanitized versions of social networking sites, which combine elements from sites like MySpace, and online fantasy games like *Myst*, are targeting children as young as 5. Some appear to be promoting creativity and individuality, because players get to decorate rooms or clothe an avatar—a symbolic representation of a persona assumed in cyberspace. But on the sites that I've looked at, such as Webkins.com, which is quite popular today, the choices are confined to choosing among predesigned objects. The pets are cute, the games are fun, and I understand the site's appeal, but there's no escaping that the underlying goal is to acquire virtual cash to make purchases. These sites, like BarbieGirls.com or Stardoll.com, don't really encourage creativity

because many seem to be designed primarily to train girls to shop—
for furniture, clothing, and accessories. Engaging with these sites isn't
like actually making doll clothes of your own design from scraps of
material, or sketching them on paper.[27] When Mattel launched
Barbiegirls.com, a toy trends expert commented that girls can "go on
the site and chat with their friends, compare outfits, rooms. It's right
on target with what girls are looking for."[28]

But are kids actually getting older younger? Girls are reaching
puberty earlier than in previous generations. There is, however, no
evidence that their cognitive, social, or emotional development, or
their judgment, is keeping pace. The frontal cortex—the area of the
brain where judgment sits—doesn't develop fully until we reach our
mid-twenties. Immersion in twenty-first-century commercial culture
encourages children to leap directly from preschool to the preoccupations of adolescence—sexuality, identity, and affiliation—before they
can possibly understand what any of them mean.

In 2007 a report from the American Psychological Association on
the sexualization of young girls stated, "Toy manufacturers produce
dolls wearing black leather miniskirts, feather boas, and thigh-high
boots and market them to 8- to 12-year-old girls. Clothing stores sell
thongs sized for 7- to 10-year-old girls (some printed with slogans
such as 'eye candy' or 'wink'); other thongs sized for women and late
adolescent girls are imprinted with characters from Dr. Seuss and the
Muppets). In the world of child beauty pageants, 5-year-old girls wear
fake teeth, hair extensions, and makeup and are encouraged to "flirt"
onstage by batting their long, false eyelashes. On prime-time television, girls can watch fashion shows in which models made to resemble little girls wear sexy lingerie (e.g., the CBS broadcast of *Victoria's
Secret Fashion Show* on December 6, 2005)."[29]

Children are gaining the trappings of maturity at a very young
age—language, clothing, and accoutrements. Toy industry executives
lament that children stop playing with toys by the age of 6—moving
on to "grown-up" products such as cell phones, video games, and
computers.[30] That they are growing up with technology means that
they may grasp the "how to" component of computers, MP3 players,
cell phones, and hand-held electronic games. But where's the evidence
that they can cope successfully with the content they encounter or that
they don't need what they're missing from spending so much time in
front of screens? Even as we marvel at children's technological acu-
men, we should be wondering: do 6-year-old children who know better than we do how to use a joy stick, surf the web, and master a
remote control also know how to make sense of, and protect them-

selves against, the ubiquitous commercialism and its attendant cynicism, sexism, and violence—to say nothing of the pornography—they encounter in virtual reality?

According to the Centers for Disease Control, in 2005 over one third of American ninth graders (boys and girls) had already had sex.[31] But the fact that many children are sexually active at age 14 doesn't mean that they are achieving emotional intimacy with their partners or handling relationships particularly well. If children were really getting older younger—if they were actually going through all of the processes of physical, cognitive, social, and emotional maturation more rapidly—then perhaps there would be little cost to them. But that doesn't seem to be the case. Psychologist David Elkind has been writing since the early 1980s about the price paid by hurrying children to grow up too fast—world-weariness, cynicism, and a lack of wonder.[32] At the same time, cultural critic Neil Postman wrote not just about the disappearance of childhood, but about the infantilization of adults.[33] Children seem to be taking longer to achieve real independence than in previous generations. About 40 percent of college graduates are now moving back home after graduation.[34] They aren't moving home, as would be the case in some cultures, to support their families. They seem to be moving home to save money and to postpone having to take care of themselves.[35]

One of the workshops offered at the 2007 Kid Power marketing conference—the largest such gathering in the United States—was called, "Can KGOY and KSYL co-exist?" For those out of the loop, the former acronym stands for "Kids are getting older younger." The latter? "Kids are *staying* younger longer."[36]

This does not tell us that children are maturing more rapidly. It implies that something is impeding their attaining adulthood. I think that one of the impediments is that we are depriving them of a chance to experience middle childhood. Perhaps 30 is now the new 20 in part because 12 is also the new 20—and 6 is the new 12. Or, to use marketing jargon, KSYL is the direct consequence of KGOY. Children are missing out on years of being able to use creative play to gain a sense of competence, explore independence, experience constructive problem solving and learn tools for making meaning.

Unlike the first 6 years of life, when enormous leaps in learning take place so quickly that children are constantly having to adjust to the precariousness of newly acquired skills, or adolescence, when body changes and issues of identity create a new self-consciousness and surging hormones affect wide swings in emotions, middle childhood is a relatively stable time when skills can be honed, imaginations can run rampant, our bodies don't seem to be out of control, and we can experience a sense of competence about interacting in the world. Children are likely to have at least rudimentary capabilities in reading and math. Their basic physical coordination has come together enough that they can run, jump, hop, and skip. They are honing their cognitive and physical capabilities—reading harder books, attempting more complicated math problems, and learning to play various sports or learning to dance or do gymnastics.

By 7 years of age, basic physical coordination is evolved enough for at least some independent play time. They are capable of cooperating and can delay gratification enough that they can execute complicated projects both alone and with friends. Adults may be in the house, but they don't have to be in the same room. If there's a safe space to play outside, they are allowed out on their own.

Middle childhood is a time when children's important influences extend beyond the home to include peers. It can be an incredibly fertile time for intellectual and creative exploration. Although girls are reaching puberty earlier than they used to, it's still a time that is relatively stable physically—at least for some portion of this time, kids aren't grappling with great hormonal surges and unwieldy body changes. It's a time when children don't have to worry about their bodies and are able to form friendships with members of the opposite sex without having to worry about sexual overtones.

One of the hallmarks of developmental psychology is the idea of scaffolding—that we evolve cognitively, emotionally, and socially by building on the skills and knowledge we acquire along the way. The developmental psychologist Erik Erikson identified stages of growth and development that revolve around focusing on negotiating specific social and emotional tasks. According to Erikson, we evolve from infancy to adolescence by acquiring a basic sense of trust in the world; building on that trust to establish our autonomy, using our newfound sense of ourselves to experiment with our own creativity; building on our creativity to establish a sense of competence by learning how to tackle and complete complex tasks; and building on our competence to establish our own identities and affiliations.

Another way to think about this is that unless we establish trust as infants, we can't establish autonomy. If we have no sense of self, we can't play creatively as preschoolers. If we can't initiate creativity, we can't learn to be competent in executing our more complex ideas in middle childhood. If we have never established a sense of ourselves as competent, we will not be able to establish a sense of identity in adolescence as separate from those who care for us.

When it comes to play, what I find most helpful about Erikson's work is that it provides a framework for understanding the content from the point of view of a child's experience and needs. For example, peek-a-boo games are a way of helping babies establish a sense that things or people don't just disappear when we can't see them. Another way to think about them is as one of many ways that babies establish a sense of trust that the world is safe and stable enough for them to begin to practice being independent.

An important component of gaining more independence and autonomy is developing a sense of control over your body. Given that children tend naturally to focus the themes of their creative play around issues of importance to them, it's not surprising that, for toddlers, bathroom play becomes endlessly enjoyable. Sarah, age 28 months and just starting to be interested in using a potty, asked her father to take down a paper dragon that had been hanging on a wall. "She wadded up some paper and made it come out of the dragon," he said. "Then she pretended to wipe its bottom. She asked me to help her make diapers for the dragon. We're constantly diapering something or placing one stuffed animal or another on the potty."

Toddlers like Sarah are at the early stages of being able to engage in creative play. Over the next few years, depending on her interests and opportunities, she may tell her own stories, make up songs, invent imaginary friends, build block constructions, paint pictures, or sculpt with clay. If her creative explorations are allowed to flourish, she will experience countless hours of pleasure as well as the exhilarating sense of power that comes from generating her own unique creations.

When girls are encouraged to act like teenagers just a few years after shedding their diapers, they miss out on the pleasures of middle childhood. And they are losing years of creative play. According to one study, American 9- to 12-year-olds only spend 1 minute a day in pretend play. In 1997—well after both Elkind and Postman began writing about a diminishing childhood—they were spending 15 minutes per day. The amount of time 6- to 8-year-olds spend in creative play decreased from 25 minutes to 16 minutes during the same time period.[37]

CONCLUSION

Creative play is essential to all children. For girls, strengthening their capacity to process and transform the world can serve as an antidote to the ubiquitous, commercialized version of successful womanhood based on the glorification of unrealistic body types, objectified sexuality, and the acquisition of material goods. Whatever time we can provide for young girls to spend away from screens and immersed in generating their own creations affords them opportunities to experience and nurture their power to create and transform in a confusing, commercialized, and often overwhelming world.

After dessert at a multigenerational family gathering, Marley, our resident 4-year-old, asked to be excused from the table while the adults remained talking over coffee. She returned a few minutes later draped in a pink, diaphanous ball gown and began to dance around the table making up a song. She started out singing softly, but as she floated and became more immersed in the process, her voice became stronger, increasing in passion and volume. Building to a final, glorious crescendo, she began belting out the song's dramatic conclusion. Flinging out her hands, she sang passionately: "I . . . am . . . God!" She held that last note for several beats. Finally, taking a deep breath, she concluded in rapid staccato, "I make up all the words!"

ACKNOWLEDGMENT

Portions of this chapter first appeared in Susan Linn, *The Case for Make Believe: Saving Play in a Commercialized World* (New York: The New Press, 2008).

4

Girls Gone Grown-Up: Why Are U.S. Girls Reaching Puberty Earlier and Earlier?

Sandra Steingraber

Don't try to make me grow up before my time, Meg: it's hard enough to have you change all of a sudden; let me be a little girl as long as I can.

—Jo, age 15, to Meg, age 16, in *Little Women*
by Louisa May Alcott (1868)

To earn a doctoral degree in biology, I followed deer around a pine forest in Minnesota for the better part of 4 years. I was trying to learn how the animals' dietary preferences were affecting the reproduction of various tree species in the understory. To do this, I needed to know something about the size of the herd and the sexual maturity of the animals within it. A doe develops distinct food habits when it is pregnant or lactating. But, among deer, sexual maturity is not a simple function of age. Yearlings and even fawns can begin ovulating if food is plentiful. If it is not, females won't become sexually mature until age 2 or older because a critical body mass is required for puberty.

In short, I discovered that the basic elements of fertility in this ecosystem were not governed by a built-in clock but were potentialities that responded to environmental signals. That understanding may shed light on a puzzling phenomenon in humans: the free-falling age at which U.S. girls are entering puberty. In February 2008 the medical journal *Pediatrics* published the findings of an expert panel convened to evaluate trends in pubertal timing among U.S. girls. Corroborating earlier findings, the panel concluded that U.S. girls as a group are reaching puberty at ever earlier ages.[1] A century ago, the average age at first menstruation, or menarche, was 14.2. By the time I began menstruating in 1972, the average age had fallen to 12.8, and it is now 12.3. There are significant racial differences: mean menarchal age is 12.6 years for white girls, 12.1 for black girls, and 12.2 for Mexican American girls.[2]

The appearance of breasts—called thelarche—also arrives earlier and earlier in the lives of American girls. Indeed the average age of thelarche is falling even faster than the age of menarche. I first sprouted breast buds when I was 11.5 years old, which, in 1970, was exactly average. By 1997, the average age for breast budding had fallen to just under 10 years for U.S. white girls and just under 9 years for black girls, with a significant portion beginning to develop breast buds before age 8.[3] In a few decades, the childhood of girls have been significantly shortened.

Researchers remain puzzled about what's causing the phenomenon. Some argue that early puberty is a distortion of a "natural" process. It could be that humans, evolving in hunter-gatherer societies, developed the ability to reproduce at younger ages in response to environmental stimuli (such as plentiful calories) and that today's environmental stimuli simply trigger that process. Increasing evidence, however, suggests that the entire hormonal system has been subtly rewired by modern stimuli, and early puberty is a coincidental nonadaptive outcome. In either case, female sexual maturation is not controlled by a ticking clock. It's more like a musical performance with girls' bodies as the keyboards and the environment as the pianist's hands.

HEALTH IMPLICATIONS OF EARLY PUBERTY

However elusive its origins, accelerated puberty has health implications. With so many third graders wearing bras, some pediatric endocrinologists have recommended lowering the age at which puberty should be considered precocious, to spare younger girls drastic hormonal interventions to halt puberty's progression.[4] Setting aside clinical questions of whether a 7-year-old with pubic hair should be treated for a disorder, public health researchers point out that what has become the norm is not necessarily normal or good.[5] Early puberty in girls is associated with a startling number of psychopathologies and health problems. Girls who are the first in their cohort of friends to reach thelarche report more negative feelings about themselves and suffer from more anxiety. Early-maturing girls are more likely to experience depression, develop eating and adjustment disorders, and are more likely to attempt suicide. Some of these effects are limited to adolescence, and others persist throughout young adult life and into middle age.[6]

According to research, early-maturing girls are more prone to early drug abuse, cigarette smoking, and alcohol use. They are more likely to be physically and violently victimized. Earlier puberty is also predictive of earlier sexual initiation with first sexual encounter following closely on the heels of puberty. The combination of early sexual intercourse and early substance use places early-maturing girls at a higher risk for teenage pregnancy. Conduct disorders and delinquency are also higher among early-maturing girls who are disproportionately represented in criminal records. Late-maturing girls were also found to perform better in school and are more likely to finish college.[7]

Early puberty also raises the risk of breast cancer in adulthood. As age of menarche decreases, overall risk of breast cancer increases. Menarche before age 12, for example, raises breast cancer risk by 50 percent when compared to menarche at age 16. Conversely, for each year menarche is delayed, the risk of breast cancer declines by 5 to 20 percent. Estrogen is the likely culprit: a woman's risk of breast cancer rises the longer she is exposed to estrogen, and early puberty increases that exposure.[8]

THE CAUSES OF EARLY PUBERTY

The link to breast cancer lends urgency to the task of understanding the causes of early puberty. The leading hypotheses fall into three categories: psychosocial factors, nutrition, and pollutants. All three represent aspects of the environment that girls inhabit. However, these groupings are not necessarily independent of each other. For example, girls who consume lots of sugary drinks and processed foods are more likely to be obese, but such a diet also exposes them to different food-borne pollutants than girls raised on, say, organic vegetarian fare. Childhood obesity may also alter interpersonal relationships and result in higher psychosocial stress. The intricate interrelationships among pubertal determinants make the tasks of isolating each variable and discussing its relative importance impossible. Hence, my analysis here is deliberately open-ended and suggestive in tone.

Psychosocial Factors

Trauma, family dysfunction, and father-daughter relationships seem to play a role in the story. Conflict and stress within families are consistently associated with early puberty. So are sexual abuse and the absence of a biological father in the household. In Poland, for example, girls exposed to prolonged familial dysfunction reached menarche

4 months earlier than girls living in families free of traumatic events. Similar results were reported in French-speaking Canada, where adverse family conditions and high anxiety were correlated with precocious puberty. Childhood sexual abuse lowered age of menarche in New Zealand girls. However, war conditions in Bosnia caused delays in menarchal ages among girls exposed to that traumatic environment. In this case, however, extreme psychological stress was also accompanied by physical injury and poverty. No one knows enough to explain these phenomena, although many have speculated about them. Some researchers, for example, have asked if girls who live with biological fathers in tight-knit families might be receiving pheromones that inhibit puberty, perhaps as an evolutionary mechanism to prevent incest.[9]

Obesity

Our obesity epidemic, which scientists have associated with changes in childhood nutrition, is almost certainly playing a role in the falling age of menarche and may also be at least partly responsible for the falling age of breast development. As a group, obese girls enter puberty earlier than lean girls. The trend of increasing body mass for U.S. girls parallels the trend for earlier puberty. On average, children eat 150 to 200 calories a day more than they did 30 years ago, and their obesity rates have tripled. Changes in body mass index (BMI) over the past 3 decades have been more pronounced in black girls than in white girls, with a higher percentage of black girls now obese or overweight. As a group, black girls also reach puberty earlier than white girls. A recent national study of preschool children from urban, low-income families found that 35 percent were overweight by the age of 3. Hispanic children were the heaviest, with 44 percent overweight or obese.[10]

Although it is certainly possible that the onset of puberty itself is triggering increased body fatness, at least four longitudinal studies have now found that body fat precedes and predicts pubertal timing. Among 181 white girls in Pennsylvania, those who were chubbier in early childhood were more likely to exhibit earlier pubertal development relative to peers at 9 years of age. A longitudinal study from Louisiana found that heavier children tended to experience menarche sooner than thinner children: each standard deviation increase in BMI doubled the odds for early menarche. High BMI during childhood also predicted earlier menarche in a cohort of Australian girls who were followed from prenatal life to adolescence. In this study, lower-than-expected birth weights coupled with rapid weight gain in childhood showed the strongest association with young age at menarche. Similarly, a Michigan study that followed 354 girls from their 3rd birthdays through 6th grade found that higher body fatness at age 3 was associated with earlier thelarche. Rate of change was also important: the faster that body fatness increased between ages 3 and 6, the greater the chances that breast budding would begin by age 9. In this study, nearly half of the girls in the cohort had entered puberty by age 9.[11]

But there are equally compelling reasons to believe that the increased heaviness of U.S. girls is not the whole story behind the falling age of puberty. For example, BMI profiles for 6- to 9-year-old children are similar in Denmark and the United States, and yet pubertal onset among Danish girls is a full year later. Fatter girls enter puberty sooner, but obesity cannot explain the marked differences between the timing of puberty of U.S. and Danish girls. Furthermore, within the United States, although early-maturing white girls are heavier at the time of puberty, this is not the case for black girls.[12]

Sexualized Culture

Many parents have wondered whether the sexualized content of television programming and other media used by children may be acting as a permissive signal to the neurohormonal apparatus that controls pubertal onset. Harvard psychologist and media watchdog Susan Linn has documented a dramatic increase in erotic marketing messages aimed at preteen girls—thong underwear for 10-year-olds, for example[13]—and researchers in North Carolina have demonstrated that early-maturing girls seek out sexual media imagery significantly more than later-maturing girls regardless of age or race. Exposure to sexy media matter is also known to accelerate sexual initiation among white adolescents.[14] However, the impact of media content on the timing of puberty itself is not a question that has been tested empirically. Indeed, it is difficult to even imagine how such a study could be designed as almost nothing is known about how sensory input of any kind modulates the pace of human sexual maturation. And, in contrast to the wealth of studies that have documented the impact of media violence on boys, scant research has been directed toward investigating the effects of sexualized media on girls.[15] A recent report by the American Psychological Association found that exposure of girls to sexualized media images raised the risk for mental health problems, but the report did not investigate its impact on pubertal timing.[16]

Certainly U.S. children are immersed in media, and their engagement has increased dramatically over the past 3 decades. Children in the United States watch an average of 3 hours of television per day.

With video games and other media format included, daily screen time can be far greater. Media use increases with age but is high in all age groups, including among children less than 2 years old, although the American Academy of Pediatrics openly discourages television viewing before the second birthday and advocates limits of less than 2 hours per day for older children. Among preschoolers, children from non-white families and low-income families watch more TV each week than white children and children from higher-income families. A national random sample revealed that children ages 8 to 18 devote more time to media than any other waking activity—about one third of each day.[17]

Television and video viewing is associated with being overweight and obesity among both preschoolers and school-aged children. The more television is watched, the higher the risk for obesity. However, the specific mechanisms are not well understood. Children who watch lots of television are more sedentary and also have lower energy expenditure while resting. Among U.S. girls, those who averaged more than 2 hours per day of television viewing had significantly higher body mass indices and were 13 times more likely to be overweight by age 11 than girls who watched less television.[18]

Sedentary Lifestyles

Not only do U.S. girls eat more calories per day than they did 3 decades ago, they exercise less. Physical activity indices are lower for black and Hispanic girls and for girls living in low-income families. Physical activity also declines as girls, both black and white, move through adolescence, but activity declines are greater for black girls. By the age of 16 or 17, half of black girls and almost one third of white girls engage in no habitual physical activity at all. The availability of a community recreation center along with participation in daily physical education (PE) classes both significantly increase moderate to vigorous activity patterns among children. However, recess and PE are less a part of school curricula now than in past decades, with only one in five adolescents now participating in at least 1 day per week of PE in their schools. Only the state of Illinois requires daily PE from kindergarten through high school. There is no federal law that requires PE to be provided in schools, nor any incentive to do so.[19]

Exercise is protective against early puberty but through mechanistic pathways that are not clearly understood. As a group, bedridden girls have earlier-than-average puberties whereas female athletes have later puberties. It is difficult to tease apart leanness from the effects of exercise. Girls with anorexia tend to have delayed puberties, as do gymnasts, runners, and ballet dancers. There is some evidence that exercise itself is protective against early puberty. Elite swimmers and ice skaters also have later puberties, and these girls are typically of normal weight. Sport competition, however, also brings with it psychological as well as physical stress, and it is difficult to isolate the relative contribution of each component to pubertal timing.[20]

HORMONE-DISRUPTING CHEMICALS

Exposures to hormone-disrupting chemicals may be part of the story of early puberty. Hormone-disrupting chemicals are substances that disregulate some aspect of the endocrine system. They can exert their effects in a number of ways: by mimicking hormones; by blocking their uptake; by altering the rate of their production; by interfering with their metabolism; or by making cells more or less sensitive to hormonal signals. Not only can endocrine disruptors sabotage any one hormonal signal through a multitude of tactics, the signaling circuits that govern the onset of puberty respond to a multitude of hormones and are therefore innately vulnerable to perturbation to hormone-mimicking chemicals. Such disruption could proceed through any number of pathways and lead to outcomes that are not easily predictable.

Recent studies demonstrate the exquisite sensitivity of children to sex hormones even during the quiescent period before adolescent puberty. Levels of estrogens in prepubertal girls are very low—100 times lower than previously thought. However, estrogen receptors are expressed in target tissues throughout childhood. Thus, prepubertal girls are highly sensitive to sex hormone exposures, which may influence the timing of pubertal maturation. Indeed, premature breast budding in girls can occur throughout the juvenile period and has been correlated with elevated estrogen levels. It is reasonable then to predict that girls would be sensitive to estrogenic environmental chemicals.[21]

Studies of children accidentally exposed to known or suspected endocrine disruptors offer important clues. One such accident occurred in Michigan in 1973 when estrogenic chemical flame retardants (polybrominated biphenyls or PBBs) were mixed into commercial cattle feed. Before the mistake was discovered, farm families and others, including pregnant and nursing mothers, consumed meat and dairy products from the poisoned cows. Their daughters—now women of reproductive age—have been followed since birth. Those exposed to the highest levels of PBBs in early life began menstruating up to a year earlier than girls with lesser exposures. High PBB exposure was also associated with earlier appearance of pubic hair. The data on timing of breast development was inconclusive.[22]

Other human studies from Puerto Rico, Italy, Belgium, and Mexico have reported links between early puberty and possible exposures to hormone-disrupting chemicals. For example, in Puerto Rico during the 1970s, researchers documented clusters of premature puberty in certain communities. Some evidence of estrogenic contamination of food was discovered, but no single culprit was ever identified.[23] Similarly, in 1977 3- to 7-year-old boys and girls who all attended the same school in Milan, Italy, developed breasts. Elevated blood estrogen levels were documented. Poultry and veal from the school cafeteria were suspected sources, but their contamination was never confirmed. Some of the girls in this cohort went on to exhibit early menarche. Also, in northwest Tuscany, researchers documented a cluster of precocious puberty among girls living in a particular geographic area with a high density of naval yards and greenhouses.[24]

Studies from the United States document cases of breast development in children accidentally exposed to estrogen creams used by their mothers as well as to ointments, hair tonics, or ingested pharmaceuticals. In most cases, symptoms regressed after use discontinued. Pubertal activation caused by hormonally active personal care products may be of particular importance in African American communities in which the use of estrogenic hair products is common. Greater use of estrogen- or placenta-containing hair preparations may partially explain the predominance of early sexual development among black girls in the United States.[25]

In addition to certain hair compounds, hormonally active agents are found in many other consumer products, including pesticides and packaging and building materials. Hence, apart from accidental one-time exposures, children are also exposed continuously to low-level endocrine disruptors in their diets, drinking water, and air supply. A recent pilot study measured hormonally active environmental agents in the urine of 90 U.S. girls 6 to 8 years old and found a wide spectrum of exposure. Levels varied significantly according to body mass and race or ethnicity.[26] Among the chemicals detected were phthalates and bisphenol-A, a chemical that was originally developed as a synthetic hormone and is now used in the manufacture of polycarbonate plastics, in the resin linings of food cans, and in dental sealants. Bisphenol-A is one of the most widely produced chemicals in the world. It easily leaches from food and beverage containers—especially during heating and washing—and has led to widespread human exposure. The U.S. Centers for Disease Control found that 95 percent of urine samples from a larger representative sample of U.S. residents contained bisphenol-A, so its discovery in the urine of young girls is troubling but unsurprising.[27]

Many parents wonder if hormones in meat and milk may be hastening puberty in girls. It is true that estrogens and synthetic hormones are still used as growth promoters in the U.S. beef industry, although their use has been forbidden in the European Union since 1989. The impact of growth-promoting hormones in food on pubertal timing of the girls who consume them remains an unanswered question. Suggesting reasons for concern, some researchers point out that federal risk assessments that have set safe threshold levels for estrogens in meat are based on overestimates of children's own endogenous production of hormones, which are now known to be many times lower than presumed by previous models.[28]

In contrast to the paucity of human data on the posited link between hormonally active chemicals and earlier puberty in girls, there is a wealth of evidence for such a link from experimental studies with laboratory animals and wildlife. Altogether, the animal data demonstrate that early exposures to environmental estrogens can advance pubertal onset—through a variety of mechanisms and at doses similar to background levels to which humans are routinely exposed.[29]

Early puberty in laboratory animals can be induced via exposure to synthetic estrogens either prenatally or shortly after birth. Low doses of estrogens very early in development appear to affect the imprinting of central processes in the brain involved in regulating the onset of sexual maturity. Similar results have been reported using barnyard animals such as piglets and lambs.[30]

Some chemicals push animals into early puberty by increasing their responsiveness to natural estrogens. These chemicals are not estrogen mimics per se but work by magnifying estrogen sensitivity. One such chemical is plastics ingredient bisphenol-A, which is used in polycarbonate bottles. Prenatal and early-life exposure to bisphenol-A can trigger early onset of sexual maturation in female rodents. Stimulation of breast development is a particular target. Prenatal and infant exposure to bisphenol-A can make breast tissue more sensitive to estrogens and alter its anatomical development.[31]

Another way that synthetic chemicals can exert feminizing effects is by interfering with the production of aromatase, an enzyme that converts male hormones (androgens) to female hormones (estrogens). One chemical that interferes with the action of aromatase is the phthalate plasticizer DEHP. (This was one of the chemicals detected in the urine samples of 6-year-old girls described above.) In laboratory experiments, DEHP has opposing effects depending on its concentration: low doses of DEHP suppress aromatase, whereas higher doses increase its activity.[32]

EARLY PUBERTY: AN ECOLOGICAL DISORDER

What we know about the falling age of puberty in U.S. girls is less than what we don't know. But some evidence-based conclusions can be drawn, and policy-based recommendations based on these conclusions can move forward as the scientific knowledge of pubertal timing continues to unfold.

The "natural hypothesis"—the idea that early humans evolved the ability to reproduce at younger ages in response to plentiful calories and that contemporary environmental stimuli have simply accelerated that trend—requires revision. Although it remains the best explanation for the falling age of menarche in U.S. and European girls throughout the nineteenth century and the first half of the twentieth century, it is no longer the best explanation for what is happening now.

During the last 50 years, additional forces seem to have been at work. The evidence suggests that children's hormonal systems are being altered by various stimuli and that early puberty is the coincidental nonadaptive outcome. The intricate hormonal circuitry that governs pubertal onset is highly vulnerable to disruption, and this disruption can take many shapes. The ongoing epidemic of childhood obesity, which can alter insulin sensitivity and increase aromatase activity, is one form of hormonal disruption that is almost certainly linked to the trend toward earlier puberty in girls. Chemical toxicants are another kind of endocrine disruptor that can lead to alterations in the timing of puberty by several pathways. Indeed, stressors of many sorts—nutritional, environmental, and psychosocial—all appear to interact in a complex manner and contribute to early sexual maturation in girls.

For these reasons, early puberty is a phenomenon best understood as an ecological disorder. As described by physician Ted Schettler, an ecological disorder does not result from a single toxicant or set of toxicants, causing a single disease through a single causal pathway. Rather, it is the consequence of multiple and interpenetrating environmental stressors that exist within a causal web and can thus be defined as an "ecological manifestation of multiple changes in the dynamic system in which people are conceived, develop, live, and grow old."[33] All of the stressors that appear to contribute to early puberty in girls—obesity, television viewing, sedentariness, family dysfunction, chemical exposures—are higher in poor communities and communities of color in which poverty, racism, unemployment, and toxic substance exposures are high and access to nourishing food and safe places to exercise is low. In particular, U.S. black children are disproportionately exposed to physical environmental stressors, and this group reaches puberty earliest.[34]

INTERVENTIONS

There is sufficient evidence for the direct or indirect contribution of body mass to pubertal timing in girls to support efforts that combat childhood obesity. Any campaign to address this problem should begin with the promotion of breastfeeding. Breast milk safeguards against obesity. At 12 months, breast-fed babies are leaner than formula-fed babies, a difference that persists into later childhood. Breastfeeding is most important for children born small for their gestational age or those who were born prematurely; for these two groups of children, rapid weight gain raises additional risks for obesity and early puberty.[35]

For older children, successful battles are being waged at local and regional levels. A number of school districts around the country have begun working to eliminate sugary high-calorie foods from cafeterias and school events—and continue doing so without federal funding or support from the school lunch program.[36] Some school-based obesity prevention programs have already demonstrated an ability to delay menarche. One is Planet Health, a school-based intervention designed to decrease television viewing and consumption of high-fat foods among schoolchildren while increasing exercise and consumption of fruits and vegetables. After two school years, 6th- and 7th-grade girls in the Boston area who attended schools randomly selected for this curriculum had lower average body mass indices, lower body fat, higher levels of physical activity, and decreased screen time compared with their counterparts at nonparticipating schools. They were also 32 percent less likely to have experienced menarche during the 19-month study than girls in control schools.[37] Such programs should be replicated widely.

The success of school-based interventions such as Healthy Planet can be carried out in the community at large. Since 2005 there has been a dramatic increase in efforts to improve access to healthy foods in urban low-income areas through the creation of farmers' markets and community gardens.[38] Persuading schools, neighborhood stores, and convenience markets to stock produce from local organic farms is part of a decentralized grassroots campaign whose efforts are relevant to protecting girls from early sexual maturation.

Strategies to lower girls' body burdens of endocrine-disruptive chemicals include phaseouts of chemicals such as bisphenol-A and phthalates. Supporting organic agriculture not only lowers the burden of hormonally active residues in food, it protects watersheds from contamination by pesticides, herbicides, animal hormones, and antibiotics, which flow from farms, ranches, and manure lagoons into rivers and streams. Buying organic thus protects drinking water, another potential source of exposure. The Healthy Schools Network has spear-headed the effort to bring nonchemical pest control practices into schools and day care centers.

The environmental justice community, with its long experience with cumulative risks and impacts, has many insights to offer here. Any meaningful attempt to mitigate the problem of early sexual maturation in girls must draw on the collective wisdom of its leadership. For example, environmental justice activists have developed methods for response that are able to ascertain and mitigate multidetermined stressors swiftly. Incorporated into their analytical framework is the recognition that health disparities, such as obesity or low birth weight, are both outcomes of and contributors to vulnerability to environmental toxicants. Known as "bias for action," this early identification and response approach, which is community-based and collaborative, holds much promise for addressing the problem of early puberty in U.S. girls.[39]

CONCLUSION

Years from now, researchers may finally elucidate just how various factors—including trauma, calories, and chemicals—interact to induce early puberty. By then, my own 9-year-old daughter will be well into puberty or beyond. I know that even now a nascent hormonal network lies somewhere under her skin and is receiving incoming signals—from tonight's dinner; from her father, brother, and me; from the farm fields that ring our village; from the smokestack across the lake. This much I know: our bodies are the mediums for a much larger message. As we change that message, it will change us.

ACKNOWLEDGMENTS

This chapter is adapted from an earlier essay "Hormonal Messages," published in *Orion* magazine in 2006, and from the monograph "The Falling Age of Puberty in U.S. Girls: What We Know: What We Need to Know," commissioned and published by the Breast Cancer Fund in August 2007. Paper copies and electronic downloads are available free of charge from www.breastcancerfund.org.

5

Something's Happening Here: Sexual Objectification, Body Image Distress, and Eating Disorders

Margo Maine

> Culture is written on the body . . . encoded on it. Fat, thin, sculpted, adorned, starved, stuffed, the female body is a kind of text which, properly deconstructed, may tell us a lot about how women are seen in the culture and what they grapple with.
>
> —Caroline Knapp

Over the past three decades, body image distress and eating disorders have become major public health issues, affecting ever increasing numbers of girls and women of all ages. Both the American Academy of Pediatrics and the Society for Adolescent Medicine have developed specific guidelines for the identification and treatment of eating disorders in children and adolescents, instructing their members to screen for these problems routinely and to develop the skills to manage them.[1] Eating disorders are now the third most common illness among adolescent females living in the United States, with an incidence as high as 5 percent.[2]

Once considered to be characteristic of upwardly mobile Caucasian adolescent females in technologically advanced nations such as those in North America and Western Europe, eating disorders are no longer restricted to certain groups in limited geographic localities. As a result of globalization, eating disorders are now prevalent among girls in every strata of American culture and in at least 40 countries worldwide.[3] The rapid spread of eating disorders both in the United States and around the world suggests that something is happening in the lives of contemporary girls and women to place them at risk. To understand, prevent, and treat these conditions, we must ask: *why girls and why now?*

This chapter explores how current cultural values, attitudes, and practices—with particular emphasis on the sexualization and objectification of women and their bodies—contribute to eating disorders and body image distress in females across the life span. In a highly charged sexual environment, girls feel pressure to look "sexy" but also fear sexual vulnerability and violence. Girls' bodies become simultaneously "hot commodities" and danger zones. Eating disorder symptoms, such as excessive dieting, exercise abuse, and purging, can become a safety net yet lead to their own risks with high costs to the physical, emotional, cognitive, social, and spiritual health of suffering females and their loved ones.

GENDER, MENTAL HEALTH, AND EATING DISORDERS

Why girls and why now? The questions are increasingly urgent as eating disorders become homogenized across class, age, race, ethnicity, and culture. In its 2000 evidence-based review of women's mental health, the World Health Organization concluded that gender is the strongest determinant of mental health and status.[4] Although overall rates of psychiatric illness are gender neutral, females suffer much higher rates of unipolar depression, anxiety, eating disorders, and somatic complaints; they are also more likely to have more persistent and debilitating depression and comorbid conditions.

The single-best predictor of risk for developing an eating disorder is being born female.[5] Although eating disorders are not the only gendered psychiatric condition, the degree of gender disparity for eating disorders is much greater than in other diagnoses. Anorexia nervosa and bulimia nervosa are 10 times more common in females than in males, and binge-eating disorder is three times more common.[6] Among psychiatric conditions, eating disorders have the highest morbidity; anorexia nervosa has an estimated 10 percent mortality rate at 10 years of symptom duration and 20 percent at 20-year follow-up.[7] Anorexia is the leading cause of death for young women from 15 to 24 years old with a general mortality rate 12 times the expected death rate for women in that age group and a suicide rate that is 75 times greater.[8] Less is known about the mortality rate associated with bulimia nervosa, due both to the potential long-lasting medical consequences and to diagnostic limitations. For example, as many as half of anorexic women will also develop bulimic symptoms but they will still be diagnosed with anorexia.[9] Even less is known about females diagnosed with unspecified eating disorders—in other words, eating disorders that don't meet the precise criteria for anorexia or bulimia— even though these disorders constitute as many as 40 percent of admissions to treatment programs and their symptoms and treatment needs are just as serious.

Subclinical eating disorders are an additional threat because they may compromise health over time or emerge into full-blown eating disorders. This term is applied to women who may be symptomatic sporadically or whose symptoms do not quite meet the criteria for a full-blown eating disorder. Still, girls and women with subclinical eating disorders suffer emotional distress, including depression, anxiety, obsessive thinking, compulsive behaviors, low self-esteem, and body shame. They may also have physical problems such as gastrointestinal disruptions, impaired immune systems, menstrual irregularities, osteopenia or osteoporosis, and general poor health.[10]

Although estimates vary, two comprehensive studies provide com- pelling data regarding the common use of pathogenic weight control techniques in teenagers whose bodies are still developing and growing. Neither report gives diagnostic information so the actual number of full clinical eating disorders or subclinical eating disorders is unclear; yet the research does speak to the fact that serious dieting and other weight loss practices are now normative in nonclinical samples of high school students. A study of more than 80,000 9th and 12th graders in the United States found that over half of the girls engaged in unsafe dieting practices, including skipping meals, restricting their caloric intake, ingesting diet pills or laxatives, inducing vomiting, smoking cigarettes (for the purpose of affecting their weight and food intake), and binge eating. Hispanic and Native American students had the highest rates.[11] The Centers for Disease Control also report epidemic rates of weight loss attempts in high school students, with 46 percent trying to lose weight, 44 percent actively dieting, and 60 percent exer- cising to lose weight or avoid gaining it.[12] Although both sexes reported significant weight concerns, the breakdown by gender shows that girls are engaging in dangerous dieting much more than boys. These trends cannot be reduced to a genetic anomaly; they can only be explained as a consequence of significant and destructive cultural atti- tudes and pressures uniquely affecting today's girls and women.

NATURE OR NURTURE? GENES OR CULTURE?

Eating disorders are multidetermined phenomena; the common final pathway for biological predispositions, psychological vulnera- bilities, painful emotional or developmental experiences, family dysfunction, psychosocial stressors, and cultural pressures. Despite these multiple contributing risk factors, a disproportionate amount of the recent research on eating disorders has focused on genes and biogenetic vulnerability. Genes, however, do not code behavior or disease; rather they code RNA and DNA, the building blocks of cells, creating variations associated with risk. Regardless of revolutionary advances, we are far from knowing how genomic variations alter protein development in the cell and affect the functional circuits of neurons.[13] In view of the speed at which eating disorders have proliferated in countries where they were previously unknown as globalization introduces Western values, the "nurture" or environment side of the nature–nurture debate appears to be the more compelling explanation. Although it is highly unlikely that a gene for eating disorders will be found, persuasive evidence exists to substantiate the impact of media images and cultural trends on the body image and eating habits of today's women regardless of their age.

A dramatic example of how quickly Western values and trends can promote eating disorders occurred in Fiji after Western television was introduced. Eating disorders were unknown there in 1995, but after less than three years of limited exposure to Western network television shows, eating disorders were rampant. In 1995 discussion about diet and weight was almost nonexistent. By 1998 11 percent of Fijian women used self-induced vomiting, 29 percent were at risk for an eating disorder, 69 percent had dieted to lose weight, and 74 percent felt "too fat." Watching popular Western programs created a desire for the lifestyles of Hollywood stars or the characters they portrayed and a commitment to change their bodies to get it. With startling speed, strong Fijian traditions and values—in which large female bodies were valued for their strength and food was celebrated and enjoyed with rich traditions and meanings—were overturned, seemingly overnight. The Fiji experience demonstrates how rapidly global influences can vanquish strong local cultural traditions and values.[14]

A compelling body of research has shown that media images and influences are a major contribution to eating disorders.[15] The more a girl is exposed to media, the more likely she is to diet and be dissatisfied with her body, her appearance, and herself, placing her at serious risk for eating disorders, depression, and anxiety. Adolescent girls who attempt suicide often report that weight and body image contributed significantly to their despair.

Female undergraduate students report more stress, depression, guilt, shame, insecurity, and body dissatisfaction after exposure to ultra-thin models, and 70 percent of college women report feeling worse about themselves after reading magazines.[16] They rarely hear the message that they (or someone who looks like them) are beautiful just as they are. And it comes as no surprise that men also see women as less attractive after exposure to magazines. A systematic review of magazine articles reveals an inordinate emphasis on women's bodies as compared to men's, the not very subtle implication being that many things may be important for men, but only the body counts for women.[17] Girls are constantly portrayed in silly positions, sometimes off balance, often passively observing others, whereas boys are active, powerful, and in control. In fact, despite increased awareness of sexism and gender equity issues, women are actually more sexualized and objectified in magazine ads today than they were in the 1980s. Female body exposure has increased with almost 53 percent of black women and 62 percent of white women scantily clad; only 25 percent of men are presented this way. More than 17 percent of ads show women in lower-status positions, such as on their knees or on the floor. Black women are particularly apt to be photographed in sexualized predatory poses, often wearing animal prints.

The female body is typically portrayed as an ornament rather than an instrument, and its objectification and sexualization are everywhere. The trend in advertising is to use a partially clad, emaciated, but often well-endowed young woman's body to advertise anything and everything. The ad could be for diamonds, men's cologne, shoes, a health club, a car: the product is irrelevant, but the message is crystal clear. A woman's naked and highly sexualized body is the gold standard for advertising, with pornographic images on highway billboards, in magazines, on family coffee-tables, in professional waiting rooms, and on our private Internet screens. The *Sports Illustrated* swimsuit issue, often the only issue in the entire year to feature a woman on the cover, has become nothing more than soft porn.

In essence, contemporary culture not only holds strict unreachable standards for girls regarding weight, shape, and appearance; it also treats their bodies as sexual objects, whose purpose is to please others, especially men. Thin means sexy, and sexy means thin; both attributes are idealized, admired, and rigorously pursued.

WHAT A GROWING GIRL SEES: SEX, SEX, SEX

No matter how hard a family or caring adults may try, it is virtually impossible to protect a growing and impressionable girl from the ubiquitous images and messages regarding the female body and how it is valued and judged. Even dolls, which were once the hallmark of innocent play, have evolved into sexual entities. Barbie dolls have become sexier, and new lines of dolls like The Scene and Bratz, marketed to girls aged 5 to 7, have a sexually provocative, tougher, and more adult edge. Clothing companies have developed thongs for little girls, some of which come complete with "eye candy" written on them, prompting a successful protest from organizations such as Dads and Daughters.

The sexualization of young girls is rampant and does not appear to be waning, despite the concerns of parents and professional organizations such as the American Psychological Association (APA). In 2007 the APA convened a task force to examine the breadth and impact of this problem, and they concluded that girls' sexualization creates a variety of harmful and lasting consequences. These include individual harm, such as: impaired cognitive functioning due to intrusive and negative thoughts, body dissatisfaction, emotional distress, negative self-image, eating disorders, and health problems. Furthermore, sexualization causes general harm because it promotes a culture that perpetuates these serious problems. Sexualization is by no means a victimless crime, and it is beginning to prey on girls at increasingly younger ages. The APA report speculates that sexualization reflects underlying sexism, a troubling tolerance for violence against women, and the ongoing exploitation of girls and women.[18]

The dangers of sexualization are ubiquitous in our culture. Beauty pageants for preschool girls introduce them to a world of sexual objectification and the crafting of a false self before they are even in school.[19] Cosmetic companies develop products specifically for little girls just past toddlerhood, and in some fashion shows and magazine layouts adult models are made up to look like little girls while wearing racy, revealing lingerie. Entertainment media is a potent vehicle for sexualization because children and teens spend more time engaged with it than any other activity with the exception of school and sleep.[20] Primetime television is rife with images and entertainment that sexualizes and denigrates women, and 85 percent of the time, this treatment occurs at the hands of male characters.[21] An analysis of situation comedies that are based in the workplace found an average of 3.3 gender harassment incidents and .5 sexual harassment incidents per show. Nearly three fourths of the shows included one or more incidents of gender harassment, most presented as jokes with laugh tracks.[22] As a result, many young women come to believe that such treatment is to be expected, and they try to deny the impact when these events occur in real life. Some of these women will suffer post-traumatic stress disorder, eating disorders, or both, as a result of this self-silencing.

A unique study that examined the presentation of gender roles and hypersexuality in the 300 top-grossing G, PG, or PG-13 films produced between 1990 and 2006 revealed troubling but predictable trends.[23] First, gender equity was found to be virtually nonexistent: Seventy-three percent of the speaking roles were male, with no change in this regard during the 16-year time span. Second, the female characters were either hypersexualized or homemakers. Females were more than five times as likely to be clad in sexually revealing outfits, typically covering a distorted, very thin body. These distortions included tiny waists and flat stomachs, suggesting no room for reproductive organs or any other biological function. Lean figures were graphically altered into lollipop or cigarette-slim shapes. Females had abnormally thin bodies three times more often than males. Third, the female roles were best described as "eye candy." Women were primarily cast as beautiful, desirable, and ornamental rather than instrumental to the plot. Finally, ethnic diversity was nearly absent: 85 percent of the identifiable characters were white, followed by black characters (8 percent), Hispanic (less than 2 percent), and other ethnicities (negligible).

Advertising that is directed at "tweens," children who are still in elementary school, exploits their desire to be seen as older and more independent by using models that look more like sexualized teens. Preteens are thus encouraged to act, dress, think, and spend money like teens.[24] The entertainment industry does the same, promoting young stars to even younger fans, pressuring them to identify with sexual images years before their bodies enter puberty.

Sex Week at Yale is an example of how pornography has become part of the mainstream. According to Gail Dines, a leader in the feminist antipornography movement, Yale University recently invited pornographer Steve Hirsch, founder of Vivid Studios, to speak about how he has contributed to mainstreaming porn.[25] His "Vivid Girls" are considered "the elite of porn," as they enjoy better pay and somewhat better working conditions than is standard for the industry. Most porn actresses have grown up in adverse conditions with damaged self-esteem and limited opportunities for advancement. Many of these women will eventually work as prostitutes, dealing with problems such as substance abuse, STDs, and sexual violence. Vivid Girls put a wholesome face on this woman-destroying industry and are used to recruit other women into it. Included in the Yale activities was the contest "Who Looks Most like a Vivid Girl?" Imagine the reactions of high school coeds and their parents visiting the campus that week.

These days attending a sporting event can feel markedly similar to going to a strip club because cheerleaders' choreographies, energy, and costumes are provocative and sexually suggestive. The National Organization for Women conducted a study of the ads featured during the 2008 Super Bowl, one of the most popular family programs of the year.[26] Advertisers paid $2.7 million for 30-second commercials. On the few occasions when women appeared, they were portrayed as passive objects rather than active players in the storyline with virtually nonexistent speaking roles, and their sexual availability to men seemed to be the primary theme or sales pitch. Most people are so desensitized to such ads and messages that they are never discussed or challenged.

SEXUALIZATION AND SELF-OBJECTIFICATION

Frederickson and Roberts explain that chronic sexual objectification has a lasting impact because it pressures girls to accept an external view of themselves and of their value as people.[27] Girls come to see themselves as objects to be looked at and judged based on their appearance. Acceptance of an external standard results in constant monitoring and self-scrutiny so that individuals have fewer and fewer resources for internal awareness and become less and less aware of internal body states and experiences. With external standards so rigid and unattainable, girls become increasingly ashamed and distressed about their bodies.[28] Bandura's groundbreaking research found that when people fail to meet cultural ideals, intrusive thoughts may undermine cognitive functions.[29] Because women earn less, have less status and power, and are more likely to be victims, failing to meet the cultural standard has a higher price, literally and figuratively, for them.[30] Intrusive and obsessive self-disparaging thoughts, absent other areas in which they feel successful, will easily compromise a growing girl's sense of self as well as her cognitive and emotional functioning.

According to Tiggemann and Slater, the cumulative effect of self-objectification creates risk for three psychological issues: depression, sexual dysfunction, and eating disorders.[31] Their study of former classical ballet dancers and nondancers found that the dancers had higher levels of self-objectification and self-surveillance and that these issues continued even when they were no longer dancing, demonstrating that self-objectification is not only a temporary state but may become an internalized and long-lasting trait. Self-objectification coexists with many of the risk factors associated with eating disorders, including diminished interoceptive awareness, poor self-esteem, body shame, and disordered eating.[32] Researchers Thompson and Stice posit that internalization of the thin ideal is among the best predictors for body image distress and disordered eating.[33]

Having internalized the negative external gaze, girls today want a body that is hardly natural or feminine; instead it is like a boy's body, but with a washboard stomach and big breasts. As a result, the number one wish of girls aged 11 to 17 is to lose weight, and plastic surgery for teens increased by nearly 50 percent in two years in the late 1990s and continues to increase each year.[34] One poll found that 25 percent of teenaged girls in the United States had already considered cosmetic plastic surgery, even before their bodies matured.[35] Taught to please others—to constantly strive to meet the cultural ideal for women while being systematically objectified and sexualized—creates constant self-doubt and insecurity, problems that the rituals and obsessions of eating disorders can temporarily mask.

DEVELOPMENTAL VULNERABILITY: AN ECOLOGICAL APPROACH

Decades ago, developmental psychologist Urie Bronfenbrenner described child development as an ecological system embedded in five layers or contexts.[36] These include:

- the child herself with her own genetic and physical traits or vulnerabilities
- the microsystem, composed of parents, siblings, and school and social experiences having a direct impact on the child
- the mesosystem, or interactions of the microsystem components, such as conflicts between family and school
- the exosystem, systems outside the family with a less direct effect on the child, including the health care system or media
- the macrosystem, composed of both the formal and informal values and beliefs of the culture

Levine and Smolak note that Bronfenbrenner's ecological system elucidates the interaction of the culture and its institutions, the family, and the individual, and creates a helpful starting point to understand the many influences on human behavior and development, especially how self-objectification can contribute to risk factors associated with eating disorders.[37]

Adolescence is always a critical time in identity formation. While absorbing as much information as possible, the teenage mission is to figure out who they are and what they want to become. Teens are keenly aware of cultural standards and ideals through intense exposure to the media and its messages in all forms, and at the same time they spend a minimum of time with their families. As a result, media exerts an immense psychological impact on them. Teenage girls, the group with the highest risk for disordered eating and body image distress, are especially vulnerable to the media and therefore to self-objectification.

The teen years are also prime time for social comparison, and the Internet has created unprecedented and relentless access to peer pressure. Girls are particularly vulnerable to peer pressure because they are socialized to place greater value on relationships and pleasing others as compared to boys. Mary Pipher elucidates the dangerous consequences of the process I describe above. Unaware of or ashamed of their own needs, values, and emotions, girls readily succumb to pressures outside of themselves.[38] The emphasis on thin sexy bodies as the vehicle for female success and admiration resonates loud and clear, often resulting in disordered eating and body image obsessions and behaviors.

Although much of the research concerning the impact of media images on youth focuses on teens and college students, a recent study demonstrated that boys and girls in grades 1 through 5 also idealize media images, and that girls are more likely to internalize the attitudes and standards projected on the screen.[39] Another study that assessed a group of children at 11 years of age and again at 13 years reported that objectification appears to affect the emotional well-being of girls but not of boys.[40] Compared to the boys, the girls suffered to a much greater degree from self-objectification, body shame, rumination, and depression.

Bronfenbrenner's ecological framework helps to shed light on how external standards evolve into internalized risks to health and well-being. The growing cultural obsession with thinness and beauty is now so pervasive that weight and body image concerns are even overheard in kindergarten playgroups. Girls' natural weight gain and change in shape preceding and during adolescence places them at odds with the cultural ideal of female beauty so that their self-monitoring, which may have started years earlier, intensifies. When puberty hits and a girl's shape drifts from a childlike to a womanly silhouette, rates of depression increase.[41] Furthermore, sexual development is starting earlier with white girls on average developing breasts and pubic hair at age 10 and African Americans at 9.[42] In a sexually charged atmosphere, with their bodies entering puberty at increasingly younger ages, girls are confused and stressed, engaging in sex earlier and also succumbing to eating disorders earlier.[43] Adding to the confusion, girls are bombarded with marketing for feminine hygiene products that wash away any true sign (or scent) of sexuality.[44] The constant subliminal message is that the natural female body must be controlled or disguised, creating an excruciating level of self-consciousness, fertile ground for the development of disordered eating and body image despair.

Girls are also more vulnerable than boys to sexual harassment and abuse, which intensifies body image concerns and can lead to self-destructive thoughts and behaviors.[45] Sexual harassment, when combined with the impact of sexualized media images, contributes to self-objectification, which can lead to body image and eating issues.[46] At every age, girls are inundated with criticisms and comments about their bodies both through media and in their personal lives. Even in elementary school, boys feel free to disparage girls' bodies in their presence.[47] With both anonymous and deeply personal messages conveying a constant stream of criticism, girls simply do not feel safe in their skin. By internalizing and trying desperately to meet external standards, they hope to find safety and self-acceptance.

YES, SOMETHING'S HAPPENING HERE

Something is indeed happening that places girls of all ages at tremendous risk. Living in a culture that is hostile to them, that sees them as sexual objects, and gives them little freedom to be themselves creates overwhelming conflicts and challenges. Taught from a young age that they should be sexy, edgy, and seek male attention, girls are burdened by sexual objectification, harassment, stereotypes, and violence. Having been raised to please others, most will attempt to meet external standards, trying desperately to become the ideal sexy, thin, perfect girl. Years of self-objectification keep girls from knowing their basic needs and feelings. Cut off from their internal voice and pressured by relentless and loud external demands, girls are vulnerable to the damage that is wrought when they attempt to craft and control their bodies by dieting.

Eating-disordered behaviors and ideas can initially function to solve the problem of the following questions: How do I succeed as a woman in this culture? How will I be accepted and valued? Who am I? What is special about me? Eating-disordered behaviors can also be ways to expose their pain, anger, uniqueness, self-control, discipline, independence, and many other important attributes or feelings. But, before long, the behaviors and beliefs associated with eating disorders create their own very serious problems, invading every aspect of their hosts' lives, robbing them of any remaining vestiges of self-confidence or happiness, compromising every organ and system in their bodies, and causing emotional, spiritual, and mental torment.

The sexualization and objectification of girls are not victimless crimes. The costs to the well-being of girls and women are far too high.

Nor is this a "woman's issue," as Frederick Douglass pointed out, in 1848, about any discrimination against or harm of women during another era:

> This cause is not altogether and exclusively women's cause. It is the cause of human brotherhood as well as human sisterhood, and both must rise and fall together. Women cannot be elevated without elevating man, and man cannot be depressed without depressing women also.[48]

We have much to learn from Douglass's words; men *and* women must rally to challenge the sexualization and objectification of women and transform modern culture so that it embraces and empowers both sexes to be equal partners, thus creating a better world for future generations. In such a world, women would no longer suffer from culturally constructed, life-threatening illnesses such as eating disorders.

6

So Sexy, So Soon: The Sexualization of Childhood

Diane E. Levin

CHANGING TIMES

The feature story in the May 2004 issue of the *New York Times Magazine* was called "Friends, Friends with Benefits and the Benefits of the Local Mall."[1] One hundred suburban teenagers were interviewed for the article. They described a world of casual sexual encounters devoid of emotions or relationships. "Hooking up" and "friends with benefits" are part of the new slang to describe casual sex with friends. The author of the story, Benoit Denizet-Lewis, reported that "the teenagers talked about hookups as matter-of-factly as they might discuss what's on the cafeteria lunch menu."[2] Sixteen-year-old Brian put it this way: "Being in a real relationship just complicates everything. When you're friends with *benefits,* you go over, hook up, then play video games or something. It rocks."[3] Formal dating relationships were frowned upon. In the words of Irene, a high school senior, "It would be so weird if a guy came up to me and said, 'Irene, I'd like to take you out on a date.' I'd probably laugh at him. It would be sweet, but it would be so weird."[4]

Three days after the *New York Times* story appeared, the *Boston Globe* published an op-ed piece by Scot Lehigh, who bemoaned the realities of the casual and unencumbered sexual behavior revealed by the teenagers. "It's truly sad to read of a high school generation too detached to date, too indifferent for romance, too distant for commitment. . . . You can't help but hope that today's teenagers will come to understand that to rob sex of romance, to divorce it from emotion, is to deny themselves exactly what makes it special."[5]

Besides describing and bemoaning a "surprising" change in adolescent sexual behavior, attitudes, and relationships, neither article paid any attention to the root cause of these changes. Nor did they connect this issue to other related concerns about the overall health, development, and well-being of today's youth, such as the growing number of children and teens who regularly view cyberporn,[6] an upsurge in teen dating violence,[7] and eating disorders.[8]

In order to address concerns about adolescents' sexual behavior, we need to start with a better understanding of the factors that are shaping their ideas about gender, sexuality, and interpersonal relationships. We also need to understand how the "casual sex epidemic" relates to other aspects of their lives. An essential starting point for developing this understanding is through an examination of the vastly expanded role of media and commercial culture in children's lives over the past 3 decades.[9]

NEW SEXUAL ISSUES IN CHILDHOOD

As I read the *New York Times* article, I was reminded of accounts that I had been hearing with increasing frequency about the changing content of sexual issues that are being raised by young children today. Here are a few particularly salient examples:

"Professional Wrestling Girls with Big Boobies"

Kara, a kindergarten teacher, showed me an entry that her student James had recently made in his "daily diary." It was a drawing of a woman with long hair and big, bright red lips with the letters *WWWWWWF* scrawled beside it. When Kara asked him to formulate a caption for the picture, he asked her to write *a professional wrestling girl with big boobies.* "At first I thought he was trying to be 'fresh,' to cause trouble," Kara told me, "but I caught myself before I reacted too harshly and asked James what he knew about 'wrestling girls.' He replied with his eyes open wide, 'I saw her on TV last night with my dad. That's how she looked!' I was pretty taken aback that his parents let him watch such a program [rated TV-14]. But it's what he's seeing that really worries me. I wonder if he made his drawing because he needed someone to talk to about it?"

Skinny Bodies Are Sexy

A couple of years ago, Shirley, the mother of 7-year-old Brenda, reported an incident that distressed her greatly. On and off for several weeks, Brenda had been asking Shirley how you "go on a diet." This had escalated into Brenda stating that she *was* going on a diet. A couple of days later, Shirley found Brenda crying in the bathtub. When she asked her what was wrong, Brenda responded, "I'm fat. I want to be sexy like Joanie, pretty like Joanie [the very thin, seemingly very popular girl in Brenda's class]!" Shirley assured me that her daughter had a normal 7-year-old girl's body. However, she didn't think it was age-appropriate for her little girl to be thinking about being "sexy" and wanting to diet. Shirley began wondering what kinds of experiences outside of her family were contributing to this problem. She felt anxious and unsure about how best to respond in the short run. Also she had heard news stories about preteen girls' precocious sexual behavior and eating disorders and worried about what the psychological and physical consequences might be for Brenda in the long run.

"What's a Blow Job?"

Recently Margie told me that her 7-year-old daughter, Eva, had asked, "Mom, what's a blow job?" Her first reaction was to tell Eva that it wasn't something for children and end it there. Instead she asked, "Where did you hear about blow jobs?" Eva replied that she had heard about them at school. Margie asked, "What did you hear about it?" Eva responded, "It's sex." Margie told me that she worked hard to protect Eva from exposure to violence and sex in the media, but now that Eva was with many children who were not as protected, she felt that she was rapidly losing control. Although she expected that she would talk to Eva about issues such as oral sex during the adolescent or even the pre-adolescent years, she was alarmed when it had come up at age 7! Furthermore, she felt very uncertain about what was appropriate to tell Eva.

Learning about Sex from the Internet

About 6 years ago, Connie, who is highly experienced at teaching sex education to 5th- and 6th-graders, called me to express concern about something that had come up in a discussion with a group of male students. She had been talking about sex as an expression of deep affection between partners in a relationship. One of her students, Gabe, challenged her by saying, "Well, you don't need to *like* the person. I saw sex on the Internet. My cousin showed me. They just do it 'cause it's fun, they like it." A couple of boys seemed surprised, but a few others said that they had seen sex on the Internet, too. Connie felt that she had entered new territory in terms of how to respond to the children and how to approach their parents about it. But she was glad that the boys had raised the issue because clearly it had been very much on their minds. I talked to Connie again 5 years later, and she said that dealing with Internet pornography has now become a regular part of her sex education work with 5th and 6th-grade boys. She finds that by this age almost all of the boys have viewed some sort of pornography on the Internet, either by coming upon it accidentally or by having another boy show it to them. And few of them have discussed what they have seen or what it means to them with an adult before Connie raised the issue.

Each of the above stories provides a snapshot of children, some at a very young age, struggling to work out ideas about things that they saw in the media or heard from friends about sex and gender. Current research and public discourse about sexual behavior and development rarely focus on children before the age of 9 or 10. Yet clearly exposure to sexual content in childhood will influence adolescent behavior.[10] The lessons that the youth in the *New York Times* article learned when they were young laid the foundation for their current sexual attitudes and behavior. What were those lessons? Where did they come from? What can we learn from them to help us raise children with healthy gender and sexual identities in the midst of the increasing sexualization of childhood?

MESSAGES ABOUT SEX AND GENDER IN OUR CULTURE

Children's ideas about gender, sex, and sexuality develop gradually and are greatly influenced by information that their environments provide. Increasingly, children's environments are dominated by unregulated electronic media.[11] A 2003 Kaiser Family Foundation report found that children aged 0 to 6 years averaged approximately 2 hours of "screen time" a day and that 30 percent of children aged 3 and under and 43 percent of children from 4 to 6 years old had a television set in their bedroom. According to the authors, "This study documented a potentially revolutionary phenomenon in American society: the immersion of our very youngest children, from a few months to a few years old, in the world of electronic and interactive media."[12]

As children are glued to the screen, they are exposed to a very large quotient of sexual material. According to a Kaiser Family Foundation survey, during the 1999–2000 television season, 68 percent of programming contained information of a sexual nature, up from 56 percent in 1997.[13] In a similar survey, 75 percent of traditional TV "family hour" programs were found to have sexual content, compared with 43 percent 20 years earlier.[14] Although studies have confirmed that children learn about sex from the media, more research is needed to fully document and understand the impact of such exposure.[15]

Although much of the graphic sexual content in the media is rated as appropriate for adolescents and adults, children are nonetheless viewing these programs much like 5-year-old James, who watches professional wrestling on TV with his father. Telling James that the sex and violence on the show are "just pretend," as many adults do, is not meaningful to young children who see real people doing real things. Other programs with sexual content that children routinely watch include soap operas, talk shows, and MTV.

A particularly alarming source of sexual content is highly accessible Internet pornography, which almost any child who does homework using Internet sources can access. Yet, on June 30, 2004, the Supreme Court rejected Congress's *Child Online Protection Act* designed to curb children's access to sexually explicit material on the Internet.[16]

Children are also exposed to sexualized toys, many of which are linked to TV shows, video games, and movies. Some of these "toys" foster associations between sex and violence. For example, Sable, a professional wrestling action figure, has large breasts and wears tight black leather pants, an unzipped bra top, and spiky red heels. She comes with a whip. On the back of Sable's box are photos of other professional wrestling action figures you can buy—including Billy Gunn, who has lipstick marks on his boxer shorts, and Al Snow, who is holding the severed head of a woman.[17] According to Sable's manufacturers, she is a suitable toy for children "ages 4 and up," whereas the professional wrestling TV programs that she is linked with are rated TV-14. Creating toys based on TV programs rated for teens and movies rated R implicitly assumes that young children are watching these shows. Programming and toys that are marketed to boys, such as professional wrestling programs and their action figures, teach boys that males should always be physically powerful and ready to fight, and that sex involves aggressive domination of beautiful women who serve as objects for male pleasure.

Girls are receiving different but equally shallow messages about being female and sexuality from toys and the media. Girls are taught that they should have skinny bodies and that they need to be consumers of clothing, makeup, and accessories in order to look "pretty," "grown-up," and "sexy."[18] We see this message expressed through *Barbie Lingerie,* a doll that comes dressed in sheer black lingerie and stockings. The packaging of the popular, sexy *Bratz* dolls contains the message "The girls with a passion for fashion." *Boston Globe* parenting reporter Barbara Meltz concluded, "There is only one [Bratz] story line: girl as sex object."[19] Bratz dolls have been enormously successful in the marketplace. In fact, Bratz sales surpassed Barbie doll sales in 2006.[20]

Sexualized images of femaleness are reinforced through the appearance and behavior of female characters on TV, in video games, and in movies—Bratz dolls now have a TV show and a much publicized movie in the summer of 2007. Even the much trusted Disney movies—should they be?—have escalated the sexualized images they show. For instance, Pocahontas has more cleavage, fewer clothes, and is much sexier than Cinderella ever was. The music and videos of pop stars such as Britney Spears and Christina Aguilera are regular features in most young girls' lives beginning in preschool. A grandmother of a 4-year-old girl laments,

> Jenna, my 4-year-old granddaughter, and I were in a store buying shoes for the new school year. The radio was playing and she said to the sales clerk, "Is that the Spice Girls singing?" He shook his head "No," and asked if she liked the Spice Girls. She nodded her head. He asked, "What's your favorite song?" Jenna looked at him coyly and said, "Let Me Be Your Lover!" When he asked if she knew the words to the song, she began to sing the song—including all the "gyrations" of her little body. I wanted to sink into a hole and cry![21]

Increasingly, young girls are encouraged to act in sexual ways in their daily lives. For instance, beauty pageants, like the ones in which JonBenet Ramsey participated, channel young girls into precocious sexual appearance and behavior. I recently heard an account of 5- to 8-year-old girls in Texas who were training as cheerleaders. They dress in clothing usually worn by much older cheerleaders. Here's an example of one of their chants:

> Like totally, for sure,
> I just got a manicure.
> The sun up there
> is bleaching out my gorgeous hair.
> 16, 24, I don't know the silly score.
> Go, go! Fight, fight!
> Gee, I hope I look all right!

The highly publicized account of Janet Jackson's exposed breast during the halftime show at the Super Bowl in 2004 served as a useful lightning rod for public concern about sexual content in the media. However, Justin Timberlake's gesture of ripping off part of her top—a sexually aggressive gesture—was far more offensive than her naked breast and yet rarely mentioned. The anger and blame directed at Janet rather than Justin speaks to deeply held cultural biases that are then amplified by the media.

THE IMPACT OF TELEVISION DEREGULATION ON THE SEXUALIZATION OF CHILDHOOD

In 1984 the Federal Communications Commission deregulated children's television, making it possible to market television programs and toys together for the first time. The television and toy industries quickly joined forces to create whole lines of toys and other products, such as bedsheets, pajamas, and breakfast cereals, which were linked to children's programs.

Increased Gender Stereotyping

Soon after the deregulation of television, I began hearing concerns voiced by parents and teachers about incidents with children involving gender stereotyping. Many of the stories, such as the one with Brenda in the bathtub above, involved girls focused on body image and appearance. Increasingly, girls were expressing the desire to be thin, pretty, sweet, and nice. At the same time, early childhood educators who had been in the field for a long time began reporting that they were seeing increased gender divisions in children's classroom play.

As I began to explore why this might be the case, I found that in the wake of deregulation, children's television programs had become highly gender divided and gender stereotyped. *My Little Pony* was one of the most popular TV programs for girls in the 1980s. The program's best-selling toy line included such items as combs, makeup, and a vanity table. Media deregulation contributed to a major setback in efforts during the 1960s and 1970s to reduce gender stereotyping in childhood culture and expand children's definitions of what it meant to be a boy or a girl.

Increased Sexual Content

In 2007 a Kaiser Family Foundation study[22] found that over half of the parents surveyed were worried about the sexual content that their children were exposed to on TV.[23] Parents and professionals alike are increasingly concerned that they are losing control over how children are introduced to ideas about sex and sexuality. Yet this issue is drawing far less attention, criticism, or controversy than violence in the popular culture does. For example, in stark contrast to extensive research on the impact of media violence, there is almost no research to date that has explored how the increasingly sexualized media and popular culture are affecting children, especially in relation to younger children.[24] One possible explanation is that talking about sex is much more complicated and less clear-cut than talking about violence. We are all in relative agreement that "violence is bad" and that it is desirable for children to use nonviolent approaches to solving their conflicts, and we have direct ways to convey and teach this message. By contrast, the messages we hope to convey about sex and sexuality are complex and age dependent.

DERAILED PSYCHOSEXUAL DEVELOPMENT

Children's psychosexual awareness and understanding are gradually constructed over time. As infants they explore their bodies, and they experience the emotional and sensory pleasures of embraces and kisses and the satisfaction of being deeply attached to a parent or other caregiver. At around 18 months they learn to refer to themselves as boys or girls, and they slowly begin working out the meanings of these labels. Learning is influenced by their developmental maturity and by the experiences and information their environment provides.[25] If there is a consistently healthy match between experiences and the information provided by their environment and their level of development, then they will likely become capable of mature and meaningful social and sexual relationships in adulthood.

However, as the stories I recounted earlier illustrate, these days there is a mismatch between young children's psychosexual maturity and the sexual information to which they are routinely exposed. Not only is the content too graphic, but portrayals of highly stereotyped maleness and femaleness, male sexual domination of women, and women as sex objects are not ones that most parents would wish children of any age to be exposed to.

HOW CHILDREN THINK AFFECTS WHAT THEY LEARN

Children between the ages of 3 and 6 years old are typically drawn to content that is visible and concrete.[26] They often use play and art as vehicles for understanding their world. We see this kind of thinking at work when James focuses on the big red lips and "big boobies" (undoubtedly a term he learned from someone older than himself) of the "wrestling girl" in his drawing. James's drawing is a vehicle with which to explore what he witnessed on television and one that helps him make contact with his teacher. We also see Brenda focusing on concrete aspects of her experience when she equates Joanie's thinness with "sexiness." The media feeds into and reinforces children's one-dimensional concrete thinking with its increasingly shallow focus on appearance, as seen in the recent deluge of "makeover" shows.

With their focus on the concrete, young children also have a hard time understanding the motives, intentions, and feelings underlying sexual behavior. When Eva asked her mother about "blow jobs," this characteristic of her thinking would lead her to focus on the sexual act and not on what her mother might say about the nature of the relationship that would result in this behavior. We see this aspect of thinking at work when Brenda focuses on how fat her body looks compared to that of Joanie, the thin, popular girl in her class. Brenda does not look at other factors that might contribute to friendship and popularity; she considers only appearance. This kind of thinking predisposes young children to think that their appearance (and not their behavior or ideas) determines what people think of them and how they treat them. Although Brenda's and Eva's thought processes are normal, we have to wonder about the normality of a culture that obligates 7-year-olds to think at all about sexiness and "blow jobs." Clearly, these precocious lessons on sex and gender are contributing to the rise in dieting and eating disorders among pre-teen and adolescent girls.[27]

Another common feature of young children's thinking is that they often attend to only one thing at a time. When Brenda thinks about being sexy, she focuses on one attribute: Joanie's thinness. When Kara asks James "what he knows about wrestling girls," he responds with one piece of information: "I saw it on TV with my dad." Often the one thing a child attends to is himself or herself. This is connected to young children's egocentrism—their failure to think about the impact of what they do on someone else. Similarly, when Jenna imitated the suggestive words and sexy gyrations of a Spice Girls song for the shoe salesman, she seemed totally oblivious about what her grandmother or others around her might think (or whether other children in her environment did such things). Because young children attend to one thing at a time, their thinking is often more like a slide than a movie. That is, they tend to deal with one static moment or a series of non-logically connected static moments. They do not focus on logical causality or relationships between events. This limits children's ability to understand the sexual behaviors they are viewing. It can also make it hard for them to sort out what is pretend and what is real.

By contrast, when Gabe talks about pornography with his 5th-grade teacher Karen, he reveals his growing ability to process two ideas at once (his and Karen's) and think about intentions that he cannot see (the nature of the relationship in which sex occurs), and he tries to make logical causal connections. Still we must feel outrage that Gabe had to process this information at the tender age of 10 and that his teachers and parents must now work so hard to provide him with a healthier understanding of mature sexuality.

THE HARM CAUSED BY BEING SO SEXY SO SOON

Certainly learning about procreation is a process that begins when children are young and continues to be elaborated on with age and an increased ability to understand. But learning about sex is not the most important part of establishing this foundation for young children. When children are young, we should be laying the foundation for later healthy sexual relationships. We do this by providing children with models of caring and affectionate relationships. We can also answer questions about such issues as physical differences between males and females or "where babies come from." However, today's children are bombarded with large doses of graphic sexual content that they cannot process and that are often frightening. While children struggle to make sense of mature sexual content, they are robbed of valuable time for age-appropriate developmental tasks. They may also begin to engage in precocious sexual behavior and learn lessons that will undermine their ability to have healthy, caring relationships in which sex plays a part when they are older.

Young children are routinely exposed to images of sexual behavior devoid of emotions, attachments, or consequences. They are learning that sex is the defining activity in relationships, to the exclusion of love and friendship. They are learning that sex is often linked to violence. Also, they are learning to associate physical appearance and buying the right accessories with being successful as a person. Such lessons will shape their gender identity, sexual attitudes, values, and their capacity for relationships.

We can see the long-term effects of these lessons in the casual sexual behavior and attitudes among the youth in the *New York Times* article. An escalation in eating disorders among preadolescent and adolescent girls is almost certainly related to images in the media and popular culture that equate thinness with sexiness and popularity. It has become common for girls to start dieting clubs in 5th grade. Seven-year-old Brenda is a prime candidate for such a club! There have also been several reports about the widespread practice of oral sex among middle school students.[28]

A TOLL ON FAMILIES AND PARENTS, TOO

Parents also pay a high price for the sexualization of childhood. In a 2002 survey by an organization called Public Agenda, it was found that 76 percent of parents believed it was a lot harder to raise children today than it was when they were growing up. When asked about the biggest challenge they faced with their children, 47 percent reported that it was trying to protect them from negative societal influences. Certainly one of those influences is the sexualization of childhood in the mainstream culture.[29]

Parents see their children drawn into the sexual content that surrounds them, but talking with children about sex often feels more difficult and more complex than talking about other complex issues such as poverty, violence, or illness. Many adults struggle to talk openly and comfortably about sex and sexuality with other adults, let alone with children, and the task becomes even more daunting in the current context. As we saw in the examples throughout this chapter, when parents see the impact of today's culture on their children (and children often see and know more than we are able to admit) and try to respond or intervene, they worry about doing or saying the wrong thing. It is easy to say things that make children feel guilty or bad, or to cut off the discussion and thereby encourage them to stop seeking their advice altogether. Parents may also begin to deny the potential harm of their children's exposure to graphic sexual content because it has become so ubiquitous in our culture and they are so helpless to stem the tide.

Parents are often told by the wider society (and especially by the industries that markets to children) that *it is their job* to decide what is appropriate for their children and to protect them from what they believe is not appropriate. Although it has never been easy, this task was less difficult for parents in the past when the prevailing cultural messages were more compatible with the values and goals they held for their children. Today parents need to fight the prevailing culture at every turn with younger and younger children. Even the best-prepared and most conscientious parents find it impossible to stem the onslaught of negative media messages.[30]

A CALL TO ACTION

By allowing children to be exposed to information about sex and sexuality that undermines their healthy sexual development, society is failing its children and their families. For too long the increasing sexualization of childhood has not been given the attention it warrants. Until we address this problem as a society and work to regain control over it from those who are motivated solely by financial gain, children, families, and ultimately all of society will pay the price.

First Amendment and free speech arguments are often used to protect industry moguls' and Internet pornographers' right to put anything they choose on the screen, even when that material negatively affects children. The arguments used generally ignore the long history in the United States of creating special policies that protect children from harm—for example, through laws against child abuse and neglect. It is time for all of us to work together to create policies and practices that will help children develop the foundation they need to become adults who are capable of forming positive, caring sexual relationships.

WHAT CAN WE DO IN THE MEANTIME?

Although there are no "magic bullet" solutions, there are many positive steps that we can take to promote healthier sexual development in the current climate.[31]

- Limit exposure to sexual imagery and content in the media and popular culture.[32]
- Establish safe channels for talking about sexual development with children when they are young. Trusted adults have a vital role to play in helping children sort out what they see and hear (no matter how uncomfortable it may make them feel) by answering questions and helping them feel safe asking them. But to open up to adults, children need to know that nothing that they bring up for discussion about what they hear or do is off limits. The more comfortable children feel about raising issues and asking about sexual content when they are young, the better able they will be to use adults to help them process the escalating content they are exposed to as they get older.
- When children are exposed to the inevitable sexual images and messages, expect them to try to work them out in their play, art, and conversations. Pay attention to children's play and art. Talk to them about it. Providing open-ended (versus highly structured) play materials—such as blocks, baby dolls, generic dress-up clothes, miniature people, a doctor's kit, a dollhouse, markers, and paper—can all support children's efforts.
- Try not to blame children or make them feel guilty or ashamed when they do or say something that feels inappropriate. Too often children are blamed and punished when they act on what makes perfect sense given their surroundings. Try to take the child's point of view and see the world through his or her eyes. This is a vital starting point for figuring out what led to an inappropriate behavior and deciding how to respond. Help children find appropriate and realistic alternative

ways to support their efforts to understand as well as alternative ways to get the information and help they need.

- When talking to children about sexual issues, take your lead from what the children do and say and what you know about them as individuals.[33] Base your responses on the age, prior experiences, specific needs, and unique concerns of individual children. Just as many of the adults did in the anecdotes throughout this chapter, try to start by finding out what children know. Before jumping in with the "right" answer, you might ask, "What have you heard about that?" The child's answer can guide what you say next.

- Answer questions and clear up misconceptions that worry or confuse children. You don't need to provide the full story. Just tell children in an age-appropriate way what they need to hear to allay their worry or confusion. Don't worry about giving "right answers" or if children have ideas that don't agree with yours. Clear up misconceptions when doing so seems helpful and appropriate. Try to calmly voice your feelings and concerns and reassure children that they are safe and that you will keep them safe.

- Teach alternative lessons to the messages in the popular culture that undermine healthy sexual development and behavior. What this means will vary with age and experience of the children. Make sure children are exposed to positive and caring relationships between adults at home, at school, and even in the media. Then they will have a foundation for gradually connecting ideas about sex to their understanding of positive adult relationships. Help them experience and express positive physical affection with appropriate people in their lives. Convey clear, age-appropriate guidelines about what is and is not appropriate.

- To the extent possible, try to engage in give-and-take discussions with children when working on all of the guidelines suggested here. Give-and-take conversation can help us decide how to respond and how much information a child actually needs. We can also use situations when sexual content comes up in the media or elsewhere as opportunities to discuss with children what they think about what they saw as well as sharing our own opinions.

- Share your values and concerns with extended family members, teachers, and other parents. The discussions that result can help you build a community of adults who share your values and who will respect rather than undermine your efforts with your child.

- Involve schools in efforts to promote healthy sexual development. In addition to parents' efforts, an important part of this task rests with the schools. Children need age-appropriate sex education programs in schools that help them build ideas about meaningful sexuality and address their real issues and concerns. The outspoken efforts of certain segments of society to preach sexual abstinence until marriage (and without the benefit of meaningful sex education), while at the same time enabling media and corporations to market sex to children more or less as they choose, are untenable and irresponsible.

- Help to create a society that is more supportive of children's healthy gender and sexual development by working to limit the power of corporations to market sex to children.[34] On a positive note, although few major efforts exist today to specifically address the sexualization of childhood, more and more individuals and groups are working at all levels to stop the commercial takeover of childhood. Several organizations have developed strategies and materials that can help you with your efforts. These organizations and their Web site addresses are listed below.

ORGANIZATIONS WORKING TO STOP THE COMMERCIAL EXPLOITATION OF CHILDHOOD

The Alliance for Childhood promotes policies and practices that support children's healthy development, learning, and play. Visit www.allianceforchildhood.net.

The *American Psychological Association* released its Task Force Report on the Sexualization of Girls in 2007. See www.apa.org/prg/pi/wpo/sexualization.html. The APA has also prepared a comprehensive position statement on the negative impact of marketing to children that calls for restrictions on marketing to children. To view the statement, visit www.apa.org/releases/childrenads.pdf.

Campaign for a Commercial-free Childhood (CCFC) is a coalition of many organizations working to reduce marketing to children. For more information, go to www.commercialfreechildhood.com.

Dads and Daughters works to help fathers make the world safe and fair for their daughters. Visit www.dadsanddaughters.org.

Geena Davis Institute on Gender in Media works to educate entertainment creators and the public about the need to decrease gender stereotyping and increase the representation of girls and women in media. See www.thegeenadavisinstitute.org.

Teachers Resisting Unhealthy Children's Entertainment (TRUCE) is a group of educators that prepares materials for parents about effective ways to resist the commercial culture and promote positive play, learning, and social relationships. See www.truceteachers.org.

7

Still on the Auction Block: The (S)exploitation of Black Adolescent Girls in Rap(e) Music and Hip-Hop Culture

Carolyn M. West

The message that young Black women's bodies can be purchased cheaply on the open market is a grim, modern-day reminder of slavery. In some ways, Black women are still on the auction block!

—Cole and Guy-Sheftall

In the early 1970s black and Latino youth in the economically depressed South Bronx created hip-hop culture, which encompassed deejaying, graffiti writing, break dancing, and rap music. Although they produced fun dance music, these marginalized young people exposed the social problems that ravaged their impoverished communities: drug abuse, poverty, police brutality, racism, and gang violence. This urban youth-based culture has grown into a multiracial, global phenomenon that permeates almost every aspect of society—from language to fashion, the dance club scene, and the general way in which young people interact with one another. Contemporary hip-hop music includes Christian and politically conscious rap music that is progressive, transformative, and even life affirming. In the 1980s when corporations began to depoliticize and financially exploit the popularity of hip-hop, rap music and music videos became the most powerful, influential, and frequently consumed product of hip-hop culture. Those that depicted violence and explicit sexual content received heavy rotation on radio and television.[1]

According to psychologists, this content can contribute to the *sexualization* of girls, which can be conceptualized as a continuum of offensive behavior, with sexualized evaluation (e.g., looking at someone in a sexual way, leering) at the less extreme end and sexual exploitation, such as childhood sexual abuse at the more extreme end. *Self-sexualization* can occur when girls think of themselves primarily or solely in sexual terms or when they equate their physical appearance with a narrow, often unattainable, standard of beauty.[2] Many concerned parents, public health experts, and social critics denounce hip-hop music lyrics and videos for hypersexualizing black adolescent girls. More specifically, they have argued that black girls may develop sexual scripts based on hip-hop culture, which in turn shapes how they express their sexuality and view themselves as sexual beings.[3]

In addition, exposure to sexualized images in hip-hop has been found to influence black girls' perception of male–female gender roles, attitudes toward sexual assault, physical dating violence, and physical attractiveness.[4] This is troubling from a public health standpoint. Music videos and lyrics that perpetuate gender inequality and glorify risky sexual behaviors but rarely provide healthy sexual messages or emphasize possible negative health consequences may increase the likelihood that black adolescent girls will have unplanned pregnancies, early sexual onset, or sexually transmitted disease (STD) acquisition, including HIV/AIDS.[5]

Displaying anonymous, nude black female bodies has a long history in Western societies, from the exhibition of enslaved women on the auction block to representations of black female bodies in contemporary hip-hop music videos.[6] The purpose of this chapter is to (1) discuss six sexual scripts that are commonly found in hip-hop culture and music videos; (2) examine possible consequences associated with exposure to hip-hop scripts for black girls; and (3) make suggestions for intervention.

SEXUAL SCRIPTS IN HIP-HOP CULTURE

When black men and women were sold as slaves, their bodies were stripped naked, examined, and then sold, traded, and bought on the open market. Unlike white women who were draped in layers of clothing during the eighteenth and nineteenth centuries, nudity among black women, although it was forced, implied that they lacked civility, morality, and sexual restraint. The systematic sexual exploitation of black women, including rape and forced breeding, was used to produce a perpetual labor force. The Jezebel stereotype, which stigmatized black women as promiscuous, was created to justify these sexual atrocities and excuse the profit-driven sexual exploitation of black women.[7]

Black women's commodified bodies continue to be exploited for profit. Put simply, corporations create the images, profit from them, and sell them back to black teens and other consumers under the guise of "authentic" black culture. African American performers, producers, and music executives also have participated in this economic exploitation.[8] For example, Black Entertainment Television (BET), the oldest and most popular 24-hour television network whose programming is targeted to African Americans, reaches more than 76 million households. On any given weekday, viewers can watch 15 hours or more of music videos.[9]

Just like their enslaved ancestors, contemporary black women's bodies are accessible, exchangeable, and expendable on the new cyber-auction block. For example, in a genre of hip-hop music commonly referred to as *booty rap*, there is a clear reference to the culture of strip clubs and pornography as scantily clad women simulate sex acts with male rappers and other female performers. These anonymous background dancers are sexualized status symbols who are owned by rap artists, similar to their luxury cars, Rolex watches, and gold medallions. *Gangster rap* glorifies pimping, senseless gunplay, an insatiable appetite for marijuana and liquor, and misogyny, in the form of physical and sexual violence against women.[10] Researchers have identified six distinct sexual scripts in popular rap music: Diva, Gold Digger, Freak, Gangster Bitch, Baby Mama, and Earth Mother.[11]

Diva

The *Diva* embodies a narrowly defined Westernized standard of physical beauty: a slender build, long hair, and lighter eye and skin color. She wears designer clothes, and her hands and feet are perfectly manicured, which gives her the appearance of an impeccably coifed middle- or upper-middle-class woman. In order to retain her social status, a Diva requires luxury cars and expensive jewelry.[12]

Gold Digger

Unlike the Diva who trades sexual favors for social status, a *Gold Digger* will sell, rent, or trade her body or sexuality for hard currency; basic needs, such as groceries; or consumer items, including manicures, new clothes, or vacations. Her relationships are typically short-term financial arrangements. When the money runs out, the Gold Digger runs out on the man, often leaving him bankrupt and bewildered.[13]

Freak

Dressed in revealing clothing and sometimes mistaken for a prostitute or stripper, a *Freak* is an insatiable sexual sensation seeker who is motivated by her own desire and pleasure. She will forgo love, emotional attachment, and even money in order to pursue a wide range of unconventional sexual activities, including group sex or sex with strangers. An "undercover" Freak is less overt and behaves like a "good girl" during the day; however, in a smoky dance club or in the bedroom, she engages in kinky wild sex.[14]

Gangster Bitch

A *Gangster Bitch* glorifies the poverty-stricken, drug-infested, violent inner-city. To illustrate, Lil' Kim, the sexy, couture-clad rapper, projects a video persona of a violence-prone, foul-mouthed, gun-toting, 40-ounce malt-liquor–guzzling bad girl who boasts about her sexual prowess and impersonal sexual encounters. Sexuality also can be used to prove her loyalty to a boyfriend. She loves her partner enough to participate in his various criminal enterprises, including theft, drug distribution, and even murder. The couple's romantic motto is "Ride or Die," which means that a Gangster Bitch will accept death or imprisonment before she would "snitch" to the police.[15]

Baby Mama

If a child is born, the *Baby Mama* script is enacted. She is the mother of a man's child(ren) whom he did not marry. Although they may occasionally have sexual contact, the couple is not currently involved. These relationships are characterized by conflict, drama, and mutual hostility. According to the script, the Baby Mama, who intentionally became pregnant to maintain a relationship with the baby's daddy, constantly begs for money, denies the father visitation with the child, interferes in his future relationships with other women, and uses the legal system to harass him. As a result, the man is justifiably angry, makes disparaging comments about the Baby Mama, denies paternity, and avoids paying child support.[16]

Earth Mother

Of course, there are hip-hop artists who do not sexualize themselves or other young black women. Artists such as Lauryn Hill, Jill Scott, and Erika Badu, project an *Earth Mother* sexual script, which is characterized by an Afrocentric, political, social, and spiritual self-awareness. These performers wear head wraps and flowing robes, style their hair in Afros or dreadlocks, exude a more subtle sexuality, and sing about female empowerment and self-acceptance.[17]

Nonetheless, the Diva, Gold Digger, Freak, Gangster Bitch, Baby Mama, and Earth Mother are pervasive scripts in music videos and hip-hop culture, which generate the lion's share of airtime and profits. And so these are the scripts that black adolescent girls are more likely to internalize or act out in their daily lives. Carla Stokes, a health educator, reviewed 27 technologically sophisticated Internet home pages constructed by black girls aged 14 to 17 who resided in southern U.S. states.[18] She discovered that the majority of these girls created hypersexualized cyber-personas. Four girls described themselves as *Down-Ass Chicks* or *Bitches*, which was analogous to the previously discussed Gangster Bitch.[19] Four girls embraced the identity of *Pimpettes* or female "players" who juggled multiple partners and manipulated men for economic gain. Nine of the sites were in keeping with the *Freaks* persona. For example, one 15-year-old girl wrote: "I am wonderful in bed . . . I am down fo whateve'."[20] Other girls posted pornographic images that depicted humans or cartoon characters engaged in sexual activity or used sexually explicit rap songs as background music, such as "MySpace Freak" by C-Side or "P-Poppin" (pussy poppin') by rapper Ludacris. Although it isn't possible to determine whether these girls' cyber-personas reflect their offline identities and behaviors, to the extent that these home pages are the stage on which they are rehearsing sexual scripts, these self-representations should raise concerns.[21]

It should be noted that seven of the 27 girls in the study rejected self-sexualization. Three girls proudly titled their Web sites *Virgin* and created home pages that highlighted their sexual purity and intelligence. Stokes referred to these seven girls who had "begun the critical process of creating independent self-definitions" as *Resisters*.[22] On their Web sites, they described themselves as well-rounded, personable, confident, self-possessed young woman. For instance, one 16-year-old wrote: "if u looking for a fashion model/u got da wrong 1 . . . /so don't read any further."[23]

Adolescents from all ethnic backgrounds must grapple with difficult questions as they make the transition from childhood to adulthood: "Who am I?" and "How do others perceive me?" Hip-hop and rap music lyrics project complex, often contradictory, multifaceted images of black adolescent girls. Black teenage girls may be torn between the expectation of respectability derived from their parents and community and sexualization that masquerades as sexual liberation. It is important to appreciate that the images projected in hip-hop videos are more than mere visual representations. Rather they can be more accurately described as sexual scripts, which can become guidelines that teach black girls why, where, when, how often, and with whom to express their sexuality.[24]

CONSEQUENCES OF HIP-HOP SCRIPTS FOR BLACK GIRLS

The process of developing a healthy sexual identity can be especially difficult for black adolescent girls as they attempt to negotiate their emerging sexuality amid conflicting and discrepant cultural scripts and images from the mainstream media, hip-hop culture, their peers, and their parents.[25] Despite immense challenges, such as poverty and negative peer influences, many black girls are able to rewrite sexualized scripts and build a healthy life.[26] However, for many girls, exposure to hip-hop culture and rap music videos and lyrics has been associated with poor body image, the normalization of using sexuality as a commodity, confusion about gender roles, the development of adversarial male–female relationships, greater acceptance of teen dating violence, and sexual risk taking.

Poor Body Image

The legacy of American slave-era beauty preferences regarding skin color, hair texture, and body type are replicated in hip-hop videos. Typically the love interests of male performers and background dancers are multiracial or lighter-complexioned black women with long, straight hair. In some cases these women are "created" with the use of colored contact lenses, hair weaves, and camera filters. Although the camera features the faces of lighter-skinned women, it lingers on the big butts of the darker-skinned women.[27] Preadolescent black boys, aged 11 to 13, clearly stated their preference for curvaceous black women with large breasts, ample thighs, and large round buttocks, particularly if the women had long hair and lighter skin color.[28] Although it seems that they enjoy an advantage in the dating game, light-complexioned girls may be highly sexualized or find themselves wondering if partners are more attracted to their physical appearance than to their personalities.[29]

Meanwhile, darker-skinned black girls appear to have a greater investment in resisting narrowly defined beauty images. In focus groups preadolescent girls expressed happiness with their overall appearance, including their brown skin. Still they believed that boys preferred girlfriends and sex partners who fit the appearance of hip-hop dancers.[30] This realization or perception can cause great pain and feelings of rejection among some brown-skinned black girls. One teenager reflected on a high school crush:

> It was obvious and evident that most if not all of the black boys in my school wanted nothing to do with black girls, which was sort of traumatizing. . . . In the final analysis, I ended up feeling that there was something wrong with him, but it was hell getting there.[31]

Sex as a Commodity

Hip-hop has glamorized pimping and prostitution by associating this form of sexual exploitation with materialism in the form of flashy attire, money, and expensive vehicles. When compared to other ethnic groups, the odds of having exchanged sex for money or drugs were higher among African American youth.[32] Although these young women (and men) may appear morally lax, many of these sex-for-money exchanges occurred in the context of "survival sex" or "compelled childhood sexual contact."[33] Typically, impoverished black girls, some as young as 12 and 13 years old, traded sex for basic necessities, such as food and shelter, which in turn left them vulnerable to pimps, pornographers, and sexual traffickers (e.g., see www.exploitedblackteens.com or www.pimpmyblackteen.com).

In addition, music videos have normalized "transactional sex" in which sexual favors are used or bartered to obtain consumer goods, such as designer clothing worn by celebrities. One Baltimore teen denied gold digging, but explained that: "If they don't have money to buy me some 'Tims' [Timberland boots], take me out . . .they don't get no rap!"[34] She and her peers preferred to date "sugar daddies" or "payloads" because these older men gave them money and gifts in exchange for sex. However, there was an obvious power imbalance between adult men and adolescent girls, which left them vulnerable to sexual assault, dating violence, and manipulation. In addition, they often felt powerless to refuse sex or other unreasonable demands, such as participation in criminal activity. These girls had learned that their value lay between their legs. Unlike men, however, female sexuality is a depletable commodity, and once expended, these young women were characterized as whores.

Gender Roles and Sexual Double Standard

Negotiating and defining femininity in the context of hip-hop images can be challenging. On one hand, black adolescent girls who viewed videos with an overabundance of stereotypical representations of masculinity and femininity expressed more traditional views about gender and sexual relationships.[35] In fact, preadolescent girls in semistructured focus groups were sexually conservative and rejected hypersexualized scripts, such as the Freak, in favor of more traditional gender roles.[36] Although male promiscuity was more accepted, and even expected, virginity or low levels of sexual activity were viewed as more desirable conduct for women. Similarly, black adolescent girls in high-school focus groups believed that women who appeared in hip-hop videos—and their female peers who imitated them—were "nasty" and dressed like "hoes."[37] Researchers have speculated that some of these girls may be adhering to the *Sister Savior* script that decreed that sex outside of marriage should be avoided for moral or religious reasons.[38] To protect their daughters from sexually transmitted diseases, early pregnancy, and sexual victimization, many black mothers caution their daughters to reject sexualized images and embrace more sexually conservative values.[39]

Interestingly, black girls in other focus groups had mixed reactions to video images. Although a few girls complained about sexualized images in music videos, others seemed oblivious and attempted to mimic the styles and mannerisms of the dancers. For example, when asked whose video they would like to appear in, they said [hard-core rapper] Jay-Z and in other videos that featured nearly naked women.[40] Other black adolescents were ambivalent. In one survey, the majority of participants felt bad about the portrayal of women (58 percent) and male–female interactions (63 percent) in rap music. Yet an equal number (59 percent) tried to act, dance, or dress like the women in rap music videos.[41] It appears that black girls recognized the value placed on female sexuality and the cultural mandate that women accentuate their femininity and beauty or risk social rejection from female friends and boyfriends. Consequently, many black girls felt compelled to strike a precarious balance between being both sweet and sexy, all while adhering to the image of the strong, independent black woman.[42]

Adversarial Relationships

It should be noted that many low-income black urban youth and young adults expressed a sincere desire to establish committed, loving intimate relationships. Unfortunately, other black male–female dating relationships are adversarial and are plagued with infidelity, lack of trust, and dishonesty.[43] Certainly many factors may contribute to these antagonistic relationships; however, exposure to rap music videos is one predictor of attitudes toward heterosexual intimate relationships. Specifically, as time spent watching rap music videos increased, so did adversarial attitudes toward male–female relationships in a sample of black adolescents.[44] Equally as troubling, more than 50 percent of black male college students agreed that rap music accurately reflected at least some of the reality of gender relations between black men and women.[45] Researchers have concluded that "in shaping students' views of sexual relationships, these videos create expectations of adversarial dynamics and of mutual disrespect."[46] When conflict becomes normative, adolescent dating relationships can quickly move to become physically or sexually violent.

Sexual and Physical Violence

Rap artists visually and lyrically beat, rape, verbally abuse, and even murder black women in their lyrics. Nearly every gangster rapper's CD has an obligatory "Beat that Ho" song, and sex has become a form of torture in which men are encouraged to break "that thing in half" and "leave some stretch marks" in a woman's mouth after oral sex. Even gang rape is depicted; in one song rappers described a line of 14 men prepared to take turns placing themselves "two on top, one on the bottom" of an underage girl.[47]

It is too simplistic to say that hip-hop or rap music *causes* violence against women. Nonetheless, this musical genre, along with other forms of musical expression, has advocated, glorified, justified, and condoned this conduct, which in turn may desensitize listeners to misogyny and violence.[48] As evidence, when compared to black male college students who disliked explicit lyrics, those who preferred this form of rap had significantly more rape-prone attitudes (e.g., "I think that many women are 'bitches'" or "Under certain circumstances date rape is understandable").[49] Are young men mimicking the behavior in music, or is music a reflection of the sexual violence in society? The temporal order is unclear. Either way an unacceptable number of black adolescent boys, 40 percent in one sample, had participated in a gang rape.[50] Some victims were as young as 13.[51]

Music videos may influence how black adolescent girls perceive violence against women. For example, even exposure to nonviolent, sexualized hip-hop music videos has been associated with greater acceptance of dating violence among black teen girls. In fact, viewing these videos brought the females' acceptance of premarital dating violence up to the level of the males' acceptance.[52] In addition, black teen girls frequently expressed victim-blaming attitudes. After listening to and discussing *Love Is Blind*, a song about a young woman who was murdered by a physically and sexually abusive boyfriend, black high-school girls expressed some sympathy but concluded that women should "just leave" an abusive partner. In addition, they read and discussed a vignette that described a case in which a young woman danced with a rap star and was subsequently raped in his hotel room. According to the participants, the hypothetical victim, and women in general, are responsible for projecting the "correct" image to men in both public and private settings. When a woman's conduct is "too sexual," she is responsible for her victimization. How should a girl respond to harassment or assault? Participants recommended wearing unfashionable oversized clothing or carrying a concealed weapon, such as a knife. Seeking help from adult authority figures, such as teachers, was perceived as ineffective.[53]

Taken together, it appears that misogynistic hip-hop may encourage boys and men to perpetrate violence against girls and possibly make girls more accepting of their victimization. This is troubling because a substantial number of black adolescent girls will be physically or sexually victimized.[54] For example, in community samples of low-income black adolescent girls, 33 percent had been raped or sexually coerced, and more than 50 percent had been pushed, shoved, or slapped by a boyfriend.[55] Victim-blaming attitudes may influence how they respond. To illustrate, mental health problems can be exacerbated if survivors endorse the Jezebel stereotype, as measured by items such as "People think black women are sexually loose." The greater endorsement of such beliefs among black rape survivors was related to increased use of victim blame attributions, which in turn was related to lower levels of self-esteem.[56]

Sexual Risk Taking

When compared to other music styles, such as rock and soul, rap and hip-hop lyrics and videos depicted more references to drugs and alcohol and multiple sexual partners.[57] Concerned parents, public health experts, and social critics have long denounced hip-hop's vulgar lyrics, videos, and dance moves as a leading cause of risky sexual behavior among adolescents. There is growing evidence to support this assertion. Researchers followed 522 black adolescent girls over a 1-year period and assessed their health behaviors, rap music video viewing habits, and perceptions of portrayals of sexual stereotypes in rap music videos (e.g., "In rap music videos, how often are black women portrayed as sex objects?"). The median hours of exposure to rap music videos, primarily gangster rap, was 14 hours per week. Girls who viewed more videos, particularly if they perceived that the videos contained sexual stereotypes of black women were twice as likely to have had multiple sex partners, more than 1.5 times as likely to have acquired a new sexually transmitted disease, used drugs, and used alcohol over the 12-month follow-up period.[58] In addition, the participants who perceived that the videos contained more sexual stereotypes of black women were more likely to engage in binge drinking, test positive for marijuana, and have a negative body image.[59]

These statistics point to complex interconnections among exposure to hip-hop culture, rap music videos and lyrics, and life circumstances. Poor body image, using sex as a commodity, confusion about gender roles and power imbalances in dating relationships, and adversarial or violent relationships have all been linked to sexual risk taking, which increases the probability of contracting STDs, including HIV. These associations are particularly troubling from a public health perspective. According to the Centers for Disease Control and Prevention, of those adolescents diagnosed with HIV in 2003, African American girls made up 72 percent of the people in the 13- to 19-year-old age group.[60]

To conclude, some black adolescent girls claim immunity from the influence of media messages.[61] Similar to secondhand cigarette smoke, which can adversely impact the health of nonsmokers, I would argue that some of the scripts in hip-hop culture can have a negative effect on the psychological well-being of black adolescent girls, even if they are nonconsumers or deny its impact. These sexualized images are so deeply embedded in our history and culture that they can obliterate individuality. Consequently, black adolescent girls expend an enormous amount of psychological energy and time trying to counter these images, ignore them, or act them out.

REBUILDING THE VILLAGE: STRATEGIES AND SOLUTIONS

Although some black girls face immense challenges, such as poverty and negative peer influences, they are not passive consumers of media images. In fact, many black girls empower themselves to rewrite sexualized scripts and build a healthy life for themselves.[62] In the sections that follow, I will offer specific ways to assist them, including research, media literacy, and parental and community involvement.

Future Research Directions

Some researchers have (mis)represented the experiences of black girls through qualitative data collected from impoverished high-risk convenience samples. Culturally sensitive measures should be developed to assess attitudes toward rap music.[63] In addition, focus groups and qualitative methodologies can be utilized to understand how black adolescent girls consume music videos and rap lyrics, interpret the images within them, and resist acting them out.[64] Among African American youth, higher levels of socioeconomic status and spiritual religious coping were associated with rejection of negative images of women in rap music videos.[65] This finding highlights the importance of surveying black girls from diverse backgrounds. For example, it would be helpful to evaluate how higher-functioning, more educated, middle-class black girls, perceive sexual scripts in hip-hop and music videos.[66] This will enable scholars to develop more complex conceptual models to understand how media contributes to the sexualization and sexual socialization of black teens.[67]

Media Literacy

Black women and girls have attempted to hold the music industry, including performers, responsible for the sexualized images that they produce. For example, in his "Tip Drill" video, rapper Nelly ran a credit card through the crack of a dancer's buttocks. The students at Spelman College, a historically black women's college in Atlanta, began a "take back the music" protest in response to objectionable song lyrics and videos. These young activists conducted community forums, wrote articles, and lobbied the music industry to change these images.[68] More recently, black feminist scholars have testified before the United States Congress about stereotypes and degrading images of black women produced by hip-hop artists and the music industry. During these congressional hearings, representatives of the music industry were clear: they are in business to entertain and to operate a profitable corporation.[69]

Black girls cannot wait for hip-hop artists or the music industry to become socially responsible. They must be equipped with media literacy skills, which will allow them to critically examine hip-hop images and to deconstruct them by asking themselves and others: Who created these images and why?, Who profits from the sexual objectification of black girls and women?, and What is the history behind these representations? These media literacy skills also are transferrable to gendered, violent, and sexualized messages in other forms of media, including television, film, magazines, video games, and music lyrics.[70] Organizations such as Helping Our Teen Girls in Real Life Situations, Inc. (HOTGIRLS.org) are designed to provide these media literacy skills.

Parental and Community Involvement

Limited parental monitoring has been associated with greater exposure to rap music videos.[71] Therefore, parents need to become involved. In fact, many children welcome their parents' input. Among black adolescents, "hands-on parenting," defined as restricting CD purchases and setting curfews, and perceived parental disapproval of teen sex reduced the likelihood that exposure to sexual content in media would be associated with early sexual onset.[72] In focus groups, black girls stated that their father's disapproval of certain sexual behavior or attire was extremely influential. Perhaps these girls would be less likely to mimic the sexual behavior in hip-hop videos. Parents may need to restrict or limit their children's media diet. Other parents can listen to the music and watch the videos with their children and try to appreciate and comprehend their content. By sharing a common language, parents and children may be able to open the lines of communication for critical discussion about sexuality, substance abuse, violence, and gender roles.[73]

Black youth in particular can no longer depend on a deeply textured network of extended families, faith communities, fraternal organizations, school clubs, sports teams, and other community associations to transmit knowledge and values. If "it takes a village to raise a child," according to an African proverb, it is now time to rebuild that village.[74] This means that parents must partner with educators, health care providers, and mentors to provide a safe space for black girls to critically analyze gender politics, their personal definitions and attitudes about sexuality, and contradictory messages presented in hip-hop culture.[75] For example, girls can explore the question: "How does one enact sensuality, beauty, and strength simultaneously without crossing one of many lines of unacceptable behavior?"[76] Parents and service professionals must be careful to avoid blaming girls for their victimization encouraging them to explore their emerging sexuality while helping them to avoid becoming sexualized, developing poor body images, or becoming so sexually repressed that they can't take pleasure in their budding sexuality. Black adolescent girls and young women who resist oppressive cultural scripts can serve as powerful peer educators. In addition, parents and service providers can collaborate with the girls they seek to help by building on the empowering aspects of hip-hop and youth culture and acknowledging their expertise about the role of media in their lives.[77]

CONCLUSION

The sexual scripts depicted in rap music and hip-hop culture are not only abstract theoretical constructs but have real, material, and tangible impact on black adolescent girls' daily lives. However, the desire to clean up the language and images in hip-hop does little to address the sexism, class oppression, and misogyny that inform the treatment of black girls within black communities or the larger society. Parents and other stakeholders must work to change the life circumstances, or in some cases the lack of life options, that facilitate the sexualization of black adolescent girls, which too often leads to unplanned pregnancies, early sexual onset, sexually transmitted disease acquisition, and victimization. In addition, there is a need to put the financial, intellectual, and creative energy into helping black girls and young women to establish their our own blogs, Web sites, podcasts, e-newsletters, and radio shows (for examples, see http:// whataboutourdaughters.blogspot.com and HOTGIRLS.org). With the support of media literacy, parents, strong communities, and their own resilience, black adolescent girls can refuse to be placed on the cyber auction block.

II

Sexualization and Child Sexual Abuse

8

The Sexual Exploitation of Children and Youth: Redefining Victimization

SHARON W. COOPER

The sexual exploitation of children and youth has certainly been a crime for centuries across many cultures. Pornography involving children from the Greek and Roman eras was often depicted in literature and art. Biblical references to prostitution are easily found in both the Old and New Testaments. The Chinese Manchu Dynasty produced literature and art promoting adult male sex with boys, encouraging the social acceptance of prostitution of boys, particularly as companions to wealthy men.[1] However, the twentieth century brought an unfathomable communication link from one culture to another with the development of Internet technology.

The Internet is often referred to as the printing press of the twenty-first century, and Web 1.0 (the World Wide Web) and more recently Web 2.0 (the World Live Web) have jettisoned the ability to share information, store data, and establish live visual contact between people at a speed that is often close to instantaneous. Web 1.0, the downloading side of Internet activity, provided the first means of criminal exploitative activity against children as offenders fine-tuned their prurient desires for children by networking. The establishment of online Usenet newsgroups available to the public in the latter part of the 1990s and early 2000 afforded like-minded people the ability to share strategies, cognitive distortion rationalizations, and plans for picture exchange of child sexual abuse.[2] The Internet truly opened Pandora's box as thousands of people in America alone began to accept a desire to relish images of the rape of children for their own sexual gratification, seeing it as normal and more importantly as a plan for action.[3] Although collectors have the greatest impact upon the supply and demand aspect of this form of abuse against children, distributors are closer to production and deserve serious attention in the war on pornography. Most noncommercial producers are family members, relatives, and acquaintances. However, distributors often take the "product" and gain immense financial benefits from ensuring that the public has access to every child victim's innermost dark secret. The landmark case of a distributor's gain that electrified the world involved a couple living in Fort Worth, Texas.

> Thomas and Janice Reedy had never been homeowners before they decided to open a Web site that marketed images of child sexual abuse in 1996. There was nothing subtle about this site, which at one point featured the words "Child Porn Here" as its banner. From 1997 until 1999, their business garnered $9,275,900, and a successful investigation by the U.S. Postal Inspection Service revealed that their business, Landslide, Inc., had a database with 100,000 names, addresses, e-mail addresses, and credit card numbers. The investigation revealed that 35,000 customers were from the United States, 7,200 were from the UK, and 2,300 were from Canada, with many others from additional countries.[4]

It became apparent that the market for Internet-based pictures of children being sexually abused and exploited would become one of the most lucrative in the history of Internet crimes.

TYPES OF SEXUAL EXPLOITATION

There are five types of child sexual exploitation: child pornography, the intrafamilial prostitution of children and youth, cyber-enticement for sexual encounters, child sex tourism, and the trafficking of children and youth for sexual slavery, labor, and civil rights violations and/or prostitution. All of these forms of child abuse existed before the Internet, but they have been seriously exacerbated by the technology that provides support for a global marketing concept of the sexuality of children.[5]

Child Pornography

> She was an 8-year-old girl, one of four children living in Germany on an American military installation with her mother and stepfather. When her 16-year-old sister left the family to return to the United States after several angry conflicts with her mother about her stepfather, everyone thought she just hadn't adjusted to the marriage. But after returning to the support of her family, her older sister alerted others about the stepfather's "picture contests," which took place every weekend while his

wife worked long shifts at a fast-food restaurant. This tip led investigators to have social workers interview the children at school and the discovery that the soldier was sexually abusing two of the daughters and
was producing and storing child pornography on the four hard drives
that he kept in his living room. The 8-year-old was able to disclose the
sexual abuse with careful questioning, but more than a year later, she
continued to deny that any pictures had been taken, despite clear evidence that she'd been photographed on numerous occasions. When the
defendant confessed to the judge during the trial that he'd "lost control
and it all happened on one day," it became necessary for the medical
expert and computer forensic team to review all of her images again and
carefully select those that showed fingernail growth, different hair
lengths, shedding teeth, and changes in body weight to assure the court
that the exploitation had occurred over months to years.

No form of child abuse has skyrocketed in incidence and public
awareness over the past decade as has that of child pornography. Even
the term "pornography" is hotly debated as being inappropriate because
it tacitly infers modeling or posing. In the situation of child pornography,
these images are clearly digital crime scenes that depict child sexual
abuse. For this reason many international agencies refer to the images on
the Internet as child abuse images or child sexual abuse images. This language allows a judge, jury, and the public to have better understanding
of the nature of the crimes depicted before their very eyes. Yet this ever-
increasing problem begs for alternative interventions because it certainly
appears that we cannot arrest our way out of this.[6]

One of the quandaries in the field of child maltreatment rests in
the lack of a realization of what child sexual abuse images actually
represent. These images are real-time evidence of child sexual abuse.
Like a security video camera in a convenience store, these pictures are
a digital crime scene.

Although all indications support a decline in the reported incidence of child sexual abuse in the United States over the past 10 years,
it is a matter of great concern that pictures of children being sexually
abused have increased exponentially and that the images are not
counted as child sexual abuse encounters.[7] It is understandable that
one is not sure how to document these images as child sexual abuse
data from a state perspective in the nonvirtual world of Child Protective Service (CPS) reports and Special Victim Unit (SVU) investigations. However, the increasing number of these images and videos
must be acknowledged as clearly one of the most egregious forms of
child victimization both in criminal justice data as well as in health
and human services information. Each child victim is revictimized
every time an offender downloads or distributes this contraband. The

most recent number of images cited by the National Center for Missing and Exploited Children, which is the federally mandated repository of child pornography images in the United States, is 12 million. The majority of children depicted in this database are as yet unknown, but there is often clear evidence that a significant percentage of the images are of American children.[8]

Another aspect of the challenges for CPS and SVU investigations in this form of sexual abuse is that in the offline world, the success of prosecution of child sexual abuse cases averages at the state level at about 72 percent. On the other hand, the success of child pornography prosecutions at the state level is 95 percent.[9] A different interpretation of these statistics reveals that, as a society, we are more likely to believe a picture than a victim.

Sexual exploitation cases involving child pornography have stymied many professionals who work in a multidisciplinary fashion typical of child abuse investigations. There are several reasons to explain the confusion aside from the difficult-to-fathom methods of sexual exploitation that have never been seen before by frontline child protection workers.

Internet crimes against children are the only type of child abuse investigations that almost exclusively begin with law enforcement as the first point of contact as compared to child protective services investigators. To complicate matters, the law enforcement professional is not usually a child abuse investigator but instead a person with specialized training in computer forensics whose secondary skill level is the interrogation of Web-based criminals. Continued training for the multidisciplinary team (MDT) members regarding the nuances of child forensic interviewing when pictures exist that memorialize a child's victimization is imperative to ensure that professionals understand that this is just one of many areas linked to violence against children in cyberspace. This realization is apparent even on an international level.[10] There are no clear guidelines at this time as to whether CPS should even accept a referral to screen children living in a home in which a custodial caretaker has been found to possess or distribute child sexual abuse images. This omission has deprived professionals of learning opportunities for several years because of the misconception that Internet child pornography was a "victimless crime," as many disciplines purported in the past. Having knowledge of the pornographic content, offenders' methods of grooming children, differences between self-exploitation and compliant victimization, and most important, explanations regarding victim nondisclosure or even denial of images are crucial tools for anyone working in child sexual abuse investigations, treatment, and prevention.

Research regarding delayed disclosure of child sexual abuse obtained from adult women has revealed that only about 12 percent of women who were sexually abused as children actually made a disclosure during childhood.[11] The overwhelming majority of female sexual abuse victims never told anyone of the abuse at the time that they were children. This information allows professionals to educate jurors that if a child did not immediately tell of sexual abuse, it doesn't mean that nothing happened. In fact, it is the rule more than the exception for a child to keep their abuse secret, often because they have had to become accommodated to the ongoing abuse.

From the victim dynamic perspective, the small percentage of children who do disclose child sexual abuse do so for specific motivating reasons, such as attempting to protect a younger sibling or feeling safe enough to tell of a parental offender because of separation or divorce. When pictures of the abuse are discovered as the first evidence that a child has been abused and the victim is not ready to tell, the end result may well be frank denial that abuse has occurred or that the contraband actually depicts someone other that the obvious child victim.

Often pornographic victimization causes a child to demonstrate a "double silencing." The victim may keep the sexual abuse a secret because of threats of exposure to loved ones or because of self-blame compounded by the secondary impact of guilt in knowing that pictures actually exist of what otherwise would have been the child's personal secret. Even worse, the victim may fear that they appeared to be cooperative or to have let it happen.[12] This realization more often than not leads to nondisclosure as a defense mechanism. The double silencing associated with pornography production has been recently highlighted in international conferences in which efforts are being made to assist in therapeutic interventions for such victims.[13] Double silencing often continues even when cognitive behavioral therapy has been provided to victims, and it is becoming clearer that alternative forms of therapy such as confrontational therapy might be more effective.

When the forensic interview involves discussion of other types of pornography with a child, skill is imperative. Relatively frequently adult and youth offenders look at adult pornography just before they assault a child. This may occur because the offender is not actually sexually excited by the child but has fantasized about a sexual assault in general. It may also give the offender an opportunity for predictable sexual arousal prior to the impending sexual assault. Children have disclosed having been shown adult pornography prior to sexual abuse. This is often done by the offender as a means of normalizing an impending sexual assault. Interviewers would typically refer to the adult pornography in derogatory terms such as "nasty, filthy, or disgusting."

Now, because of the increasing incidence of pornography production as part of child sexual abuse, interviewers must refrain from such characterizations of any images simply because a child is far less likely to disclose if he knows that the interviewer has great disdain for something that the child may also have experienced as a victim.

The role of extortion in child pornography victimization cannot be underestimated. Many victims express extreme distress that if they tell of pornography production as part of their abuse, images stored on cell phones or video cameras will be distributed on the Internet. Such blackmail is very effective in convincing a youth to avoid all appearances that they've reported the sexual offenses.

> She saw the mirror as her enemy. Every time she wanted to brush her hair or apply her makeup, the obese 16-year-old teen recalled having to recite her "script" over and over in front of her mirror. The offender was nearby, always correcting her and telling her to say it his way. For 3 years, her stepfather had forced her to have sex with him and to perform nude erotic dances in front of a video camera, reciting the script describing that all of her actions were her idea and a means to get even with an overly strict father. She'd had to say it more than a thousand times. He's assaulted her sexually more than 200 times. . . . . she knew because she'd kept count on a secret calendar. He would videotape his sexual abuse of her at the end of her "stripper routine." She believed his threat that he would send one of the hundreds of DVDs that he'd made of her to a contact in another state with instructions to flood the Internet with her videos if he failed to call by a certain date every month. Over the 3 years, the videos reflected her worsening weight gain.

Many professionals are just becoming competent in computer-based skills, so that they can understand that the sheer volume of child pornography on the Internet as well as the amount in the possession of an offender precludes the possibility that all of the images are morphed virtual avatars, that they were acquired serendipitously while an offender was "Web surfing," or that all of the images are adults posing as children. All of these presumptions have been previously posed rationalizations, even in courts of law. The rescue of known victims has revealed that on many occasions no efforts were made by the offenders to disguise the child or make them appear to be older than they actually were. In addition, information regarding known victims of child sexual abuse images reveals that nearly 70 percent of the images were made by immediate family members, relatives, or close acquaintances.[14]

An additional quandary in child pornography cases entails the techniques of forensic interviewing when pictures are involved. When careful questioning has allowed a young child to disclose historical aspects of sexual abuse, but child pornography is omitted even though this contraband sparked the investigation, interviewers must recognize that at times the child's defense mechanisms are too great to acknowledge this aspect of their victimization. Interviewers must be very careful not to place the child in a position to deny the existence of images because this is often the only aspect of the investigation in which there is objective evidence. Much research has confirmed that the actual physical examination of the child is likely to be normal, despite visual pornographic confirmation of repeated vaginal, oral, or anal penetration by an adult male.[15]

Pornography and Cyber-Enticement

The classical presentation of a cyber-enticement case involves a minor who met a person in an online chat room and after a time began to dialogue privately either through instant messaging or eventually by telephone. The offender usually steers the conversation to sexual topics and then initiates frequent contact with the youth, eventually encouraging an offline meeting. The offender typically minimizes the age difference and focuses on the developing relationship. In one report, 83 percent of victims went with the offender somewhere, and in 73 percent of cases, they met for a sexual encounter more than once. In 50 percent of cases, the offender traveled more than 50 miles to meet the victim. However, the research also revealed that 64 percent of offenders communicated online with the victim for 6 months or more before meeting for a sexual encounter.[16]

It is easy to understand why a young person would develop trust in a person who is contacting them in a nurturing, mature, concerned, and eventually provocative manner several times a day for many weeks or months. Almost anyone could fall prey to such attention but especially teens who are typically struggling with parental discipline as they strive to emancipate themselves from their families as a normal developmental behavior. Autobiographical testimony to the U.S. Congress underlined these facts when it was provided by Justin Berry, a youth who was lured, groomed, enticed to leave his home for sexual contacts, and eventually paid money via credit cards as he became a compliant victim to more than a thousand men.[17]

Adult and or child pornography in cyber-enticement is sometimes transmitted as a means of desensitizing the youth to the sexual nature of the relationship and sometimes as a means of educating the youth regarding desired sexual acts. In 40 percent of cases, youth who were victimized in computer-initiated sex crimes were given illegal drugs or alcohol upon meeting the offender offline.[18]

A 13-year-old teen met a 14-year-old girl online, and for nearly 6 months they chatted and became the best of friends. They exchanged pictures and talked about their deepest concerns. Little did the 13-year-old know that her "friend" was an adult male who ultimately introduced to her to another "friend," a man who would continue the masquerade until he too had the victim's ultimate trust. On a cold winter night, the coatless teen went to the end of her driveway just to finally catch a glimpse of her online friend. She certainly didn't expect to be forced into his car and driven several states away from her home where she was placed in a dog kennel, forced to wear a dog collar and heavy chain, and was repeatedly raped, beaten, and videotaped over the next several days. She was electrocuted, starved, and handcuffed to a bed while she remained aware that images of her sadistic abuse were being shared with others online. Her rescue couldn't have come a day too soon because the offender announced that he was growing too fond of her and he would be taking her somewhere after he returned from work that day. Her courageous words to Congress several years later were, "Just because you don't put up a fight doesn't mean that you went willingly."[19]

Recent contacts have been made through social networking sites instead of online chat rooms. This venue affords the offender the opportunity to see photos of the potential victim, and the offender can post images of whomever he chooses to be to his selected viewer. Numerous cases include adults who at first describe themselves as being 17 or 18 years of age; then as the victim becomes more comfortable with blogging, chatting, or text messaging, they gradually admit that they are older (although they are usually never being candid about their true age). Caught up in an exhibitionistic society, youth have been swept into virtual communities such as MySpace.com and Second Life, resorting to role-playing and taking on new identities. Online video gaming represents another influence, especially for males to see girls as sexual objects rather than people worthy of their care and concern. This sexual objectification can eventually affect a youth's self-image, leading to additional online risk-taking behaviors.[20]

The victimization caused by Internet pornography, with or without enticement, presents significant challenges to the field of therapeutic interventions. Because of the degree of guilt and self-blame associated with child pornography, children are seemingly loath to discuss this aspect of their victimization.

In addition, many youth are truly in love with the offenders who always agree with their adolescent angst and who seem to be their most consistent support system. When asked specifically why children won't tell about the pornographic component of their abuse, researchers in the UK documented responses from 80 victims. The results revealed that:

- Children felt that they appeared to let it [pornography production and sexual abuse] happen.
- They cooperated when made to smile during the abuse.
- They were at times recruiters for other children who were often their friends and who were ultimately sexually abused and photographed.
- They participated in autoerotic exhibitionism by masturbating or had sexual encounters with other children as they were coerced to do.
- They were threatened that other family members would be shown the images if they were not cooperative.[21]

For these reasons and the resultant paranoia that children and youth have when they know that these images are on the Internet, therapists may need to be more assertive in discussing sexual exploitation with a child. The therapist also must be alert to computer aversion because this problem could have serious education implications for a young person. Finally, therapists have a "need to know" regarding the content of pornographic contraband so that they can tailor their treatment accordingly. There is a significant difference between victimization associated with a child masturbating in images as compared to being sadistically abused with bondage and rape by multiple offenders.

New terms that are emerging in social science, adolescent behavior, and criminal juvenile justice research include compliant victimization and self-exploitation. Although it is believed that the vast majority of youth online and in social networking sites are safe and practice appropriate behaviors, some teens and tweens are lured and groomed into autoerotic exhibitionism, often via Web cameras.[22] Such youth are compliant victims because their grooming into sexually explicit behaviors was offender driven. It is important to understand the gradual seduction so often seen in online grooming. When an offender has this understanding, he will carefully link with youth, and with great patience gain their trust and not infrequently their love.

Taken out of context, videos and still images of autoerotic exhibitionism would certainly be interpreted as self-exploitation when, in fact, the images may well be the result of weeks to months of grooming conversations with an offender who uses this opportunity to not only acquire personal pornography produced by the child, but also to gain physical access when the child is enticed to leave their home for what they perceive to be a date. This meeting is almost undoubtedly going to result in at least statutory rape and perhaps sadistic abuse and murder. The youth usually is aware that the encounter will be with an older online "friend" and that the anticipated offline activity will be at least a rendezvous with the possibility of an eventual sexual encounter.[23] At times the images of child pornography are used as extortion to compliance, and at other times they are placed on the Internet without the youth's knowledge.

Research regarding the age of onset and completion of puberty of American children reveals that girls are physically completely mature as early as 14 years, depending on their race (Table 8.1). If a child is overweight, as so many American children are, puberty begins even earlier.[24]

This data affirms that there are undoubtedly thousands more teens whose sexually explicit images and videos are on the Internet although they have not been counted as underaged victims. Often sexual maturation of teens makes it difficult to know that a 15- or 16-year-old is the subject in child sexual abuse images. This is particularly true when pornography is used for the advertising of teens for prostitution. These images often are not even included in the estimated 20,000 child pornography images posted on the Internet each week.

On the other hand, many youth who give into peer-driven pressures and begin to self-exploit may fail to recognize that they are producing and distributing child pornography and consequently committing federal offenses. Internet, Web camera, and cellular telephone technology have made this type of victimization much more prevalent and exceedingly worrisome. Newspaper reports of self-exploitation by youth, especially in the context of consensual teen sexual behaviors, are increasing.

The classic scenario of a teen consensual sexual relationship "keepsake" is digital photographic memorialization of fellatio in which a male has possession of the images on his cell phone. Later, if the couple should dissolve the relationship under less than amicable circumstances, the male can seek retribution by distributing his ex-girlfriend's images to friends and even strangers on an Internet social networking site or via the 3G technology that allows transfer of pictures from one cell-phone camera to another.

Determining the consequences for such behaviors remains difficult as legal scholars seek to define terms such as self-produced child pornography.[25] The 3G technology, which was developed in Japan and has provided the platform for cellular telephone companies to offer the ability to take a picture with a camera phone and then transmit it

Table 8.1 Sexual Maturation Ratings and Ages of American Children

	Non-Hispanic white	Non-Hispanic black	Mexican American
Male Children			
Pubic hair			
PH2	11.98 (11.69–12.29)	11.16 (10.89–11.43)	12.30 (12.06–12.56)
PH3	12.65 (12.37–12.95)	12.51 (12.26–12.77)	13.06 (12.79–13.36)
PH4	13.56 (13.27–13.86)	13.73 (13.49–13.99)	14.08 (13.83–14.32)
PH5	15.67 (15.30–16.05)	15.32 (14.99–15.67)	15.75 (15.46–16.03)
Genitalia development			
G2	10.03 (9.61–10.40)	9.20 (8.62–9.64)	10.29 (9.94–10.60)
G3	12.32 (12.00–12.67)	11.78 (11.50–12.08)	12.53 (12.29–12.79)
G4	13.52 (13.22–13.83)	13.40 (13.15–13.66)	13.77 (13.51–14.03)
G5	16.01 (15.57–16.50)	15.00 (14.70–15.32)	15.76 (15.39–16.14)
Female Children			
Pubic hair			
PH2	10.57 (10.29–10.85)	9.43 (9.05–9.74)	10.39 (–)
PH3	11.80 (11.54–12.07)	10.57 (10.30–10.83)	11.70 (11.14–12.27)
PH4	13.00 (12.71–13.30)	11.90 (11.38–12.42)	13.19 (12.88–13.52)
PH5	16.33 (15.86–16.88)	14.70 (14.32–15.11)	16.30 (15.90–16.76)
Breast development			
B2	10.38 (10.11–10.65)	9.48 (9.14–9.76)	9.80 (0–11.78)
B3	11.75 (11.49–12.02)	10.79 (10.50–11.08)	11.43 (8.64–14.50)
B4	13.29 (12.97–13.61)	12.24 (11.87–12.61)	13.07 (12.79–13.36)
B5	15.47 (15.04–15.94)	13.92 (13.57–14.29)	14.70 (14.37–15.04)

Source: Sun, S. S., Schubert, C. M., Chumlea, W. C., Roche, A. F., Kulin, H. E., Lee, P. A., Himes, J. H., and Ryan, A. S. National estimates of the timing of sexual maturation and racial differences among U.S. children. *Pediatrics* 2002;110:911–19.

to another telephone without ever using the Internet. This technology is the reason that the United Nations Study on Violence against Children in 2005 says that the term "Internet crimes against children" is already becoming somewhat antiquated because issues of new communication technologies must be included as well.[26]

Intrafamilial and Commercial Child Sexual Exploitation through Prostitution

The 12-year-old sister watched as her mother checked "yes" to the photography contract that she believed was her key to a career in modeling. It surprised her when her mother gave permission not only to swimsuit modeling and evening gown modeling, but also to topless modeling and nude modeling. And so it began for the oldest, her 10-year-old sister, and the 8-year-old baby girl every weekend at the home of the family friend who promised that his camera would make them famous. Instead the three girls were victims of child sexual abuse, pornographic memorialization of the abuse, and the emotional abuse that accompanies being extorted and threatened that if they ever told, they would be killed. After dozens of weekends during which the girls were victimized and paid at the rate of $20 for the oldest girl, $15 for the 10-year-old, and $10 for the baby girl, the 12-year-old finally told her principal when she was banished from the classroom for sexually explicit behaviors. The investigation confirmed what the children told, and the prosecutors proceeded to what should have been a straightforward court case. However, 2 years later, when the 12-year-old was 14 and pregnant and preparing to testify, she requested a visit once more with her doctor from 2 years ago who had so carefully documented all of her statements about the death threats, the Viagra, and the other Polaroid pictures of child pornography of other girls that she never knew. The victim asked the doctor if she should tell about the money. She was reassured that certainly she should tell because it was the truth and besides the medical records were clear about the money that was given each time the children were sexually abused. The victim seemed relieved but still apprehensive. When she was asked what else was bothering her, she hesitantly stated that she hadn't revealed everything. She stated that she had omitted the fact that "When we got home, we had to give the money to Momma and not tell Daddy."

Intrafamilial child sexual exploitation doesn't only include sexual abuse with pornography production. Prostitution is also clearly on the list of terrible mistreatment of children. Intrafamilial prostitution was discovered to be far more common when researchers interviewed hundreds of youth housed in juvenile detention centers for prostitution. Internet facilitation of such prostitution has revealed some of the numerous ways in which this form of abuse occurs. An example is seen with mothers who are dialoguing with unknown men in chat rooms and who offer their children in a sex-for-money meeting. Another scenario is a woman who is marketing herself online who throws in a 10-year-old child as an additional benefit to the highest bidder. One father sent pornographic pictures of his 7-year-old daughter to men as he negotiated their coming to his home to have sex with her. He used the computers in the local public library. But long before computers, social workers had seen the tip of the iceberg in parental facilitation of prostitution. Consider the crack-addicted mother who takes her two young children to the crack house to buy drugs. Then there is the abusive drug-dealer father who gains custody of his daughters who are in their early teens after the death of his estranged wife from cancer. He begins to rent out rooms in his trailer to recently released convicted sex offenders. Consider the child who tells a social worker that she had told her mother about the sexual abuse committed by her live-in boyfriend, who was paying all of the bills in the home, but her mother refused to believe her. Then there's the overlooked 6-year-old child whose mother is doing a 6-month stint in the local jail, so her child is given to a neighbor who immediately begins to prostitute the child from her home. If such children are rescued and placed in one of the many foster-care homes or residential treatment facilities because of the mental health impact of such abuse, runaway behaviors begin the tragic story of commercial sexual exploitation on the streets.[27]

When faced with sexual exploitation through out-of-home prostitution and trafficking, multidisciplinary professionals have failed to understand the links between child sexual abuse, out-of-home placement, runaway behaviors, homelessness, and prostitution recruitment, often performed by other exploited youth. Such professionals also have minimal understanding of the ultimate terrible victimization of being marketed on the streets, in strip clubs, and sexually oriented businesses, at private parties and hotels and online. The preconceived notion of such youth as the key offenders in prostitution has prevailed for such a long time that demystification of child welfare workers, law enforcement, mental health professionals, health care providers, and the criminal justice system has only recently begun. Fortunately, the U.S. federal justice system has taken on the important role of investigating and prosecuting domestic and international human trafficking cases. However, ECPAT, an extraordinary international nongovernmental organization, has highlighted that many more services were offered to internationally trafficked victims as compared to American youth who are being domestically trafficked from one side of the country to the other for the purpose of sexual abuse and exploitation. Victim blaming has been the rule more than the exception in this form of child abuse.[28]

The landmark work of Richard Estes from the School of Social Work at the University of Pennsylvania has transformed the world with respect to understanding the demographics and risk issues associated with the commercial sexual exploitation of children (CSEC). Estes has provided profiles of children and exploiters from the United States and assisted in providing a better understanding of the links between poverty and exploitation. Together with Elena Azaola from Mexico, Estes's research provides a much better picture of international trafficking of children, children as chattel, and especially corruption of law enforcement as another barrier to effective intervention and prevention methods.[29]

Although it is still believed that most commercial sexual exploitation of children takes place offline, the use of online classified services, such as www.Craiglist.com and www.Eros.com, is increasing access to children and youth in a manner not previously reported. The role of technology allows for more covert means of trafficking of youth and requires knowledge of how destinations are communicated by means of the Internet and cellular telephones, as well as the accepting of online payments. It is presently felt that www.Craigslist.com is the most common means of online marketing of children and youth for prostitution.

Sexual exploitation investigations involving trafficking have often failed to provide adequate victim medical assessments both for forensic purposes and to evaluate the degree of intimate-partner violence victimization, which is a constant in this form of abuse. The severe multi-traumas of physical, emotional and sexual abuse in these types of cases actually are tantamount to torture in many instances and have long-term ramifications for mental health, women's health, and general well-being.[30] In addition, efforts to bring traffickers to justice are sometimes thwarted because of witness tampering and extortion. Some prosecutions have had to provide witness protection. Because of the organized nature even of street pimps, who have their own territories and networks and follow the underworld rules of engagement associated with pimping, the identities of victims are occasionally protected in court records. Professionals in the child abuse field have been inadequately trained in this area, likely because of the false notion that children and youth in this situation are simply demonstrating delinquent behaviors.

> The exploited youth, now turned adult, sat nervously in the quiet room as she told of being pistol whipped in the front seat of the Lexus. She described having her head slammed against the dashboard repeatedly

because she did not bring home her quota of money and had consumed alcohol in order to prepare for the consequences of the infraction. She pulled back the top of her blouse to reveal the large, poorly healed scar on her shoulder, which was the continuation of a slash from her scalp to the top of her hand. She recalled the saturation of the plush white leather of the car when she was thrown into the back seat by the pimp. She related that this offender was what many called a gorilla pimp, and the interviewer knew that this was a term used to denote a sadistic and brutally violent man who often beat women on a random basis and coerced them to beat each other. The lure of romance is not a typical behavior of such a pimp, but instead he would obtain his victims through frank abduction, false imprisonment, date rape, or by having bought them from another pimp.

The major medical problems so commonly seen in the commercial sexual exploitation of children are substance abuse, consequences of intimate partner violence, sexually transmitted diseases, women's health consequences, and severe mental health problems.

The substance-abuse addiction concerns include illegal drugs as well as alcoholism, conditions that do not usually abate without treatment. Often the addiction occurs as the offender intentionally provides illegal drugs to youth to foster dependence on both the drugs and the dealer. At other times, substance abuse is a coping mechanism for youth who are totally overwhelmed by the circumstances of multiple sexual encounters, beatings by perpetrators (johns), and the extreme endangerment to which they are exposed every day. Chronic liver disease is a common sequela often associated with hepatitis B and C.

The consequences of intimate partner violence (IPV) include battering injuries, closed head trauma, sexual assault, social isolation, deprivation, starvation, and extreme psychological abuse, which often includes unfathomable conditioning to control tactics by the pimp. Homicide is the leading cause of death in the prostitution of youth; thus such abuse requires the most attention when youth are rescued from the streets.[31] The fear of repercussions from the offender is so severe that the same "domestic violence" dynamics exist that prevent women from leaving abusive marital relationships. Careful questioning is mandatory to assess the possibility of traumatic brain injury as many survivors provide positive clinical histories and evidence of mental dysfunction as a consequence of their abuse.

The most severe impact on sexual and reproductive health is seen in commercial sexual exploitation of children and youth. Multiple sexually transmitted diseases, unwanted pregnancy, ectopic pregnancies because of scarring in the fallopian tubes, pelvic inflammatory disease (a leading cause of infertility), anal and rectal trauma, intravaginal injuries from foreign bodies, cervical dysplasia, and most important, an early exposure to the human papilloma virus, the most significant virus associated with cervical cancer. HIV/AIDs is certainly an additional concern of rescued persons who do not always have the last word regarding condom use with perpetrators. HIV/AIDs is the second most common cause of death in prostitution. There is also an increased incidence of anal and genital trauma and battering to male youth related to sadistic perpetrators and offenders.

The final victim impact of the commercial sexual exploitation of children rests within the limbic system of the brain and includes the subsequent issues of post-traumatic stress disorder (PTSD), depression, anxiety, and other mental health problems. Research involving American women who were victimized by prostitution revealed a general rate of PTSD of 68 percent, and my clinical evaluations have demonstrated an associated high incidence of depression as well. The likelihood of these problems was worsened if there was additional pornography exposure or production.[32] Just as Iraq and Afghanistan war veterans have a high incidence of PTSD (as high as 44 percent), the PTSD of abuse victims is permanent and requires therapeutic interventions, which are impossible to access in a juvenile detention setting and difficult to access within the mental health system of the United States.[33]

SUMMARY

The Internet has many uses—not the least of which is the sexual exploitation of children and youth. Child sexual abuse images are a common thread through all of the types of sexual exploitation. For years to come, professionals in fields relating to child maltreatment will try to pick up the pieces of lives devastated by information and communication technology. Youth are natives in this world of technology, and adults are still, by and large, the immigrants. It is imperative that we continue to navigate the landscape so that we can also be knowledgeable about newer technologies used in of the sexual abuse of children and the consequences of their exploitation.

9

Childified Women: How the Mainstream Porn Industry Sells Child Pornography to Men

GAIL DINES

In a March 2006 special edition of *Vanity Fair*, 30-year-old Reese Witherspoon is photographed looking wide-eyed and innocent in a girl's party dress. In her left hand she is holding a little girl's doll. Earlier in the magazine is a photo of then 12-year-old Dakota Fanning, wearing makeup, an off-the-shoulder evening gown and a "bed head" hairdo. In the middle of these two images is a bare-breasted Sienna Miller, lounging on a chair and wearing only skimpy panties and very high-heeled strappy shoes, otherwise known as "FM shoes" in pop culture—the FM being short for "fuck me." Captured in just three images is the essence of the visual landscape that surrounds us, a landscape that has become so pornographic as to not warrant even a second glance when we see sexualized childified women, sexualized adultified children, and a whole bevy of sexualized young women whose body language, gaze, and (lack of) clothes scream "fuck me" to the spectator.

These images, together with the thousands and thousands of others that bombard us daily, are part of what media scholars call "image-based culture;"[1] a term used to describe a society in which images have replaced the spoken or written word as the major form of communication. From billboards to 24-hour-television, the staple of this image-based culture is the youthful, sexualized female body. Advertisements, movies, TV shows, music videos, and pornography are just some of the ways that this image is delivered to us, and as we become more and more desensitized to such depictions, the producers need to ramp up the degree to which the female body is sexualized as a way to get our attention. This has led to an increasingly pornographic media landscape in which the codes and conventions that inform pornography filter down to mainstream imagery to such a degree that the images we now see in mainstream media are almost on a par with those that were found in soft-core porn just a decade ago.

One way the fashion and advertising industry has tried to capture the attention of viewers in this image-saturated culture is through the sexualization of younger and younger girls.[2] One of the pioneers of this type of advertising was Calvin Klein, who in the early 1980s used 15-year-old Brooke Shields in ads for his jeans with the famous tagline "Do you wanna know what comes between me and my Calvins? Nothing." In the mid-1990s Klein ratcheted up the imagery by using mostly underage teenagers in poses that looked so much like actual child pornography that the Justice Department started to investigate him for possible violation of the law. Klein escaped prosecution, only to come back a few years later with ads for his children's underwear line that featured prepubescent boys and girls wearing only underwear. This time Klein was forced to pull his ads almost overnight due to public outcry. Around the same time, a 17-year-old Britney Spears released a debut single called "Baby, One More Time" which became an instant international success. In the accompanying video, Spears sports a schoolgirl image with braided hair, socks, and a school uniform with a knotted shirt that revealed a bare midriff as she writhes around asking her ex-boyfriend to "Hit me baby one more time." Spears later went on to employ Gregory Dark, a long-time porn director whose films include *The Devil in Miss Jones*, *New Wave Hookers*, and *Let Me Tell Ya 'Bout Black Chicks*, to direct her videos.

As pop culture begins to look more and more pornographic, the actual porn industry has had to become more hard-core as a way to distinguish its products from those images found on MTV, in *Cosmopolitan*, and on billboards. Because today's boys and men are brought up in this pornified[3] culture, they are going to want their porn to look very different from their father's *Playboy*; a young naked woman smiling provocatively with her legs spread is hardly going to catch the attention of an already desensitized generation. Moreover, from childhood these consumers have also been fed a steady diet of violence by an increasingly deregulated media industry that offers up murder and mayhem as entertainment. Put these two together and you have a generation of men who need and expect more extreme and hard-core imagery than ever before, so much so today that even porn directors and producers are somewhat surprised by the demands of users. Porn director Mitchell Spinelli is quoted as saying "People want more. They want to know how many dicks you can shove up an ass. . . . Make it more hard, make it more nasty, make it more relentless."[4] And indeed porn today is more hard, more nasty, and more relentless than ever before with mainstream Internet porn depicting sex act after sex act that are devised to push the woman's body to the limit of physical endurance. Whether it be sites specializing in gagging the woman with a penis (for example, *Gagonmycock.com*, *GagFactor.com*, *GagtheBitch.com*) or pounding anal sex (AlteredAssholes.com, AssPlundering.com, AnalSluts.com), image after image shows a level of misogyny and cruelty that is breathtaking, even for the porn industry.

The problem for pornographers is that they are fast running out of new ways to keep users interested even as they have created subgenres of pornography that show just about every type of degradation, humiliation, and violence you can subject a woman to short of killing her.[5] Given this direction, there are really not many subgenres left for them to develop that both push the limits of hard-core porn and yet remain within the law. Porn director Jules Jordan, who is known for a particularly violent brand of porn, said that even he is "always trying to figure out ways to do something different" because the fans "are becoming a lot more demanding about wanting to see the more extreme stuff." So one of the big questions pornographers have to grapple with today is how to keep maximizing their profits in an already glutted market in which consumers are becoming increasingly desensitized to their products. The solutions for them are the same as for all capitalists: find innovative ways to both expand market shares and revenues in existing markets, to bring in new customers, and to find new market segments and distribution channels. Thus the major task for the porn industry is to keep looking for new niche markets and consumer bases to open up and exploit while making sure they stay within the law or alternatively work to change the law; an option that the now mainstream pornography industry increasingly employs.

The main body charged with lobbying lawmakers on behalf of the porn industry is the Free Speech Coalition, an organization which, although it was founded in 1991, had to wait until 2002 for its first big legal victory in the case of Ashcroft v. Free Speech Coalition. Here the Supreme Court ruled in favor of the coalition when it declared the 1996 Child Porn Prevention Act unconstitutional because its definition of child pornography (any visual depiction that appears to be a minor engaging in sexually explicit conduct) was ruled to be overly broad. The law was narrowed to cover only those images in which an actual person (rather than one that appears to be) under the age of 18 was involved in making the porn, thus opening the way for the porn industry to use either computer-generated images of children or real porn performers who, although they are 18 and over, are childified to look much younger.

Following the court's decision, there has been an explosion in the number of sites that childify women, as well as those that use computer-generated imagery. In the former category, the pioneer was Hustler's *Barely Legal* porn magazine that started in 1974 and is now a very popular Web site and video series with *Barely Legal 79* released in February 2008. Hustler is owned by Larry Flynt, a multimillionaire who is known in the porn world for being a risk taker and somewhat of a maverick. It is not surprising that it took the Supreme Court's 2002 decision to open the gates to this new genre since before then sites such as *Barely Legal* were vulnerable to prosecution, and few pornographers had either Flynt's money or will to fight a legal battle. Now that the chance of prosecution has been eliminated, sites with childified women[6] have sprung up all over the Web. Consequently more men than ever now have the opportunity to masturbate to pseudo child pornography (PCP)[7] images of "girls"[8] being penetrated by any number of men masquerading as fathers, teachers, employers, coaches, and just plain old anonymous child molesters.[9]

Because pornography that uses children (defined by the law as persons under 18) is still illegal, PCP sites that use adults (defined by the law as persons over 18) to represent children is never called child pornography by the industry. Instead almost all of those sites that childify the female porn performer are found in the subgenre called "teen-porn" or "teen-sex" by the industry. There are any number of ways to access these sites, the most obvious one being Google. Typing "Teen Porn" into Google yields over 13 million hits, and the user has his[10] choice of thousands of porn sites. A number of the 13 million hits are actually for porn portals where "teen porn" is one subcategory of many, and when the user clicks on that category, a list of sites come up that runs for over 90 pages. Moreover, teen porn has it very own portal,[11] which lists hundreds of sub-subgenres such as "Pissing Teens," "Drunk Teens," "Teen Anal Sluts" and "Asian Teens."

Even though these sites are also becoming increasingly popular with porn users, with nearly 14 million Internet searches for "teen sex" in 2006, an increase of 61 percent in just 2 years, and 6 million Internet searches for "teen porn," an increase of 45 percent[12] over the same period, there is very little research on either the content or effects of such sites. One of the main reasons for this could be that those who research the field of child pornography and child sexual abuse prevention have been overwhelmed by the flood of real child pornography that followed the growth of the Internet. Because an actual child is used in the making of such imagery, there is an urgent need to both track the producers and consumers of such pornography and to infiltrate the many international child porn rings that swap thousands of child pornography pictures in the relatively safe and anonymous space created by the Internet. To get some idea of the scope of the problem, one Internet ring that was raided in 1998, called the Wonderland Club, operated in over 12 countries, and to join each prospective member had to have at least 10,000 child pornography images to swap.[13]

Obviously, next to such a mind-boggling level of actual child abuse, researching PCP images appears less pressing because the woman is 18 and, according to the law, no actual crime is taking place. But if we shift our attention away from production and toward consumption, then we can begin to ask questions regarding the possible effects that PCP and actual child pornography may have in common because both aim to sexually arouse men to images of sexualized "children." If, as researchers argue,[14] actual child pornography is used by some men to prepare them for actual assault on a child by both desensitizing them to the harm done to children and arousing them while at the same time offering a blueprint on how to commit the crime, then is it not possible that PCP sites could play a similar role? The answer to such a question depends to a large degree on just how successful the PCP sites are in constructing a reality for the user that he is in fact masturbating to images of sexualized children and not to adults, because he presumably goes to these sites with the goal of gazing at females who look or behave somewhat differently from the thousands of females that populate the regular porn sites. So the first step in developing an analysis of effects is actually an investigation into how PCP sites borrow, employ, and mobilize symbols, codes, conventions, and narratives that are found in actual child pornography. It is only after developing such a map of content that we can begin to ask questions about the ways that PCP images leak into the real world attitudes and behaviors of users.

MAPPING THE CONTENT OF PCP SITES

As the goal is to explore the linkages between PCP sites and actual child pornography, it makes sense to develop a classification system for the former from the typologies developed to classify the latter. One of the most popular of these is, according to Tony Krone,[15] a well-known researcher in the field, a five-point typology of child pornography drawn from the 10-point typology developed by COPINE.[16] Using this typology not only helps to distill the thousands of PCP sites into a workable number of categories, it also provides a way of understanding how users may seamlessly move between the two genres.

The five categories of child pornography described by Krone are:

1. Images depicting nudity or erotic posing with no sexual activity
2. Sexual activity between children or solo masturbation by a child
3. Nonpenetrative sexual activity between adult(s) and child(ren)
4. Penetrative sexual activity between adult(s) and child(ren)
5. Sadism or bestiality

Although there are PCP sites that fall into all five categories, the vast majority fit into categories 2, 4, and 5. The acts, narratives, and visual techniques of the PCP sites in 2, 4, and 5 are drawn from the adult genre of pornography; solo masturbation, penetrative sexual activity, and sadism (not bestiality)[17] are common types of sex acts in mainstream pornography. What follows is a descriptive analysis of those PCP sites that fall into each of the three categories and a discussion on how the sites move from being relatively nonviolent (images of girls masturbating) to images of girls being used sexually in ways that are sadistic and abusive.

Type 2: Sexual Activity between Children, or Solo Masturbation by a Child

The competition for customers is fierce in the porn industry because the user, sitting at his computer and eager to begin his masturbatory session, has a cornucopia of sites, themes, images, and narratives to choose from. The pornographers know this so they attempt to pull the user in quickly by giving the sites names that are short, to the point, and unambiguous. It is therefore not surprising that many of the sites in this category actually have the word solo in the name, along with a word that cues the user into the youthfulness of the females depicted: *Solo Teen, Solo Teen Babe, Sexy Girl Solo, Solo Cuties, Solo Gals, Solo Teen Girls*. When the user clicks on any one of these sites, the first and most striking feature is the body shape of the female porn performers. In place of the large-breasted, curvaceous bodies that populate regular porn Web sites are small-breasted, slightly built women with adolescent-looking faces that are relatively free of makeup. Many of these performers do look younger than 18, but they do not look like children, so the pornographers use a range of techniques to make them appear more childlike than they actually are. Primary among these is the use of childhood clothes and props, such as stuffed animals, lollipops, pigtails, pastel-colored ribbons, ankle socks, braces on their teeth, and, of course, the school uniform. It is not unusual to see a female porn performer wearing a school uniform, sucking a lollipop, and hugging a teddy bear as she masturbates with a dildo.

Another technique for childifying the woman's body is the removal of all the pubic hair so the external genitalia looks like that of a prepubescent female. It is interesting that over the years this technique has lost much of its signifying power as it is now commonplace in porn for women to remove all their pubic hair. The result is that today virtually every female porn performer looks like a child, a shift that in itself is cause for concern as those porn users who are not looking for pseudo-child images nonetheless are exposed to them when they surf the porn sites. This normalization of a shaved pubic area is increasingly filtering down into mainstream pop culture. Regular articles in women's magazines discuss the best way to remove pubic hair; TV shows such as *Sex and the City* publicize and eroticize the Brazilian bikini wax; and beauty salons across the country promote the Brazilian as a way to spice up sex.[18] The effect this is having on adolescent girls was made evident to me when I spoke to the Sexual Assault Nurse Examiner (SANE) conference in Boston in 2007. These nurses administer rape kits on adolescents who are the victims of sexual assault, and one of their tasks is to check for the markers of puberty with pubic hair being a key marker. However, I was informed that this is no longer effective because girls are removing the hair as soon as it grows in, something that the nurses had never seen before. In my interviews with college-age females, I repeatedly hear that pubic hair is considered unhygienic and a sexual turnoff by their boyfriends so they now wax or shave. This is probably one of the clearest examples of how a porn-generated practice slips into the lives of real women, no doubt because a good percentage of the male partners have become accustomed to and aroused by images of women in porn.

For all of the visual clues of childhood surrounding the women in PCP sites, however, it is the written text accompanying the images that does most of the work in convincing the user that he is masturbating to images of sexual activity involving a minor. The words used to describe the women's bodies (including their vaginas)—tiny, small, petite, tight, cute, teeny—not only stress their youthfulness, but also work to separate them from women on other sites because these adjectives are rarely used to describe women in regular porn. Most striking is how many of these PCP sites refer to females as sweeties, sweethearts, little darlings, cutie pies, or honeys; these terms of endearment starkly contrast with the abusive names the women on other sites are called—slut, whore, cumdumpster, and cunt being the most popular slurs. The use of kinder terms on the PCP sites is a method of preserving the notion for the user that these girls are somehow different from the rest of the women who populate the world of porn in that they are not yet used-up whores deserving of verbal abuse. This would explain why so many of these Web sites have the word "innocent" in their name—for example, *Innocent Cute, Innocent Dream, Innocent Love,* and *Petite Innocent.*

The reason that innocence is so central to the marketing of the sites and the reason the girls are portrayed as not yet sullied, dirtied, soiled, or tainted by sex is that the promise offered on the Website is to witness their loss of innocence. One fan of this genre, writing to a porn discussion forum, calls this a "knowing innocence," which he defines as "the illusion of innocence giving way to unbridled sexuality. Essentially, this is the old throwback of the Madonna and the whore. Therein lies the vast majority of my attraction to this genre."[19] This fan, and indeed many others, if their posts are to be believed, make clear that for them the pleasure is in watching the (sweet, cute, petite) Madonna being coaxed, encouraged, and manipulated by adult men into revealing the whore that lies beneath the (illusionary) innocence. The pornographers reveal their understanding of the nature of this spectatorial pleasure when they offer the guarantee to their consumers that the "girls" they are watching are "first-timers," having their "first sexual experience," which, of course, leads to their "first orgasm ever." The *Solo Teen* site goes so far as to promise that "Here you will ONLY find the cutest teen girls. . . . Our girls are fresh and inexperienced and very sexy in an innocent kind of way."[20] It is thus no surprise that most of these sites advertise "fresh girls added each week" because using the same performer twice would cut into the sexual excitement of the viewer. How, after all, does one defile an already defiled girl?

The story of the "defilement" told on these sites is genre-bound in that it almost always starts with an eager but innocent girl who is gently and playfully coaxed by off-camera adult men into sexually performing for the pleasure of the viewer. This is the narrative informing most of the images on the *SoloTeengirls.com* site, which has hundreds of movies available to members, as well as hundreds of still photographs posted on their site as a teaser for nonmembers. Each woman has five photographs and a written text detailing her supposed first sexual experience. For "Natasha," the story goes as follows:

> This lil cutie came in pretending that she couldn't wait to be naked in front of the camera. And . . . we couldn't wait to see her. As she started to take off her clothes and show off, she giggled and smiled, but we could tell she was nervous, and when she found out that naked meant showing off her snug little teen pussy, she blushed! But showing off her pussy proved to be too much of a turn-on, and when *we encouraged* her to play with it, she could not resist. This beautiful teen girl really *did have her first time* on camera, and we got to watch her stroke that velvety teen pussy. (emphasis added)[21]

The message that the written text conveys in this story can be found throughout the Web sites in this category as it embodies the way the pornographers carefully craft a story of who is really innocent and who is really culpable in the scenario. For all the supposed innocence of the "lil cutie," as evidenced by her nervousness, giggling, smiling, and blushing, it really only took a bit of encouragement to get her to masturbate for the camera, which in porn-world language is another way of saying that it didn't take much for her to reveal the slut she really is. It is this very culpability on the part of the girl that simultaneously divests the user of his culpability in masturbating to what would be, in reality, a scenario of adult men manipulating a naïve girl into masturbating for the pleasure of other adult men, himself included.

The solo teen sites are a gentle way to introduce the user to PCP because the absence of adult male performers in these sites means that the pornographers can construct a story for the user that avoids talking about heterosexual sex with underage girls and instead talks about a hot girl who, on the cusp of discovering her sexuality, needs just a little gentle verbal encouragement to finally take the plunge. The following classification of sites, those which have actual penetrative sex by a man, construct the male performer as both active and visible, and yet still manage to create a narrative that allows the user to believe he is watching consensual, nonexploitive sex, and not the sexual abuse of a minor.

Type 4: Penetrative Sexual Activity between Adult(s) and Child(ren)

The overriding theme on those PCP sites that show nonsadistic sexual activity between a "child" and an adult is her supposed loss of virginity, a loss that the user gets to witness in excruciating clarity. With names such as *Bloody Virgins*, *First Time Sex*, *Real Virgins*, and *Defloration*, these sites make it very clear to the user just what he is getting. I have included these sites in the nonsadistic category, not because they don't include images of women in pain—many do as the women clearly experience pain as they are being penetrated for the first time—but because the sex acts in and of themselves are not of the body-punishing, abusive type that is standard in the more hard-core sites described in the sadistic category below.

The sex depicted in these sites differs markedly from much of the sex on regular porn sites as the adult male displays affection for the female in the form of kissing and caressing. This is a real departure from most porn sex as even in feature movies,[22] where there is some perfunctory kissing and touching, signs of affection give way very quickly to the usual mind-numbing penetration of the female's orifices. In these

PCP sites the kissing and touching actually lasts through much of the movie, and rarely is the woman called a slut or a whore. What is also striking to anyone who is familiar with the codes and conventions of Internet porn is that the male actually keeps asking the female in a tender way if the sex feels okay, or if he should slow down in case he is hurting her.

But rather than seeing these differences as a positive step toward a less violent type of porn, what they actually represent are techniques aimed to authenticate representation of the consensual loss of virginity by a younger female to an adult male. On these sites there is no mention of coercion or even subtle manipulation as the performer is depicted as eager to lose her virginity. Moreover, as the male performer is clearly older and more mature, were he to behave like most men in porn, he would reveal himself to be a violent and manipulative exploiter of underage girls; an image that would destroy the carefully crafted story of him as a tender teacher, gently leading an innocent but ripe and ready girl through this major rite of passage. On these sites, any type of text, image, or sex act that remotely suggests coercion would situate the user as a co-conspirator in a scenario that could be read as the rape of a minor; a role that many men may find uncomfortable and that might prevent them from coming back for more.

One site that seems to be very popular, given its top billing on many of the teen porn Web portals, and its constant pop-up advertisement that appears while on other teen porn sites, is *Defloration.com*. Claiming to be "The first website about virginity since 1998," and promising the user "real acts of defloration," the home page is dominated by a picture of two hands stretching open a vagina so the user can get a clear view of the internal genitalia, which depicts, the site claims, an "intact hymen."[23] Alongside this picture are four smaller images; one has a doll resting on a woman's thigh, and a second has a lollipop placed inside a stretched vagina. The text by the side of the picture explains that the hymen is:

> A mysterious body part that is lost by young girls when they have sexual intercourse for the first time. Few people have ever seen what this fragile object looks like. A girl who has never had sexual intercourse (a virgin) is supposed to have her hymen intact. In many societies, a girl's virginity until marriage is considered a great virtue. For a girl who possesses such chastity, getting married becomes easy.

Once the pornographers have eroticized the hymen with its "mysterious" quality and "fragile" state that is "stretched and ruptured by the erect penis," they explain to the user that the "girl" may experience "discomfort and bleeding" during intercourse. For many porn users, this is too good an offer to miss because they get to anticipate seeing something real unfold before them, rather than a staged performance by a "whore."

For $38 a month, the user gets a cornucopia of images on the site to choose from as there are pages and pages of Eastern European girls, and for each you can click on a selection of stills or an actual movie that is split into two segments: "Hymen Performance" and "Losing of Virginity." In the first, a male masturbates the girl and then stretches her vagina open so the viewer gets a clear internal shot. The second segment is a long and drawn-out documentation of her being penetrated as she is grimacing and often asking her penetrator to be careful because the act is painful. This continues, sometimes for 10 to 15 minutes, until he withdraws his blood-stained penis. The camera lingers on the penis, showing the user clear evidence of the "defloration," and then the male performer takes his penis and smears the blood over the buttocks and thighs of the female, an act that mirrors the usual "money shot" in porn where the semen is rubbed all over the woman's body.

On this site and others of this type, the techniques used to childify the women are not so much childhood clothes or props, but the actual behavior of the women during sex. For those men accustomed to seeing mainstream adult porn, the women in these sites look inexperienced by comparison. In place of the writhing, oiled, voluptuous women who look like they know exactly what they are doing, these women look like younger females who are unsure of how to perform sex for the camera. Their bodies are not arched enough, their moans are not throaty enough, and their movements are awkward, sometimes to the point of being clumsy. Given the nature of the porn industry, it is unlikely that these women are acting the part because they are not top-tier porn performers, but just a few of the many thousands of women who move in and out of the industry at an alarming rate. It is much more likely that the viewer is witnessing not only the girl's first porn movie ever, but much worse, the first time she is being penetrated vaginally so these girls are indeed having the loss of their virginity documented by the porn industry, to be circulated over and over again for men's masturbatory pleasure.

No matter how much these girls grimace, they say they are enjoying the sex, and they moan intermittently as a way to mimic arousal. This actually reflects what goes on in real child pornography, according to Kenneth Lanning,[24] as much of the illegal child pornography he has investigated does show the child looking somewhat like a willing accomplice, appearing as if they are eagerly consenting to the experience. Of course, this is a lie but one that Lanning argues many perpetrators, and indeed some lawyers, social workers, and police believe, because they view the image as a truth teller rather than a carefully constructed representation of reality that is produced with specific goals in mind. In their research on men convicted of downloading child pornography, Quayle and Taylor found that these men looked for "superficial clues which allowed the viewer to believe that the children in the pictures were consenting and enjoyed being photographed."[25] One such user, a man convicted of downloading child pornography, explained that he was just looking for "images of girls mainly. Girls actually having sex. And they had to look happy . . . I mean I wasn't looking for rape or anything."[26]

In the next type of sites to be discussed, those that can be classed as sadistic, the girls also look as if they are enjoying the sex, even though in this category, we are watching physical, sexual and verbal abuse being perpetrated against them.

Type 5: Sadism

Before describing these sites, there are some definitional problems that need to be explored. Although the term "sadism" may seem obvious, it does in fact take on a polysemic quality when it is used to describe what is happening to women in pornography. In the typology above, sadism is defined as "sexual images involving pain," but in pornography, no matter how cruel and abusive the sex act, the woman is instructed to look as if she is experiencing pleasure, not pain. In addition to the gagging and pounding anal sex mentioned above, pornography that falls into this category, called Gonzo or wall-to-wall[27] by the industry, includes acts in which the woman is slapped, has her hair pulled, her throat grabbed, and objects are used to stretch open her orifices.[28] As all this is happening, she is not only being called any number of names, including bitch, whore, slut, cumdumpster, and cunt, she is also begging for more abuse. This, of course, is the narrative of porn; women love to be used and abused, and if female porn performers want to work in the industry, they have to act in ways that conform to this narrative. Although porn users tend to take the images at face value and claim that such acts are not sadistic because they do not cause pain, antiporn feminists argue that these acts are an assault on the body of the performer. Regardless of how the woman is acting, they believe such acts are sadistic.[29] This is the position I am taking in this article; hence porn with these types of acts will be classed as sadistic.

These PCP sites dispense with any attempt to project the girls as innocent yet ready to be gently introduced into the world of adult sex. These females, although they are also depicted as being new to sex, are portrayed as wanting it as rough and as hard as all the other women in Gonzo porn. The site *Teen Dirt Bags*,[30] for example, boasts that its "slutty girls are taking cock in their fresh unused pussies!" so the viewer can see "the cutest little tramps suck, fuck, swallow, and beg for more." Mention is often made of how innocent these girls look, but this is described as being a ruse because just below the surface is a raging slut for whom nothing is too painful, demeaning, debasing, or dehumanizing. This is illustrated in the following description of Keri who, according to the text surrounding the images, is:

> such a sweet young thing, you'd never believe that she has the mind of a pervert! She looks so innocent and prude, but don't let her fool you, this little slut is a dirty little whore! Keri demonstrated that as she spread her ass cheeks apart and begged him to drill her tight little ass! He granted her wish and gave her an anal pounding like she never had before![31]

The use of so-called teens in Gonzo porn allows the pornographer to layer yet another level of abuse on the already abusive Gonzo genre. The physical and emotional immaturity of teens makes space for a whole range of scenarios that heighten and intensify the violence because they can be easily manipulated into doing just about anything, no matter how painful and cruel. Moreover, their bodies, which have not yet fully developed, have more potential to be damaged. Not surprisingly, throughout these sites, constant mention is made of the teen's small vagina and anus, but unlike the solo porn sites, the goal here is not to stress her "innocence" but to highlight the damage that will be done to her body when she is penetrated by an adult male's penis. The men's penises are described as being extra large, having the power to "break," "rip," tear," and "split" her orifices, which are not yet mature. On the site *I Am Eighteen*, the reader is invited to "watch us break her tiny body with some hard, pussy-splitting fucking!" while over on the *Ass Plundering* site,[32] the tagline boasts that "we plunder these tight little virgin asses." The level of cruelty depicted in the movies is made apparent by the accompanying text, which promises all kinds of injuries that the user gets to witness, some so severe that the "bitches wouldn't be able to walk for a week after the utter anal demolishing." The site is littered with pictures of "hot, little, innocent girls" with red, raw anuses. Although these are standard images in non-teen Gonzo, they have greater authenticity when they are attached to a "teen" or a "virgin" because their bodies are less able to deal with such violent penetration.

Many of these sites pair the teen with much older men and highlight the age difference in their names—sites such as *Old Farts Young*

Tarts, Old and Young Gang Bang, Old and Young Porn, Old Men Fucking.
These older men, some of them in their sixties and seventies, are
depicted as using some form of manipulation and trickery to get the
teen. The teen, depicted as naive and unsophisticated, is easily fooled.
Not content with just eroticizing the age imbalance between the girl
and the man, the pornographers throw in the economic inequality that
exists between young and older people as a way to provide the male
with even more power over her. On one such popular site, aptly
named *Teens for Cash,* the site banner reads: They're Young, They're
Dumb and They'll Do Anything for Money. Here, scenario after scenario depicts teens offering to do odd jobs for extra cash, only to be
seduced into prostituting themselves by the promise of real money.
A typical scenario reads:

> Tatiana arrives to give the guy's house a thorough cleaning. However,
> housekeeping doesn't pay much, so when Dick and Rod offer her cash
> to clean her carpet Tatiana is all over them. Once she vacuums the dust
> off their old pussy punishers, Tatiana is the one left cleaning up the
> mess![33]

Surrounding the text are images of "Tatiana" gleefully holding
money as she is anally, vaginally, and orally penetrated by men who
look to be at least in their sixties.

Another scenario that offers much potential for exploitation by
the pornographers is the teen girl as babysitter. Here the females are
not only younger, but they are also in his home in an
employer–employee relationship. Given the multiple power imbalances here, it is no surprise that the teen porn genre is full of sites
with titles such as *Fuck the Babysitter, Drunk Baby Sitter, Gag the
Babysitter, Dirty Babysitter, Babysitter Lust,* and *Banged Babysitter.*
Although the scenarios may differ at the margins, they are all ultimately the same. They all tell the story of a young hot babysitter who
is seduced by an older man, the result being a thrilling sexual
encounter for all parties involved. This desire on the part of users to
convince themselves that they are masturbating to images of consensual thrilling sex explains the narrative found in another popular
Gonzo PCP subgenre, namely incest porn. The sites that sexualize
and legitimize incest run the gamut of possible incestuous pairings
(mother and son, sibling on sibling, extended family, etc.) but, without doubt, the most common portrayal is of father and daughter.
Although it is clear that any sexual relationship between a father and
his minor daughter is rape, the sites go to great lengths to provide the
user with an alternative framing of father–daughter incest. This is

especially clear on the site *YoungDaughter.com*. The first thing on the home page is the following "explanation":

> The disapproval of incest, especially between father and daughter, is a classic example of projection. The alleged reason for diasproval (sic) is that incest is the same as sexual abuse, aggression and violence. These are all rational arguments, but they are used to justify an irrational opinion. In fact, most cases of incest have little to do with violence.[34]

Indeed, if these sites were to be believed, incest is what happens when a seductive and manipulative "daughter" finally gets her reluctant "father" to succumb to her sexual advances. On the site *Daddy's Whore*, the reader is invited to watch "sexy naughty girls seducing their own fathers," and on *My Sexy Daughter* the female performers are defined as, "sweet, irresistible angels teasing and tempting their own daddies."[35] The site *First Time with Daddy* asks the user to "check out forbidden love stories," in which sexually curious daughters are eying their fathers' bodies with lust. A typical story line reads:

> I have fancied my father for years. I thought it was a perversion and was afraid to reveal my emotions. . . . Once I saw him in a wet dream. This was a sign. Still half a sleep (sic) I went into his room and jumped onto his bed.[36]

Of course, it doesn't take much to get the father to acquiesce. Surrounding the text are images of the "daughter" being penetrated orally, anally, and vaginally by the "father."

In those stories in which the father is seen as the active seducer, the girls are generally only too happy to oblige. Once the sexual "relationship" begins, it is clear that the sex was better than either could ever have imagined. Even in those occasional stories in which the daughter is somewhat afraid, the end result is orgasmic sex. In one story a "daughter" explains that:

> my mom died 3 years ago. Since then dad never brought home a woman. Soon I started noticing very strange looks he gave me. I was even a little afraid. One evening dad came to my room. I was sitting on my bed. He approached me and. . . . [37]

A sequence of eight images surrounding the text tells the story of a clothed anxious girl succumbing to the sexual advances of the father, ending up naked and orgasmic on a bed. What stands out in this story, and indeed in most of the scenarios in these sites, is the absence of a mother to protect the daughter from the father's abuse. Some of the scenarios, such as the one described above, say that the mother is dead, but most make no reference to a mother at all, creating a family scene in which the girl is isolated and at the mercy of the perpetrating father. This lack of a mother is actually not unusual in cases of father–daughter incest. In her study,[38] Judith Herman found that over half the sexually abused girls she interviewed had mothers who were absent from the daily routine of the family due to ill health or death. In these families Herman describes fathers who are controlling and patriarchal; "as the family providers, they felt they had the right to be nurtured and served at home, if not by their wives, then by their daughters."[39] For some of these fathers being "nurtured" extended to being sexually serviced by their daughters who were turned into surrogate wives, even though they were children physically and mentally. Of course, the real-life consequences of such abuse look nothing like the fairy tale world of incest porn; these girls all exhibited many symptoms consistent with PTSD.

The reduction of the daughter to an object to be used by the father is most stark on the UseMyDaughter.com site (the banner reads: "Want to Fuck My Daughter?"), which tells the story of a drunken father pimping out his daughter to any man who will pay. The images and the sex in the films are standard Gonzo porn, but the narrative that contextualizes the images tells a story of economic degradation and poverty, with the way out being the daughter's prostitution. The text introducing the site reads:

> Meet my daughter Janessa, she's 19 years old and like her mom, she is so freakin' hot. And its no fucking secret to the world that she loves to fuck. What a fucking slut! i think she got that from her mom. God damn her womb is so polluted . . . aaanyways. My daughter fucks some stupid guys anywhere she goes. I was like WTF!? for free? Shit! I didn't raise her to get fucked for free! Well, im a bum old, and im always fucking wasted so fuck that, now i let her fuck any guy she wants as long as the guy pays me some cash bucks. . . . Aww fuck that, why dont you hit join now!!! Watch this slut take cocks for cash in my pockets.[40]

The "daughter" or slut, as the father constantly refers to her, is depicted as an active and willing player in the scenarios, often leaving her father by the roadside as she speeds off with the latest john. The text makes constant reference to the father's drinking and poverty as a way to minimize his culpability in turning his daughter into a prostitute and also finds a way to put the blame on the absent mother by mentioning her "polluted" womb.

All the sites discussed so far, even the Gonzo ones, depict scenarios in which the men do not use overt force to get the girl to comply with their sexual demands. Rather the fathers seduce, manipulate, and cajole the girl into submission. This picture actually mirrors what goes on in the real world of child molestation as most of the victims are subject to a seasoning process in which the perpetrator first seduces the child with gifts, affection, calculated acts of kindness, and offers of friendship or mentoring. Having forged a bond, the perpetrator then manipulates and exploits the emotional connection to erode the child's resistance to sexual activity and to ensure the child's silence. For perpetrators this is a safer way than overt force because it does not leave visible scars, and because it is an act of breaking the child's will, the victim is more likely to keep the abuse hidden for fear of appearing disloyal to the perpetrator. Moreover, the bond acts as a kind of glue for the child, keeping her or him connected even when the adult is perpetrating awful acts of sexual violence. The pornographers are well aware of this seasoning process, and they do an excellent job of depicting it in their movies by showing a whole range of techniques: from gift giving to strategic acts of kindness, in which the perpetrator poses as a kind (sexual) mentor. Always brazen, the pornographers constantly use the word "breaking" to refer to what they are doing to the girls, and one site even calls itself "Breaking Them In."

Probably the most detailed, graphic, and violent example of PCP porn that acts as an instructional manual on how to break a girl is the *Cherry Poppers* series, produced and directed by one of the founders of Gonzo porn, Max Hardcore. Known for his brutality and use of bizarre objects (such as dental tools) to torture women, Hardcore has reached almost legendary status in the industry as a man willing to take porn to ever more extreme levels. In the *Cherry Poppers* series of 11 episodes, Hardcore shows the user in unbearable detail how to physically and emotionally season a girl (often dressed in school uniform and knee-high socks) into compliance and silence. As a way to illustrate this, I will describe a scene from *Cherry Poppers* Vol. 10, in which Hardcore, on finding the younger sister of his girlfriend alone in her house, proceeds to show her "what boys like" and warns her not to tell her sister what happened as "she'll get mad."

Hardcore begins by showing the girl how to fondle his penis, instructing her to "give it a little kiss, don't be afraid to suck it. Just like a sucker, just like a lollipop." He continues to instruct her in a soft, gentle voice. She removes her clothes and continues to perform fellatio on him; "take a deep breath," he tells her, taking his penis out of her mouth at times to let her breathe. He also shows her how to produce enough saliva to make the oral sex pleasurable for him. After Hardcore puts her on the sink and shaves her pubic area, he penetrates her with his fingers before vaginal intercourse, something

rapists of girls often find necessary in order to stretch the child's
vagina so that it won't be torn or ruptured by an adult penis. He then
does the same with her anus. Throughout the sexual activity, Hardcore
alternates gentle talk of her being a "good girl" with rougher
reminders that she is a cunt. "Say it," he demands, yelling at her, and
she repeats, not looking at him, "I'm a little cunt." Alternation
between being gentle and abusive goes on throughout the film and is
a strategy pedophiles use to terrify, seduce, and confuse the victim.
The very last scene is Max Hardcore taking a picture of the naked and
semen-covered girl as she smiles for the camera.

At the very moment when Hardcore takes a picture of his victim,
he reveals, intentionally or unintentionally, possible links between
PCP, real child porn, and molestation. Studies show that a good proportion of pedophiles take pictures of their victims to document the
abuse for (1) their own or other pedophiles' future masturbation, (2) to
blackmail the child into silence as they threaten to show the photos to
friends if the child reveals the abuse, and (3) to show future victims
how to perform sex. Max Hardcore's behavior in *Cherry Poppers* looks
like a studied account of how to season and rape a child, and any man
watching him will be well schooled in the nuts and bolts of perpetrator behavior. *Cherry Poppers*, and indeed all the other sites mentioned,
are carefully crafted to give the user a sense that the girls depicted are
indeed girls and not women, but how these images play out in the real
world has yet to be researched. These sites have not been the focus of
empirical analysis. We can explore, however, how these sites may act
as socializing agents for their users by constructing a particular set of
ideologies that normalize children as legitimate sexual partners for
adult men.

IMAGES AND IDEOLOGY: THE WORLD ACCORDING TO PCP

Once he clicks on these sites, the user is bombarded through
images and words with an internally consistent ideology that legit-
imizes, condones, and celebrates a sexual desire for children. The
norms and values that circulate in society that define adult–child sex
as deviant and abusive are wholly absent in PCP, and in their place is
a cornucopia of sites that deliver the message (to his brain via the
penis) that sex with children is hot fun for all. As the user clicks on the
PCP sites, he enters a pseudo-virtual community that welcomes him
in through constant usage of the word "we," rather than the singular
"I" or "you." In identifying with the others implicit in the word "we,"
he gets to participate in a ready-made group of like-minded men who
actually know him so well that they can anticipate his likes and needs,

as in the teaser for *MySexyDaughter.com:* "We know you enjoy rough and bewildering incest action, so we have a very special thing for you."[41]

For those men whose primary sexual interest is children, PCP is an obvious first step into the world of child pornography because it is a relatively safe way to access images that can be used for masturbatory purposes. With their use of uninitiated porn performers who look young, the strategic placing of childhood props, and a written text that highlights and sexualizes the girl's supposed child status, the PCP sites are a workable substitute for those men not yet ready to break the law and open themselves up to possible prison time, not to mention the stigma of being caught with such material. This "community" he has found by typing into Google a collection of words that speak to his most secret sexual desires plays an important role in validating his feelings and desires because the sites constantly highlight just how much the object of his lust enjoys the sex.[42] For these men PCP sites can be seen as kind of a low-stakes primer, nudging, encouraging, and in a way seducing them into joining the club with promises of community, friendship, and understanding, the very things that a nascent pedophile may lack the most. In a perverse way the sites are seasoning the would-be-user in much the same way a professional predator seasons his prey. They first find out what the mark lacks and then tease and manipulate him into compliance with the promise of fulfilling these deeply felt needs.

Sometime these sites reel in the user by tossing out a challenge to his masculinity, a sure way to get most porn users to bite because pornography is after all ultimately about pumping up masculinity through the debasement of everything that is coded as female—in this case children. Nowhere is this clearer than on the animated incest site, which tells the men that incest is "an amazing way of learning about yourself and your dearest people!" But then the site tells the user that if "he is not yet brave enough to try," the next best thing is "our hand-drawn group incest stories based on totally crazy things real people tried."[43] The implicit question here is: are you man enough to take the first step and masturbate to images that are truly so deviant and transgressive that it takes someone really brave to do the real thing?

Although these PCP sites may satisfy the user for a time, desensitization eventually leads to boredom and the need for harder and more extreme porn. The obvious next place to go is real child pornography. Here a real child is used, and the truly illegal and hence secretive nature of the porn is only going to add an even greater erotic thrill to the user, who has been somewhat desensitized by now. Indeed Quayle and Taylor[44] found in their study of men convicted of downloading child pornography that even the real thing became boring after a while, with men seeking out more overtly violent images of younger and younger children. Although this descent into utterly abusive and violent child porn is not a given for PCP users, these sites may only whet his appetite for more, not fewer, images of real child pornography because they will always fall short on delivering their promise of watching a real child turned into a whore as their legality means that she was not a child.

But what about those men who are not looking for a substitute to the real thing? Rather they prefer to have sex with adult women, yet they masturbate to the PCP sites. It is obvious that such men are visiting these sites. The sheer volume of traffic makes clear that these sites are generating interest across a broad range of men. Why would they go to these sites rather than the thousands of others that offer a dizzying and increasingly cruel array of sex acts that are played out on the adult female body? The answer is the same for these men as it is for pedophiles: desensitization. In one of the few studies on men's use of pornography in the age of the Internet, Pamela Paul[45] spoke to a cross section of porn users, many of whom expressed shock at just how quickly their viewing preferences had turned to increasingly violent and bizarre porn genres that they previously had found distasteful. Now, however, they actively sought out these sites. Many of these genres featured adult women—including urination, bestiality, and heavy bondage—but for some men, children became the object of their sexual desire, especially after they clicked on the pop-up ads for teen porn, which led them into the PCP sites and eventually into real child porn. For some men the teen sites were just a stepping-stone to the real thing, as they moved seamlessly from adult women to children. David G. Heffler, a psychotherapist who counsels child pornography offenders, was recently quoted in a story in the *Buffalo News*. In the article, he stated that in his clinical work he has had many men who revealed that "after looking at adult porn a long time, they get bored. They want something different. They start looking at children. Then, they can't get enough of it."[46]

This slide from adult to child pornography flies in the face of conventional wisdom. We tend to think of men who are sexually aroused by children as pedophiles who form a distinct and separate group from other men by virtue of their deviant sexual interests and behavior. However, after a thorough analysis of the empirical literature, sociologist Diana Russell[47] argues that the research on pedophiles points not to a model of two clearly defined groups (pedophiles and non-pedophiles), but rather to a continuum with some men clearly situated at either end, and others are not only scattered along the continuum but also subject to shifts, depending on the particular constellation of their life experiences, at any one time. Russell notes that although past researchers have pointed to unusual life experiences, such as the loss of a spouse, substance abuse, and unemployment as contributory factors, today studies suggest that ongoing use of pornography increasingly plays a role in shifting men along the continuum.

Russell's analysis of how men can be socialized into eroticizing and sexualizing children through PCP leads her to the profoundly disturbing conclusion that for both pedophiles and non-pedophiles alike, this type of pornography "can serve as a bridge between adult pornography and child pornography." Because there are no actual large-scale empirical studies on this subject, it is impossible to point to any findings. But if Russell is correct, and the anecdotal evidence suggests that she is, then the continued and increasing popularity of PCP will have devastating implications for child sexual abuse. First, the demand for real child pornography will increase, which will mean a greater number of children being abused for the purpose of production, and second, a greater number of children will be at risk of being sexually abused by men who use the pornography as a stepping-stone to contact sex with a child. The research on the relationship between consuming pornography and actual contact sex with a child suggests that a percentage of men will act out their desires on real children after viewing child porn. Quayle and Taylor found in their study of convicted child offenders that "for some respondents, pornography was used as a substitute for actual offending, whereas for others, it acted as both blueprint and stimulus for contact offense."[48] Although the actual percentage of child porn users who also sexually victimize children varies from study to study, with some putting the number as low as 40 percent[49] and others as high as 80 percent,[50] the weight of the evidence is that masturbation to images of sexualized children is linked to actual child sexual abuse for a significant proportion of men.

In addition to the psychological literature on the effects of child pornography on individual men's behaviors and attitudes, there is a wealth of research within media studies that show that people construct their notions of reality from the media they consume, and the more consistent and coherent the message, the more people believe it to be true.[51] Thus the images of girls in PCP does not operate within a social vacuum; rather they are produced and consumed in a society in which the dominant pop culture images are of childified women, adultified children, and hyper-sexualized youthful female bodies. Encoded within all of these images is an ideology that encourages the sexual objectification of the female body; an ideology that is internalized by both males and females and has become so widespread that it normalizes the sexual use and abuse of females. This does not mean that all men who read PCP will rape a child, or even be sexually attracted to a child. It does mean, however, that on a cultural level, when we sexualize the female child, we chip away at the norms that define children as off limits to male sexual use. The more we undermine such cultural norms, the more we drag girls into the category of "woman," and in a porn-saturated world, to be a woman is to be a sexual object deserving of male contempt, use, and abuse.

With the advent of the Internet and the resultant mass explosion of porn production and consumption, we entered into an experimental zone. Never before has pornography been so accessible and anonymous, the two key factors that make it especially attractive to men. If the porn industry wants to keep increasing its consumer base and revenue, it will have to continue to ramp up its images because its consumers are easily bored and always on the lookout for more extreme images. No one can predict where all this will lead, but we do know that images of childified women are a big moneymaker, and in the porn industry, as in all other industries, maximizing profit is the only thing that matters. For those of us who put the welfare of children above profits, it will take a well-organized movement to stem the legal, political, and cultural power of this multibillion-dollar–industry. Without any such protest, pornographers will continue to do business as usual, and our culture will become an even more pornified and hostile place for women and children.

10

Prostitution and the Sexualization of Children

Melissa Farley

The process of imposing a sexualized subordinate identity on women begins in childhood. Men's dominance over women is established by sexual objectification, a dehumanizing process that is at the psychological core of violence against women.[1] Sexual objectification subordinates women to men by exaggerating differences and by treating women and girls with contempt, ridicule, and violence, thus placing them in an inferior status. It also paves the way for sexual violence against women and children: incest, rape, sexual harassment, battering, prostitution, pornography, and sex trafficking.

Not merely the display of images, sexual objectification is an active, engaged, ongoing process that harms women and girls in a myriad of complex interactions on the street, in homes, at jobs, in schools, and in relationships with partners and families. For example, one woman described the intrusive sexual objectification of hate speech euphemistically termed "catcalls:"

> While it is true that for these men I am nothing but, let us say, a "nice piece of ass," there is more involved in this encounter than their mere fragmented perception of me. They could, after all, have enjoyed me in silence. I could have passed by without being turned to stone. But I must be made to know that I am a "nice piece of ass": I must be made to see myself as they see me.[2]

Prostitution is "ground zero"[3] for the sexual objectification of women. As Andrea Dworkin wrote,

> When men use women in prostitution, they are expressing a pure hatred for the female body. It is as pure as anything on this earth ever is or ever has been. It is a contempt so deep, so deep, that a whole human life is reduced to a few sexual orifices, and he can do anything he wants.[4]

Prostitution of children is best understood as commercialized rape of children. Children typically enter prostitution, an organized form of child sexual abuse, as a result of sexual or physical abuse by caregivers. They are then recruited by pimps, kidnapped, or sold into prostitution by parents or caregivers.

Girls are sexualized when they are very young. A 2007 report by the American Psychological Association documented the sexualization of girls as young as 4 years who were targeted by every form of media, including television, music videos, music lyrics, movies, magazines, sports media, video games, the Internet, and advertising.[5] The APA report noted that the sexualization of girls was linked to low self-esteem, depression, and eating disorders.

Today, popular culture markets prostitution to girls as glamorous, fun, sexy, and an easy source of income. Girls who are poor or who are marginalized on the basis of their race or ethnicity or who lack alternatives are especially vulnerable to these messages. As a result children and their parents spend lots of money helping girls mimic smiling strippers and escorts—the mainstreamed mask of prostitution.

As girls are becoming increasingly sexualized by popular culture, they are more likely to be the object of men's sexual fantasies, and because children are more easily controlled than adults, children are a lucrative sector of the prostitution market.

THE POWERFUL EFFECT OF THE MEDIA ON CHILDREN'S ATTITUDES AND BEHAVIOR

What is it that corporations are selling to children? Is it simply a thong here, a grossly sexualized doll there? Corporations project rigid and stereotyped ideas of femininity and sexuality onto children who are not able to analyze or reject that objectification of themselves, according to columnist Cynthia Peters. In her analysis of a fashion layout titled *Babes in Coutureland*,[6] which featured 6- to 10-year-olds striking sexual poses, Peters writes that corporations:

> want to colonize the farthest reaches of our souls in order to better make money off of us. Sexuality is a potentially dangerous independent

island nation—a rogue state that must be brought into service of the marketplace from a very early age. Teach 7-year-olds that sexual expression is a matter of accessorizing and you've secured a lifetime of purchases in the lingerie department. Dissociate sex from nonmarket feelings (pleasure, desire, intimacy) and associate it instead with consumable superficialities, and you'll not only keep the rabble in line, you'll have them lined up at the mall.[7]

U.S. culture is market-driven, and corporations don't hesitate to employ deeply sexist and racist advertising to children as long as those messages sell products. In *Brandchild: Remarkable Insights into the Minds of Today's Global Kids and their Relationships to Brands*, Allen Kanner, co-founder of Campaign for a Commercial-Free Childhood, noted that the 2002 global market share of products sold to teenagers was $202 billion.[8] Television, social networking Web sites such as YouTube and MySpace, movies, music videos, video games, and magazines aimed at children convey powerful messages that are psychologically incorporated, directly influencing children's attitudes and behavior. Many of these messages have damaging effects on children:

Excessive media use, particularly where the content is violent, gender-stereotyped, sexually explicit, drug- or-alcohol-influenced, or filled with human tragedy, skews the child's world view . . . and alters his/her capacity for successful, sustained human relationships.[9]

A 10-year review of research on the effects of media on children documented that media exposure resulted in increased violent and aggressive behavior, increased high-risk behaviors, and accelerated onset of sexual activity. Adolescent psychiatrist Villani recommended that health care professionals inquire about children's media history in order to assess the extent of exposure to toxic messages, their degree of internalization, and risk.[10]

For the most part, the extensive research regarding damaging media influences on children has been ignored. Analyzing the public's response to scientific facts about media violence and media disinformation about the violence in its own industry, psychologists Bushman and Anderson conclude,

Fifty years of news coverage on the link between media violence and aggression have left the U.S. public confused. Typical news articles pit researchers and child advocates against entertainment industry representatives, frequently giving equal weight to the arguments of both sides. A comparison of news reports and scientific knowledge about media effects reveals a disturbing discontinuity: Over the past 50 years, the average news report has changed from claims of a weak link to a moderate link and then back to a weak link between media violence and aggression. However, since 1975, the scientific confidence and statistical magnitude of this link have been clearly positive and have consistently increased over time. Reasons for this discontinuity between news reports and the actual state of scientific knowledge include the vested interests of the news, *a misapplied fairness doctrine in news reporting*, and the failure of the research community to effectively argue the scientific case.[11]

Bushman and Anderson suggest that a parallel exists between the arguments of the tobacco industry against the scientific evidence for the harms of smoking on the one hand, and the arguments of the entertainment industry against the scientific evidence for the connections between media violence and aggressive behavior. They describe the struggle between science and corporate interests as a "war of deception" by the tobacco industry, which is heavily invested in peoples' continued smoking.[12] A misapplied fairness doctrine is operative when media coverage of the harms of prostitution pits research evidence "balanced" by interviews with sex industry advocates who insist that prostitution is a job choice.

We have not yet seen as many years of research on the effects of the sexualization of girls as we have on the effects of media violence. Nonetheless there is compelling evidence that girls are adversely impacted by images of their own commodification and sexualization.[13] Smith and colleagues summarized behavioral effects of the sexualization of girls, including the earlier age of sexual activity, risky sexual behavior, viewing prostitution as humorous and enjoyable, noting that "the media acts as an advertising agent for prostitution."[14]

The message sent by the media to girls is that they *should always be sexually available, always have sex on their minds, be willing to be dominated and even sexually aggressed against*.[15] Although Merskin was describing the sexualization of girls in the media, this statement is also precisely what is expected of women in prostitution. Prostitution itself is part of what it means to be female today. When femaleness is commodified and turned into a commercial product, girls are in effect transformed into prostitutes. They are turned into their sexual characteristics alone, genitals marked by "wink, wink" thongs, breasts marked by shirts saying "hooters," mouths marked by garish lipstick. Girls become sex and nothing else, as analyzed by feminist scholars Catharine MacKinnon and Andrea Dworkin.[16]

CULTURAL MAINSTREAMING OF PROSTITUTION VIA THE SEXUALIZATION OF GIRLS, RAUNCH CULTURE, AND PORNOGRAPHY

Contemporary U.S. culture is saturated with pornography that humiliates and injures women. *New York Times* columnist Bob Herbert noted that the "disrespectful, degrading, contemptuous treatment of women is so pervasive and so mainstream that it has just about lost its ability to shock."[17] Advertisers for Clinique skin moisturizer, for example, using the pornographic gaze, display a woman with lotion spattered like semen across her face to simulate the john's triumphant, humiliating ejaculation into her eyes and nose.[18]

Pornography is intensively and deliberately distributed to Internet consumers, particularly young boys who are systematically groomed as the next generation of pay-for-porn customers and johns. The graphic, brutal, and demeaning exploitation of women whose photographs are on the Internet remove any hint of tenderness or intimacy in sexual relationships.[19] One in three children who are online receive unwanted pornography. "I go to Web sites about racing dirt bikes," commented one boy, "and when I'm on there pop-up ads come up with naked pictures of girls and guys."[20]

According to tracking data compiled by familysafemedia.com, 68 million daily pornography search engine requests are made. These requests represent 25 percent of all Web searches. There are 1.5 billion pornography downloads a month, representing 35 percent of all Web downloads.[21] Revenue from online pornography is greater than the combined revenues of the top technology companies: Microsoft, Google, Amazon, eBay, Yahoo!, Apple, Netflix, and EarthLink.[22]

Prostitution of girls was a marginalized concept as recently as 25 years ago. Only superficially addressing the prostitution of children, Hollywood produced films in the 1970s with 12-year-olds as prostitutes—Brooke Shields in *Pretty Baby* (1978) and Jodie Foster in *Taxi Driver* (1976). Soon after, films began to glamorize prostitution. In 1984 the protagonist in the film *Angel* was a girl who was "high school honor student by day, Hollywood hooker by night." By 1990 *Pretty Woman* mainstreamed pimps' messages about the glamour of prostitution to teens. Today prostitution itself is defined as female sexuality,[23] and girls are paying close attention.

In the 1990s pop singer Madonna and Britney Spears brought prostitution from the fringes to the mainstream.[24] Yet some analysts make futile attempts to split off real prostitution from pretend prostitution. A reviewer wrote, "The girls were emulating pop stars like Christina Aguilera and Britney Spears, not porn stars like Jenna Jameson."[25] Where has that reviewer been hiding out? Any previously existing boundary between "pop stars" and "porn stars" has been deliberately obscured.

For example, Britney Spears, like JonBenet Ramsey, grew up as a child beauty pageant star. At the age of 17, she became the middle aged man's fantasy of the schoolgirl who is secretly a slut. The man who pornographized Spears in her music videos had previously directed humiliating and violent pornography.[26] Spears has been described as "the canary in the coal mine of U.S. culture."[27] The cultural coal mine is the sexualization and commodification of girls who are presented as consenting participants in their own sexual exploitation.[28] The largely invisible creators of the coal mines are corporations who supply the market created by johns, pedophiles, and other predators who demand that women, girls, or prostitutes should be continually sexually available to them, happy to be subordinate, turned on by rape. At Spears's 2004 wedding to Kevin Federline, all male guests were told to wear tracksuits with the word "Pimp" on the back; Federline's father wore a suit reading "Pimp Daddy." Women and girls attending the wedding wore tracksuits that read "Maids."[29]

The culture itself has become a compelling force for the sexualization of girls and the mainstreaming of prostitution. Today prostitution is marketed on the Internet and via cell phones. Distribution of pornography and advertising for prostitution via cell phones is a common corporate practice. Criddle has described the use of cell phones by pedophiles. Because some cell phones have no fixed IP address and are untraceable, pedophiles watch the current-time rape of children via cell phone, sometimes paying an additional fee for their own participation in the child rape and pornography by text-messaging demands for specific crimes to be committed against children. They then dispose of the phones.[30]

Young women's magazines advertise pornified girls inviting sex, from *Seventeen's* 2002 ads for Hotkiss and Candies[31] to *Vanity Fair's* 2008 topless-but-holding-a-sheet cover photo of 15-year-old Miley Cyrus (Disney's "Hannah Montana"), who tearfully told reporters that she was manipulated into the pose by photographer Annie Leibowitz.[32] Young women's magazine *Marie-Claire* ran an article in 2002 about women's sexuality with tips from a prostitute in a Nevada legal brothel and also from Jenna Jameson, a woman who had prostituted in more than 50 videos.[33] Several years later the magazine ran a second article, "Prostitution Gives Me Power,"[34] mainstreaming prostitution as an excellent job for young women. Describing prostitution as social work, the author, a legal Dutch prostitute, boasted that she could set her own work hours, carefully select her johns, and keep all the profits.

Young women are taught the sexuality of prostitution, which in essence means that they ignore their own sexual feelings (or lack of them) and learn that their role is to service john-like boyfriends who have learned about sex via pornography. Thirteen-year-old girls who are Jenna Jameson fans attend her book tour for readings from *How to Make Love like a Porn Star*.[35] Today 15-year-old girls ask Cosmogirl sex advice columnists if they can get pregnant from anal sex.[36] This question likely results from pressure from a boyfriend who had seen anal sex, common in today's pornography. Yet the answer from CosmoGirl simply addressed the physiology of anal sex rather than the social context of the question and the possibility that the child was experiencing sexual coercion as a result of pornography seen by a boyfriend.

The World Wide Web's most frequent use is accessing pornography that is indistinguishable from prostitution and trafficking. Pornography consists of actual photographs of real women and children in prostitution that are used to traffic women and girls.[37] So-called "soft pornography" or "amateur pornography" and videos that mainstream prostitution and prostitution-like activities such as *Girls Gone Wild* generate billions of dollars. For *Girls Gone Wild* footage, Joe Francis takes his film crew to clubs where teenagers are partying. After girls are drunk, Francis persuades and entices them into being filmed. Francis has been jailed on charges of child abuse subsequent to his production of child pornography.[38]

The pornographification of young women has been described as raunch culture by Ariel Levy who provides a depressing volume of evidence that some women today have embraced their own degrading objectification.[39] Seeming to have abandoned the hope of real equality with men, women and girls enact prostitution. Lap dancing and pole dancing have become mainstreamed as women's and girls' sexuality. Pole dancing, once the exclusive province of women prostituting in strip clubs, has moved to women's homes and exercise classes. Classes in pole dancing are now advertised as fitness exercises to girls 7 to 11 years old.[40] Stripper-chic outfits mainstream prostitution for young women and girls although it is not called prostitution. In the following example from an Internet teen dating advice column at allexperts.com, a girl is specifically taught how to prostitute by doing a lap dance for her boyfriend:

Question: hi jen, well i have a lil problem its not really a problem but it is for me. . . . i wanna give my boyfriend a lap dance, bc he wants me 2 and i think it would be fun but i cant dance and have no idea how to lap dance, i cant go and buy ne videos or ne thing bc im not 18 so i would have to use my parents credit card to buy it online and that wouldnt work and i dont wanna buy it at some store and i dont think i would be able to buy it. please help.

   Answer: Hey Holly, well to give a lap dance you have to feel sexy. so wear your sexist [sic] undies and bra, and provocitive clothing. you should start by giving him sexy looks and winks and little teasing kisses. its all about dominating. put on some music you can grind too. you start off infront of him and just dance kinda dirty. if you can't dance and can't get a friend to show you, just rub yourself infront of him. spread your legs slightly and rub your chest your neck, down ur stomach and ur inner thighs. lick ur finger, look really sexy. thats when you start stripping. start with shirt. after you take it off, get on top of him and rub your chest all in his face and roll your body against his. *he has to be sitting up* have your hair down and flowing around, so it looks wild. and continue from there. everytime you take something off, make sure it looks sexy and rub against him like ur life depended on it. make him want you. give him a hardon by watching you strip and rub against him. get on top of him kiss down his body. do everything and anything you want. remember you are in control and thats why your making him want you. its your show, make him beg. hope i helped bye bye love Jen[41]

   In 2001 *Hustler* began marketing prostitution to teens with makeup kits to teens marked with the *Hustler* logo.[42] Although *Hustler* was understood as hard-core misogyny in the 1980s, according to *AdultVideo News*, today T-shirts with the *Hustler* logo are hip and trendy for children.[43] Girls' panties that said "Who needs credit cards . . . " on the front and "When you have Santa" on the rear were removed by Walgreens only after consumer protests. Feminist activist Jessica Valenti commented, "There's nothing quite like telling adolescent girls that they don't need to worry about finances since they have their very own moneypot between their legs."[44] Another indicator of the mainstreaming of prostitution to girls is adolescents' waxing their pubic hair to emulate pornography actresses.[45]

   Not satisfied with just the teenage market, corporations have initiated campaigns designed to sell eroticized products to preteens, children, and even toddlers. Underpants labeled "hottie" or "wink, wink," and other articles of clothing linked with stripping are designed for girls. Clothing stores sell thongs to girls that read "feeling lucky?," which is a line used by prostitutes while soliciting johns. And stores sell sparkly T-shirts that say "porn star."

   Prostitution is glamorized and marketed to girls as a fun and glamorous activity with products such as eroticized Halloween costumes[46] and dolls. The prostitute-like Bratz dolls, dressed in stripper outfits with miniskirts, fishnet stockings, feather boas, and collagen-injected lips are marketed to 7- to 10-year-olds. Bratz dolls have dissociated, deadened expressions that appear world weary and used up—the same expression seen on the faces of sexually assaulted children and prostituted women. Bratz product designer Paula Treantafelles acknowledged the corporation's pursuit of the preteen market. At the age of 7 to 10 years, "they're very different from four-to-six year-olds." Using the same language that pimps use to sell sex to johns, she proudly noted that Bratz "are about self-expression, self-identity," and even promote "girl power."[47]

Other Bratz dolls sexualize female infants. Marketed to toddlers, Bratz Babyz, with painted toenails as well as bottles, are advertised as infants who "already know how to flaunt it, and they're keepin' it real in the crib!"[48]

PROSTITUTION IS MARKETED TO GIRLS AND YOUNG WOMEN AS POLE DANCING, STRIPPING, OR EXERCISE

School systems throughout the United States are highly restrictive regarding the content of sex education courses, sometimes not permitting education about sexual intimacy at all. Yet at the same time girls are receiving powerful messages about prostitution via popular culture. Sexualized content on Black Entertainment Television (BET) and Music Television (MTV) was analyzed by an organization of parents promoting corporate responsibility in entertainment. In a 4-month period of time from December 2007 to March 2008, depictions of strippers increased dramatically.[49]

As recently as 30 years ago, stripping was a sexy dance on a stage. Today stripping is usually indistinguishable from prostitution. Stages still exist, but most stripping is done via lap dances in which a stripper grinds herself against a john's crotch in a club, often in a "private dance" where acts of prostitution are purchased via a $500 bottle of champagne in the VIP room.

Middle school students at a 2005 career day in California were told that stripping and exotic dancing were excellent careers for girls. A smiling job counselor told a group of students that strippers can earn very good salaries, especially if they have breast enlargement surgery. "For every two inches up there, it's another $50,000," he enthusiastically told the girls.[50] An Abercrombie & Fitch (A&F) marketing catalog included a pseudo-advice column that explicitly promoted stripping/prostitution as an empowering summer job for students. In addition to photos of pornography and prostitution, the A&F catalog included images of teacher–student sex.[51]

In Taiwan a similar mainstreaming of sex industry careers for teenage girls is taking place. Prostitution of Taiwanese girls was described by a postmodernist as "simply another form of sexual exploration."[52] Justifying enjo-kosai (casual prostitution) for teenagers, Ho reasoned that because the girls had already been exposed to a surround of sexuality in the media, and because they were sexually adventurous at adolesence anyway—they might as well benefit from prostitution because they would learn management skills and make money.

Stripper clothing is popular with girls. Pamela Anderson, the star of a TV cartoon show *Striperella* is also a pornography actress. Anderson is a role model for girls who flock to her book readings.[53] A preadolescent girl demonstrated stripper maneuvers on a pole installed in one of the bedrooms in the home she lives in on *Keeping Up with the Kardashians*, which ran on E! television.[54]

Pole-dancing toys were marketed to 4- to 5-year-olds by Tesco, the largest chain in the United Kingdom. Tesco sold a pole-dancing kit complete with instructions for mimicking prostitution: "Unleash the sex kitten inside . . . simply extend the Peekaboo pole inside the tube, slip on the sexy tunes and away you go! Soon you'll be flaunting it to the world and earning a fortune in Peekaboo Dance Dollars."[55] Other prostitution-themed items sold by Tesco included T-shirts for 6-year-old girls with the words "so many boys, so little time."[56] Another company offered older teens classes in pole dancing, advertised as fitness. "By putting children in a pole-dancing exercise class, you're teaching children a sexual body language that they don't know the meaning of but adults do," stated a critic of the classes.[57]

RACISM, HIP-HOP AND PROSTITUTION

A 2006 RAND study of 1,461 12- to 17-year olds found that degrading lyrics—but not sexual lyrics that were not degrading—influenced adolescents' sexual behavior. The study's authors described prostitution-like roles for girls as degraded hoes and roles for boys as pimp-like or john-like sexual studs in popular teen music.[58]

Although the sexual objectification of girls occurs in many forms of music, not exclusively in hip-hop,[59] it is especially toxic in hip-hop's misogynist and racist lyrics in which women are hoes and bitches deserving of contempt and violence.[60] The misogynist racism that labels women as hoes has a powerful effect on girls' lives, especially African American girls' lives. Thulani Davis noted that African American girls have been especially harmed by rap culture, which stereotypes them as hypersexual, sexually irresponsible, and uninterested in intimate relationships.[61]

Many hip-hop songs teach children that the value of women, especially black women, is between their legs.[62] Pimping has been glamorized for boys, as in the cartoon Lil Pimp, in which a white 9-year-old boy runs a stable of hoes with his pimping pals.[63] Pimping is increasingly seen as a positive role for young men. A Dolce & Gabbana fashion ad showed a 20-something male model wearing a T shirt saying "I Sell Sex."[64] Maternity tops and children's clothing have been imprinted with the word "pimp."[65]

Abused as a child, Karrine Steffans has written about her teenage relationships with much older hip-hop bosses. Pimplike if not an actual pimp, one man required her to get on her knees when he decided that she needed to "suck Daddy's dick and Daddy won't be mad at you no more. That's what a good girl is supposed to do." Steffans learned from painful experience that women in rap videos who smilingly tolerate rappers' racist and misogynist epithets are there because of a lack of self-esteem and a lack of educational and job opportunities in their communities.[66]

Although sometimes billed as the incarnation of sexual liberation, Lil' Kim's lyrics glamorize prostitution. Goldberg aptly described Lil' Kim's music as "permeated by the malice and despair of sport fucking" and reflecting a "defeatist 'ho mentality."[67]

> Now I'm back to my old ways, like in the old days
> Flirtin, not givin a fuck, what?
> Got you lookin in the mirror sayin, "Damn!"
> Sick thinkin bout the next man fuckin this tight pussy
> Niggaz want me, even though they got a honey
> If I'ma be number two, they givin me some hush money[68]

In his documentary *Beyond Beats and Rhymes*, Byron Hurt interviewed young women about rap music. Unsurprised or perhaps silenced by the misogyny of men in the rap music world, the young women seemed to accept the misogynist words 'ho and bitch as definitions of themselves.[69]

VIDEO GAMES NORMALIZE BEING A JOHN FOR BOYS AND BEING BOUGHT FOR SEX FOR GIRLS

Video games run the gamut from fun and instructional games to those that mainstream violence, rape, and increasingly prostitution. The best known of these games is Grand Theft Auto published by Take Two Interactive and Rockstar Games. Several versions of the game exist, all involving use of a prostitute. In some versions players who are overwhelmingly teenaged boys have the option to sexually exploit a prostitute, beat her up, run her over, or shoot her in order to earn points in the game. Points are also earned in GTA Vice City by owning a strip club or a pornography production studio.

"Next time, I'm going to just run them over," said a 16-year-old boy as he selected a Grand Theft Auto III mission on his PlayStation 2. He loves the game. "What you can't do in real life, you can do in the game, like carjack people and shoot police," he said. And, in that version, he can also kill prostitutes for points in the game.[70] In 2008 Take Two and Rockstar have established a trafficker as the GTA IV protagonist.[71]

"Of course we have an ethical responsibility, individually, collectively as companies, and collectively as an industry," said game designer Steve Meretzky, "We can't, on the one hand, crow about the power of software as a learning tool, and on the other hand say the immersion in realistic graphic violence has no impact on a player."[72] Echoing these sentiments, game designer Richard Garriott explained,

> I am a devout believer that "role playing" is one of the most powerful teaching tools in the world. Think about young kids out on playgrounds playing imaginary games, be it pretend warfare, or tea parties in the clubhouse. In all these cases, kids are trying out interpersonal actions and honing their interpersonal skills. They find out that when you don't play well, others won't play with you. They find out that pulling someone's hair makes that person cry, and hopefully that makes the aggressor sad. To unleash a game that does not respond with the real world's countermeasures to player behavior, means that the game really does have a risk of "teaching" bad behavior, or at least misses the opportunity to reinforce "right" and "wrong."[73]

Brenda Brathwaite, who designed the game *Playboy: the Mansion*, has written about the emergent sex occurring in video games such as GTA. Virtual prostitution was one of the first emergent behaviors in video games.[74] For example, a skateboard video game is encoded with software that permits the gamer to unlock videos of women who are stripping.[75] Boys are likely to access sex simulation games such as VirtuallyJenna, which was created with real-time 3-D game technology. According to the game's designer, the goal is to simulate sex so that gamers' sexual needs are satisfied in a few minutes.[76]

The video-game rating system fails to protect children from content that has been shown to adversely affect them. For example, *Tony Hawk's Underground*, rated T for teen-appropriate, includes use of a strip club,[77] and *Playboy: the Mansion*, rated M for 17 and older, features a prostitution-like mission in the game in which the player—who enacts game protagonist Hugh Hefner—meets a rock star and his twin girlfriends. If the player succeeds in seducing and sleeping with the twins, they send their friends Brazilian triplets for the next mission.[78] These games are played by young children as well as teenagers.

SOCIAL NETWORKING SITES AND THE PROSTITUTION OF CHILDREN

Children grow up using the Internet for games, educational resources, for social information about music and movie stars, and they also use the World Wide Web to post information about themselves and to network with other youth. Sexual boundaries have disappeared on Youtube, MySpace and other social networking sites. Promoting a pseudointimacy that facilitates the dissemination of private sexual thoughts and photographs, the social networking sites can be used by any child with a computer. On several sites the fine print grants the Web site owner permission to use or modify the child's photo in perpetuity in any medium chosen.[79]

Sexual boundaries have disappeared on many social networking sites. Popular social networking sites MySpace, Facebook, Flickr, Stickam, and Yahoo host adult pornography, child pornography, and solicitation for prostitution. MySpace, for example, lists thinly veiled prostitution advertising, such as "Find a Booty Call."[80] Stickam, another socially risky Web site used by teenagers, encourages them to post live Web-cam sexual behaviors.[81]

Espin-the-bottle, a social networking site aimed at teenagers, is owned by the Hearst Corporation. *Espin* is advertised as a sexualized "flirting and dating" site for persons aged 13 to 57. The *Espin* site accepts advertising from companies that promote ways to help children hide their Internet use from parents. The site targets children with sexualized quizzes that encourage sexualized responses that are then posted on the site.[82] Another site, MissBimbo.com, encourages girls to compete to become the "hottest, coolest, most famous bimbo in the whole world."[83]

Today the sale and purchase of prostitution takes place online. Johns today use the Internet more frequently than the street to find women and girls for prostitution. Pimps, johns, and other sex predators use the social networking Web sites to groom children for prostitution. Children are then rented out on commonly used prostitution Web sites such as redbook.com, eros.com or Craigslist. Pimps use the same tactics online that they use on the street: enticement, persuasion, grooming, coercion, denial and minimization of harm, social isolation, intimidation, and violent threats.[84] They entice, persuade, and coerce vulnerable runaway or homeless girls into prostitution, then instruct them in the use of an escort service cell phone, and show them the nearest Internet café or public library where the girls post ads and answer calls from johns.

Craigslist originated as an online community bulletin board but now releases 25,000 new advertisements every 10 days for "erotic services," which is code for prostitution.[85] In Sacramento, California, a crossroads for organized criminals who sell girls in Seattle, Los Angeles, San Francisco, and Las Vegas, hundreds of ads for prostitution a day are posted on Craigslist.[86] Because Craigslist is free and content is not filtered prior to being displayed on the site, pimps advertise for prostitution via bulk e-mails.

In 2008 a 15-year-old ran away from her home in western Wisconsin and was subsequently pimped out on Craigslist where 15 separate ads offered her for sale to Milwaukee johns. In another case, a 16-year-old girl was pimped by a man who raped her, took photographs of her while she was naked, and posted them on Craigslist. At the time of his arrest, the girl told police that he had beaten her and threatened her at gunpoint.[87] In 2008 federal agents arrested two Detroit pimps who had placed 2,800 ads for prostitution on Craigslist, MySpace, and other social networking sites. The pimps were charged with sexual exploitation and sex trafficking of children. The children were transported by organized crime networks in Detroit, Chicago, New York, Cleveland, Milwaukee, Houston, and College Park Maryland.[88] The girls' prostitution was photographed and sold as pornography.

In 2007 an attorney demanded that MySpace provide information on how many registered sex offenders were using the popular teenage social networking site. It was soon discovered that 29,000 registered sex offenders had profiles listed on MySpace.com.[89] One sex offender lived in San Bruno, California. According to his MySpace page, the 41-year-old San Bruno resident was single, a Sagittarius, a nonsmoker and nondrinker, and he listed a woman who stripped online among his six MySpace friends. California's online database of registered sex offenders offered a different profile of the same man who had convictions for forced sodomy, oral sex, and "lewd and lascivious acts" with a person under the age of 14. A 22-year-old San Francisco man created a typical MySpace college student persona, professing a love for poetry, nature, and obscure coffeehouse bands. His profile failed to mention that he was a convicted child molester.[90]

SEXUAL ABUSE AND PROSTITUTION OF CHILDREN

Girls and young women are vulnerable to prostitution because of a relentless confluence of oppressive forces in their lives. Sexism, racist or ethnic discrimination, poverty, and the sexualized culture itself are coercive social influences that push girls and young women into prostitution.

The relationship between a sexualized culture and girls' vulnerability to prostitution is particularly clear in Las Vegas, epicenter of the North American sex industry. "There's this whole generation of girls growing up in Las Vegas, surrounded by the sex industry and they naturally fall into it. It's a normal everyday thing."[91] A woman reported that her 18-year-old daughter served soft drinks in Las Vegas clubs. She believed that her daughter was being groomed by club owners for prostitution. Watching out for her daughter's safety in Las Vegas, she said, felt like "standing in the middle of a river, trying to hold it back."[92] Her fears were well founded. In Las Vegas the prostitution and trafficking of 11- to 17-year-old girls is "rampant," according to the police.[93] A strip-club manger told me that he recruited women for stripping by first placing them in waitress or bartending jobs. Once they were accustomed to the sex industry subculture and they saw how much money passed through women's hands, he persuaded young women to strip. Stripping often included prostitution in the VIP room or champagne rooms of the strip club.

As girls are sexualized in the media and in their lives, men's sexual abuse of them is facilitated, and a market for sex with children is cultivated.[94] As a result girls of increasingly younger ages are at risk for sexual abuse not only by pedophiles but by men who have been culturally conditioned to sexual arousal by children. Pedophiles' niche in the sex industry is a result of the massive expansion of online pornography, an increasing emphasis on sexualized images of children and "amateurs," and children's extensive use of the Internet.[95]

There is an invisible continuum between sexual abuse of children, their internalization of the perpetrator's objectification of them, and their subsequent entry into prostitution. Most women enter the sex industry as adolescents. Boyer and colleagues interviewed 60 women prostituting in escort, street, strip club, phone sex, and massage parlors (brothels) in Seattle, Washington. All of them began prostituting between the ages of 12 and 14.[96] In another study, 89 percent of young women had begun prostitution before the age of 16.[97] In other studies, 78 percent of 200 adult women in prostitution began prostituting as juveniles, and 68 percent began prostitution when they were younger than 16 years of age.[98] Two Canadian studies indicated that most women enter prostitution by age 15.[99]

Adult and child "prostitutes" thus are not two different classes of people, but *the same people at two different points in time.* The expression "child prostitution" itself is a misnomer because child prostitution is, in fact, the crime of sexual assault of a child. Yet in many parts of the

world, including the United States, "protection [of children in prosti-
tution] is administered through incarceration, and punishment is sym-
bolically transformed into welfare." Arresting children for prostitution
instead of offering them shelter, emergency services, and long-term
safety is a crime.[100]

Almost all women in prostitution have a history of childhood sexual abuse. Having been sexually assaulted once, usually by someone
she knows, girls are 28 times more likely to enter into prostitution than
non-sexually assaulted children.[101] In Canada, 82 percent of 100 women
prostituting in Vancouver had a history of childhood sexual abuse.
The women told us that they had suffered sexual abuse from an average of four perpetrators.[102] In a large-scale study of age of entry into
prostitution, 70 percent of adult women said that their childhood
sexual abuse affected their entry into prostitution.[103]

Familial sexual abuse functions as a training ground for prostitution. Andrea Dworkin has described sexual abuse of children as "boot
camp" for prostitution.[104] The sad statement of Ashley Youmans, "I
know what my purpose is," referring to her sale of sex to Spitzer
reflects her own history of abuse.[105] As one young woman told Silbert
and Pines, "I started turning tricks to show my father what he made
me."[106] Growing up with sexual abuse and parental neglect, Nora
Kuzma (known as Traci Lords in pornography made of her when she
was 15), named her pornography "scripted prostitution."[107]

Which girls are most vulnerable to prostitution? Childhood sexual
abuse increases the likelihood of prostitution for girls and women.
Women who have survived severe assaults from multiple sexual
abuse perpetrators in childhood were more likely to enter prostitution
as young women.[108] Marginalization because of race, ethnicity or
poverty also increases the likelihood that a girl will be prostituted.

West and colleagues found that being sexually abused as a child
not only increased black women's risk of being assaulted again as
adults, it also increased their risk of prostitution. Sexual abuse survivors who were later revictimized as adults were three times more
likely to have been involved in prostitution than women who had not
been revictimized as adults.[109]

The most extreme poverty creates girls' most extreme vulnerability to prostitution. A girl from Guatemala described her life before and
after joining a gang for survival. She was abandoned at age 6 and lived
on the street with her brother, who was shot. She then joined the rival
gang that had not killed her brother. Sexual abuse, abandonment by
families, and abandonment by the state led to her entry into the gang.
The gangs then continued the abuse under the pretense of protecting
her from even worse harms. Girls are frequently gang raped as initiation

to gang life and later prostituted to raise money for the gang. They are expected to transport drugs or guns. One girl was given a choice between what the gang called group sex and a group beating for her gang initiation. She chose the beating.[110]

DISTINCTIONS BETWEEN CHILD PROSTITUTION AND ADULT PROSTITUTION THAT DON'T EXIST IN REALITY

Unlike familial child abuse and rape, the commercial use of children for sex generates enormous profits. Yet there are splits in peoples' understanding of prostitution because of propaganda from johns and pimps. In many peoples' minds, there is a split between adult and child prostitution, a split between indoor and outdoor prostitution, a split between legal and illegal prostitution, and a split between prostitution and sex trafficking.

This compartmentalization of sexual violence benefits a perpetrator, whether he is a hip, friendly child pornographer like Joe Francis, an Abercrombie executive justifying thongs for 6-year-olds, or an arrested pedophile. All of these forms of exploitation are part of a continuum of abuse, some more extreme than others. It is a tragic tactical error to split them off from each other—thereby permitting sex predators the "right" to exploit someone who is defined as less harmed than someone else.

Johns and pimps promote distinctions between good and bad prostitution. They tell us that there are nice johns who buy consenting adult women and bad johns who buy children. They tell us that there are nice johns who buy voluntary prostitutes and bad johns who buy trafficked women. They say that there's a world of difference between high-class escorts and sex slaves, and that there's a big difference between street and indoor prostitution. Their message is that although there are a few real victims, for the most part prostitution is a victimless activity. The johns and pimps inform us that it is our task to figure out who are the "real victims." If the john pays enough, they tell us, if the woman he buys is over 18, if she's indoors, if she smiles and says "I consent," then he can use her for sex.

Drawing distinctions between who is hurt the most or the least in prostitution is much the same as saying that a battered woman was only black and blue and that her arm wasn't broken; therefore she is not a serious battering victim. It's like making a distinction between a slave who had the "privilege" of working in the master's house and another slave who was treated worse in the master's fields. When we make these distinctions regarding the severity of battering, slavery, and prostitution, we in effect set aside a subclass of oppressed people whose suffering we agree to ignore.

Johns benefit when we separate out a group of women in prostitution whom we concede can be offered up for sale—the older teens who are turning tricks in the VIP room of the strip club, the ones doing hand jobs in the massage parlors, the ones who are paid more, the ones in the legal brothels. Pimps benefit when we spend time making spurious distinctions between internationally trafficked victims and home-grown victims of domestic trafficking, and when we spend inordinate amounts of time and resources to determine whether or not she has had her 18th birthday. When some kinds of prostitution are labeled "high-end" or "voluntary," prostitution is mainstreamed and business prospers.

ALTERNATIVES TO MAINSTREAMING PROSTITUTION TO CHILDREN: INTERNET LITERACY, MEDIA LITERACY, AND EDUCATION ABOUT SEXUAL INTIMACY

Learning from pornography, children frequently attempt sex that is casual or nonrelational, without consequences or commitments. Levy described the "imaginary licentiousness" that girls enact in order to be grown-up. One girl explained, "Sexually, we didn't really do anything, but you wanted to *look* like you did."[111] Trained by popular Western culture, girls learn to present a hypersexualized, prostitution-like version of themselves to the world. When boys then treat girls as pornography teaches them to, girls are frozen or automaton-like, hyper-aggressive, or hyper-passive.

In 2000 PBS *Frontline* staff asked girls questions about sex and relationships. Their responses were compelling.

> *Interviewer:* You said the girls are getting to be more like boys. Can you explain that a little bit?
> *Heather:* Like how guys will like have this girl and go have sex with her or somethin'. And then they'll just completely drop her you know. Some girls are startin' to act like that. Like, "I just wanted to have sex with him. Now it's over." And there's just girls that are just startin' to feel the same way about guys, because guys have done that so many times to them they just start doin' the same, you know.
> *Nicole:* It's kind of like the girls are comin' back and treatin' the guys like they treated us. Like playin' 'em and goin' out with three different guys at a time instead of the guy goin' out with three different girls at a time.
> *Brandi:* Sex sucks actually. So I think only guys are gonna benefit from it. I think sex was made for guys, because you just lay there and you're just like, Get off me, what are you doing?
> *Interviewer:* Do you think that girls enjoy sex as much as guys do?
> *Nicole:* No. No. I would give anything to be a guy for one day and have sex.

Heather: I mean the first time that you have sex you think it's cause it means somethin'. But then you realize it doesn't. You just don't really care anymore. So that's pretty much how it is now. I mean for most girls it—there's still like a few feelings involved, but not like it used to be at all. Girls are startin' to get like guys like, "Hey, that's all I wanted from you. Next."

Interviewer: It's kinda sad.

Heather: It really is.

Interviewer: It seems like girls who have a lot of sex have a worse reputation than guys. Is that true?

Katy: If a guy does that then they're considered a pimp cause they get all these girls. A girl does that and they're considered a slut.

Brandi: Yeah, girls can sleep with the same amount of guys that guys can sleep with girls and they will be called the biggest slut, the biggest ho, but the guy is the pimp and the yeah, you know, you're the man. They get props for it but we get lowered for it. So it's not fair.

Katy: A slut's worse than a pimp. A pimp's good. Like, if you're like walkin' down the street and you see a guy with like four girls around him you're like, "man, that that guy's probably got somethin' goin' on" you know. "He's real cool. He got he he" ah, excuse me. "He's got all these girls." A girl walks around with like four guys it's like "look at that little slut." That's that's not good.

Interviewer: That doesn't seem fair.

Katy: It's not. *Girls can't stand it, but that's how we have to live.*[112]

Some children understand that their sexualization is linked to pornography.

Okay I am under 16 and I will tell you why so many teens wanna have sex. I am definitely not one of them! But all the guys in my class watch porn and are having all these sexual fantasies and a few of them even touch you in places which aren't suitable. They are growing up too fast and, personally, I think a lot of it is down to those horrible porn magazines like playboy etc.[113]

Children receive their sex education from online pornography. A 2001 Kaiser Family Foundation study found that 70 percent of 15- to 17-year-olds saw online pornography. Girls (25 percent) were significantly more likely than boys (6 percent) to report that they were very upset by the experience of accidentally encountering Web pornography.[114] Child psychologist Michael Carr-Gregg expressed concern that adolescent girls mimicked group and anal sex because they assumed the normalcy of sex acts seen online.[115]

Children blog about their need for sex education, and not only regarding the anatomy and physiology of sex. They describe a need for education in how to develop intimate relationships. A 16-year-old complained,

> If you want to blame anyone for the underage promiscuity blame schools. if they spent more time goin into the ins and outs as it were of sex and all aspects based around it maybe kids wouldnt be so interested. the schools are so regimented on what they will and wont say that they leave too much up to the imagination. From experience if schools actually taught sex education properly instead of throwin in a 50 min lesson about "how sex is when the penis penetrates the vagina" and actlly taught about the emotions, experiences and body parts, us kids wouldn't need to find out for ourselfs.[116]

An Australian boy complained about sex education that did not teach him anything about sexual intimacy. He commented, "They should warn you in school about how bad you feel after a one-night stand!"[117]

A 2007 study validated these children's descriptions of what sex was like for them. Surveying 618 9th- and 10th-grade adolescents about their sexual behaviors and attitudes, the authors found that adolescent girls who engaged in oral sex were likely to feel used and to feel bad about themselves. The authors recommended that sex education include discussion of the social and emotional aspects of sexual intimacy in addition to the physiology of sex and STD risks.[118]

Blogs and Web sites that monitor social networking sites have appeared, some more sophisticated than others. Some sites compile listings of arrests of sex predators on Web sites and generally raise social awareness of the use of social networking sites for sexualization of children, including prostitution of children. See, for example, http://blog.blogblocker.com/category/facebook/ and http://myspacemurders.org/ or Linda Criddle's *Look Both Ways: Help Protect Your Family on the Internet.*[119]

Children need media literacy education so they can counteract toxic messages about their sexuality. Today media literacy resource material must include not only resources on sex stereotyping, but specific education on the damaging effects of the media's sexualization of children, with recommendations for ways to discuss these issues with children of different ages. Smith and colleagues suggested that parents and pediatricians challenge corporations that promote the sexualization of children.[120] Galician and Merskin provide a model for evaluation of common myths about sexuality and love, providing examples for parents and teachers of the deconstruction of these myths in movies and television.[121] Media Awareness Network provides extensive resources for educating children about pornography and sexual advertising.[122] MediaWatch is another site offering media literacy materials and a feminist analysis of sexism and violence in the media.[123] There are many tools available to decrease or eliminate the toxic intensity of media sexualization of girls. Many of these tools will benefit parents and teachers, as well as children. Hopefully, these resources will raise everyone's awareness about prostitution. And, hopefully, some girls will manage to grow up with an autonomous sexuality that is their own rather than a sexuality imposed on them by a culture dominated by pimps and johns.

Series Afterword

The rich diversity of cultures created by humankind is testament to our ability to develop and adapt in diverse ways. But however varied different cultures may be, children are not endlessly malleable—they all share basic psychological and physical needs that must be met to ensure healthy development. The Childhood in America series examines the extent to which American culture meets children's irreducible needs. Without question, many children growing up in the United States lead privileged lives. They have been spared the ravages of war, poverty, malnourishment, sexism, and racism. However, despite our nation's resources, not all children share these privileges. Additionally, values that are central to American culture—such as self-reliance, individualism, privacy of family life, and consumerism—have created a climate in which parenting has become intolerably labor-intensive, and children are being taxed beyond their capacity for healthy adaptation. Record levels of violence, psychiatric disturbance, poverty, apathy, and despair among our children speak to our current cultural crisis.

Although our elected officials profess their commitment to "family values," policies that support family life are woefully lacking and are inferior to those in other industrialized nations. American families are burdened by inadequate parental leave, a health care system that does not provide universal coverage for children, a minimum wage that is not a living wage, "welfare to work" policies that require parents to leave their children for long stretches of time, unregulated and inadequately subsidized day care, an unregulated entertainment

industry that exposes children to sex and violence, and a two-tiered
public education system that delivers inferior education to poor children and frequently ignores individual differences in learning styles
and profiles of intelligence. As a result, many families are taxed to the
breaking point. In addition, our fascination with technological inno-
vation is creating a family lifestyle that is dominated by the screen
rather than human interaction.

The Childhood in America series seeks out leading childhood
experts from across the disciplines to promote dialogue, research, and
understanding regarding how best to raise and educate psychologically
healthy children and to ensure that they will acquire the wisdom, heart,
and courage needed to make choices for the betterment of society.

Sharna Olfman, PhD
Series Editor

Notes

CHAPTER 2

1. Johnson, A. G. (2005). *The Gender Knot: Unraveling Our Patriarchal Legacy,* 2nd ed. Philadelphia: Temple University Press.

2. For a review of statistics and arguments concerning the rape culture, see: Buchwald, E., Fletcher, P., and Roth, M. (2005). *Transforming a Rape Culture,* 2nd ed. Minneapolis: Milkweed Editions.

3. See Warshaw, R. (1994). *I Never Called It Rape: The Ms. Report on Recognizing, Fighting, and Surviving Date and Acquaintance Rape.* New York: Harper & Row.

4. See Anderson, C. A., Gentile, D. A., and Buckley, K. E. (2007). *Violent Video Game Effects on Children and Adolescents.* New York: Oxford University Press.

5. IAB Internet Advertising Revenue Report; PricewaterhouseCoopersLLP; Universal McCann: http://www.iab.net/media/file/resources_adrevenue_pdf_IAB_PwC_2005.pdf.

6. Paragraph 4, Joint Statement on the Impact of Entertainment Violence on Children, Congressional Public Health Summit (July 26, 2000). Retrieved online on April 20, 2008 from http://www.aap.org/advocacy/releases/jstmtevc.htm.

7. See, for example, Anderson, C. A., and Bushman, B. (2002). "Human aggression." *Annual Review of Psychology* 53: 27–51; and Anderson, C. A., Berkowitz, L., Donnerstein, L., Huesmann, L. R., Johnson, J. D., Linz, D., Malamuth, N. M., & Wartella, E. (2003). "The influence of media violence on youth." *Psychological Science in the Public Interest* 4 (3): 81–110.

8. See Schwalbe, M. (2005). *The Sociologically Examined Life: Pieces of the Conversation,* 3rd ed. New York: McGraw-Hill; also, see McQuail, D. (2005). *Mass Communication Theory,* 5th ed. Thousand Oaks, CA: Sage Publications, Ltd.

9. Page 2, American Psychological Association (APA). (2007). Report of the APA Task Force on the Sexualization of Girls: Executive Summary. Available online at www.apa.org/pi/wpo/sexualization.html.

10. See Sutton, M. J., Brown, J. D., Wilson, K. M., and Klein, J. D. (2002). "Shaking the Tree of Knowledge for Forbidden Fruit: Where Adolescents Learn about Sexuality and Contraception." Pages 25–55 in Brown, J. D., Steele, J. R., and Walsh-Childers, K., eds. *Sexual Teens, Sexual Media. Investigation Media's Influence on Adolescent Sexuality.* Mahway, NJ: Lawrence Erlbaum Associates.

11. See Brown, J. D., L'Engle, K. L., Pardun, C. J., Guo, G., Kenneavy, K., and Jackson, C. (2006). Sexy media matter: Exposure to sexual content in music, movies, television, and magazines predicts black and white adolescents' sexual behavior. *Pediatrics* 117: 1018–1027.

12. The APA report cited above highlights cognitive, emotional, physical, and sexual consequences for girls and women living in such an environment, including feelings of shame and depression, disordered eating and eating disorders, diminished sexual health, and increased emphasis on physical appearance as the core of women's value. These issues are discussed extensively throughout this volume.

13. The researchers connected this finding to the patriarchal emphasis on masculine risk taking, aggression, and the suppression of emotions. For a report on this study, see: http://news.healingwell.com/index.php?p=news1&id= 527968.

14. Pages 1 and 2, "Boys will be men: Guiding your sons from boyhood to manhood," by Paul Kivel (2006). Available online at: http://paulkivel.com/ articles/boyswillbemen.pdf.

15. See www.toptenreviews.com/pornography; and www.mediabynumbers. com.

16. See Dines, this volume.

17. See, notably, Dines, this volume, in addition to the following: Quayle, E., and Taylor, M. Child pornography and the internet: Perpetuating a cycle of abuse. *Deviant Behavior* 23(4): 331–361 (2002); Johnson, C. F. (2004). Child sexual abuse. *The Lancet* 364: 462–470 (2004).

18. See Wolak, J., Mithcell, K., and Finkelhor, D. (2006). Online victimization of youth: Five years later. *National Center for Missing & Exploited Children.* Available online at: http://www.missingkids.com/en_US/publications/NC167.pdf.

19. *ScienceDaily.* One in three boys heavy porn users, study shows. Retrieved April 26, 2008, from http://www.sciencedaily.com/releases/2007/02/ 070223142813 .htm.

20. Carroll, J. S., Padilla-Walker, L. M., Nelson, L. J., Olson, C. D., Barry, C. M., and Madsen, S. D. (2008). Generation XXX: Pornography acceptance and use among emerging adults. *Journal of Adolescent Research* 23(1): 6–30.

21. Jensen, R. (2007). *Getting Off: Pornography and the End of Masculinity.* Cambridge, MA: South End Press. Pages 56–57.

22. Jensen (ibid.), p. 59.

23. www.lukeisback.com.

24. http://www.acidrainvideo.com/.

25. From http://www.lukeisback.com/stars/stars/mitchell_spinelli.htm, accessed on April 27, 2008.

26. From http://www.lukeisback.com/stars/stars/mitchell_spinelli.htm, accessed on April 27, 2008.

27. Albo, M. (2008, February 14). "Max Hardcore: Spreading the love," AVN Media Network. Retrieved on May 2, 2008, from http://www.avn.com/performer/ articles/616.html.

28. See www.tontenreviews.com/pornography.

29. Page 5, Paul, P. (2005). *Pornified: How Pornography Is Transforming Our Lives, Our Relationships, and Our Families.* New York: Times Books.

30. Laramie Taylor notes that the closest U.S. equivalent may be "frat boy"; see Taylor, L. D. (2006). College men, their magazines, and sex. *Sex Roles* 55: 693–702.

31. Much of this information can be found online at http://www.magforum.com/mens.htm.

32. See www.loaded.co.uk.

33. http://www.magforum.com/mens2.htm.

34. See Stableford, D. (2008, February 11). Magazines take a huge hit at the newsstand. *Folio.* Retrieved April 29, 2008, accessed online at http://www.foliomag.com/2008/magazines-take-hit-newsstand.

35. See NetRatings UK Ltd (2007, March 13). Who's winning the battle of the Men's Magazines Online?

36. See Taylor, ibid.; also Taylor, L. D. (2005). All for him: Articles about sex in American lad magazines. *Sex Roles* 52 (3/4): 153–163; and Morrison, L. (2008). "Dominate everything: *Maxim Magazine's* advice on how to be a real man." UNC-CH honors thesis, School of Journalism and Mass Communication.

37. See Morrison, ibid.

38. See Taylor (2005 and 2006), cited above.

39. Thomas, S. (2006, June 19). Maxim: My part in its triumph. *The First Post.* Retrieved on April 29, 2008, from http://www.thefirstpost.co.uk/2607,features,maxim-my-part-in-its-triumph.

40. See the text of this article at www.maximonline.com/articles/index.aspx?a_id=5498, retrieved on April 8, 2007.

41. Paragraphs 1 and 4, www.maximonline.com/articles/index.aspx?a_id=5498.

42. Retrieved on April 29, 2008, from http://www.maxim.co.uk/maxim girls/realgirls/3733/fresh_off_the_boat.html.

43. See Web site listed above.

44. See www.prostitutionresearch.com.

45. See a list at www.maximmag.co.uk/search/?words=voyeur&searchby=maxim, retrieved on April 8, 2007.

46. www.maximmag.co.uk/maximgirls/realgirls/292/you_are_the_voyeur.html, retrieved on April 8, 2007.

47. NPD Group (2008, January 31). "2007 U.S. Video Game and PC Game Sales Exceed $18.8 Billion Marking Third Consecutive Year of Record-Breaking Sale." Retrieved on May 1, 2008, from http://www.npd.com/press/releases/press_080131b.html.

48. GameDaily.com (2008, April 3). Video Games Explode: Global Revenues Now on Par with Box Office. Retrieved on May 1, 2008, from http://www.gamedaily.com/articles/news/video-games-explode-global-revenues-now-on-par-with-box-office/?biz=1.

49. Mazel, J. (2008, April 30). Grand Theft Auto 4 Sells ~2.5 million in the Americas on Day 1. VGChartz.com, retrieved on May 1, 2008, from http://www.vgchartz.com/news/news.php?id=1102.

50. Magrino, T. (2008, April 28). Q&A: GTAIV—Big, or Huge. GameSpot.com, retrieved on May 1, 2008, from http://www.gamespot.com/news/6190011.html.

51. See Richtel, M. (2008, April 29). Grand Theft Auto IV and real-world billions. *New York Times.* Retrieved on May 1, 2008, from http://bits.blogs.nytimes.com/2008/04/29/grand-theft-auto-iv-and-real-world-billions/?ref=technology.

52. Gentile, D. A., Lynch, P. J., Linder, J. R., and Walsh, D. A. (2004). The effects of violent video game habits on adolescent hostility, aggressive behaviors, and school performance. *Journal of Adolescence* 27: 5–22. See also Robert, D., and Foehr, U. (2004). *Kids and Media in America.* Cambridge: Cambridge University Press.

53. See Anderson, C. A., Gentile, D. A., and Buckley, K. E. (2007). *Violent Video Game Effects on Children and Adolescents.* New York: Oxford University Press; also Dill, K. E., Gentile, D. A., Richter, W. A., and Dill, J. C. (2005). Violence, sex, race, and age in popular games: A content analysis, pages 115–130 in Cole, E., and Daniel, J. H. (eds.), *Featuring Females: Feminist Analyses of Media.* Washington, DC: American Psychology Association.

54. See www.esrb.org.

55. See paragraph 6, Lang, D. J. (2008, April 30). MADD attacks "Grand Theft Auto IV", *News and Observer.* Retrieved on May 1, 2008, from http://www.newsobserver.com/1569/story/1056137.html.

56. Walsh, D. A., Gentile, D. A., Walsh, E., Bennett, N., Robidea, B., Walsh, M., Strickland, S., and McFadden, D. (2005). Tenth annual MediaWise video game report card. Minneapolis: National Institute on Media and the Family.

57. Anderson, C. A., and Gentile, D. A. (2008). Media violence, aggression, and public policy. Pages 281–300 in Borgida, E., and Fiske, S. (eds.). *Beyond Common Sense: Psychological Science in the Courtroom.* Malden, MA: Blackwell.

58. For a review of this aspect of the game, see the "prostitute trick" on http://www.gamespp.com/playstation2/hintscheatcodes/GrandTheftAuto GTA3.html.

59. See www.gameindustry.biz for articles related to the series.

60. For a review of this controversy, see Thorson, T. (2005, July 15). Confirmed: Sex minigame in PS2 San Andreas, *Gamespot News.* Retrieved on May 2, 2008, from http://www.gamespot.com/news/2005/07/15/news_6129301.html.

61. Paragraph 5, Adams, D. (2006, June 8). Rockstar, FTC settle over Hot Coffee." *IGN.com.* Retrieved on May 2, 2008, from http://ps2.ign.com/articles/711/711788p1.html.

62. Paragraph 4, Schiesel, S. (2008, April 28). Grand Theft Auto take on New York." *New York Times.* Retrieved on May 1, 2008, from http://www.nytimes.com/2008/04/28/arts/28auto.html.

63. Paragraph 5, Schiesel, S. (ibid.).

64. www.ign.com.

65. For a review of the release and retracting of this video by IGN, see Totilo, S. (2008, April 30). "IGN yanks 'GTA IV' sex and hooker-shooting video: 'We crossed a line,' company says." *MTV Multiplayer Blog.* Retrieved on May 1, 2008, from http://multiplayerblog.mtv.com/2008/04/30/ign-yanks-gta-iv-sex-and-hooker-shooting-video/.

66. Paragraph 3, Kuchera, B. (2008, April 28). "GTA IV sex video gives Thompson, other critics fresh ammo." *Ars Technica.* Retrieved on May 1, 2008, from http://arstechnica.com/news.ars/post/20080428-jack-thompson-targets-gta-iv-with-an-unlikely-ally-ign.html.

67. Paragraph 3, Totilo, S. (ibid.).

68. Anderson, C. A., and Gentile, D. A. (ibid.).

69. Radd, D. (2006, May 8). Controversially executed. *GameDaily*. Retrieved on May 2, 2008, from http://www.gamedaily.com/articles/features/controversially-executed/68910/?biz=1.

70. Paragraph 1, Lewis, E. (2004, December 3). Playboy: The mansion—Hands all over. IGN.com. Retrieved on May 2, 2008, from http://ps2.ign.com/articles/570/570049p1.html.

71. http://www.dreamstripper.com/.

72. http://www.virtuallyjenna.com/.

73. http://www.virtualhottie2.com/.

74. Wallace, M. (2007, May 10). Playboy magazine enters second life. 3pointD.com. Retrieved on April 16, 2008, from http://www.3pointd.com/20070510/playboy-magazine-enters-second-life/.

75. Morris, C. (2004, August 25). Video game gals take it off for Playboy. CNNMoney.com. Retrieved on April 13, 2008, from http://money.cnn.com/2004/08/25/commentary/game_over/column_gaming/.

76. See http://www.cduniverse.com/productinfo.asp?pid=7485282&style=ice. Retrieved on May 2, 2008.

77. For a review of these studies, see Dill, K. E., and Dill, J. C. (1998). Video game violence: A review of the empirical literature. *Aggression and Violent Behavior* 3(4): 407–428.

78. Jensen (2007), p. 102.

79. Malamuth, N. M., Addison, A., and Koss, M. (2000). Pornography and sexual aggression: Are there reliable effects and can we understand them? *Annual Review of Sex Research* 11: 26–91.

80. Page 743, Greenfield, P. M. (2004). Inadvertent exposure to pornography on the Internet: Implications of peer-to-peer file sharing networks for child development and families. *Applied Developmental Psychology* 25: 741–750.

81. Page 748, Greenfield (ibid.).

82. Peter, J., and Valkenburg, P. M. (2006). Adolescents' exposure to sexually explicit online material and recreational attitudes about sex. *Journal of Communication* 56: 639–660.

83. Peter, J., and Valkenburg, P. M. (2007). Adolescents' exposure to a sexualized media environment and their notions of women as sex objects. *Sex Roles* 56: 381–395.

84. For coverage of this study, see *The Local: Sweden's News in English* (2006, April 25). One in ten Swedish boys views porn daily. Retrieved on May 4, 2008, from http://www.thelocal.se/3641/20060425/.

85. Lo, V., and Wei, R. (2005). Exposure to internet pornography and Taiwanese adolescents' sexual attitudes and behavior. *Journal of Broadcasting & Electronic Media* 49(2): 221–237.

86. Page 394, Peter and Volkenburg (2007).

87. Page 700, Taylor (2006).

88. Giles, D. C., and Close, J. (2008). Exposure to "lad magazines" and drive for muscularity in dating and non-dating men. *Personality and Individual Differences* 44: 1610–1616.

89. Dill and Dill (ibid.), p. 424.

90. Dill's work on these issues is extensive. For a review, please see her Web page: http://www.lrc.edu/psy/dillk/.

91. Dietz, T. L. (1998). An examinination of violence and gender role portrayal in video games: Implications for gender socialization and aggressive behavior. *Sex Roles* 38(5/6): 425–442.

92. Yao, M., Mahood, C., and Linz, D. (2006, June 16). Sexual priming, gender stereotyping, and likelihood to sexually harass: Examining the effects of playing a sexually-explicit video game. Paper submitted to the Game Studies Interest Group of the International Communication Association, Dresden International Congress Centre, Dresden, Germany. Retrieved on April 15, 2008, from http://www.allacademic.com/meta/p92539_index.html.

93. Page 21–22, Yao et al. (ibid.).

94. For example, they are more likely to believe that women want or deserve to be raped, that women "cry rape" for attention, that rape victims are promiscuous, and that rape is a way to teach uppity women a lesson.

95. For example, they are more likely to believe that women's place is in the home, that men should have authority over women, and that women are inferior. These findings are reported in: Dill, K. E. (in press). Do anti-social video games foster sexism and violence against women? Research on sexist and pro-rape attitudes among gamers. In Stark, E., and Buzawa, E. S. (eds). *Violence against Women in Families and Relationships*. Westport, CT: Greenwood Press. A draft copy of this manuscript was retrieved on May 6, 2008, from http://www.lrc.edu/psy/dillk/Articles/Sexist%20and%20Pro-Rape%20Attitudes%20Among%20Video%20Gamers-Draft%202-Karen%20Dill%20pdf.pdf.

96. Dill, K. E., and Thill, K. P. (2007). Video game characters and the socialization of gender roles: Young people's perceptions mirror sexist media depictions. *Sex Roles* 57: 851–864.

97. Page 861, Dill and Thill (ibid.).

98. Page 105, Jensen (2007).

99. Silbert, M. H., and Pines, A. M. (1984). Pornography and sexual abuse of women. *Sex Roles* 10: 864; quoted on page 105, Jensen (2007).

100. Paul (ibid.).

101. Page 81 in Paul (ibid.).

102. Page 86 in Paul (ibid.).

103. Page 93 in Paul (ibid.).

104. Page 96 in Paul (ibid.).

105. Page 96 in Paul (ibid.).

106. Page 98 in Paul (ibid.).

107. Page 101 in Paul (ibid.).

108. Page 104 in Paul (ibid.).

109. Page 182 in Paul (ibid.).

110. Crampton, T., and Foderaro, L. W. (2004, June 25). Sexual video by students prompts inquiry in Scarsdale. *New York Times*. Retrieved on May 6, 2008, from http://query.nytimes.com/gst/fullpage.html?res=9404E5DB1F39F936A15755C0A9629C8B63.

111. *Local6.com*. (2005, January 7). Police: Boys videotaped sex with unconscious girl. Retrieved on May 6, 2008, from http://www.local6.com/news/4063269/detail.html.

112. Associated Press. (2007, January 25). Teens accused in taped sex assault. *Pantagraph.com*. Retrieved on May 6, 2008, from http://www.pantagraph.com/articles/2007/01/26/news/doc45b92ab3df0f5430168720.txt.

113. Page 182–183 in Paul (ibid.).

114. See Jensen (ibid.), pages 114-116, for more on this.

115. For more on this idea, see Galloway, A. R. (2004). Social realism in gaming. *Game Studies* 4(1). Retrieved on May 14, 2008, from http://www.gamestudies.org/0401/galloway/.

116. Retrieved on May 14, 2008, from http://www.virtuallyjenna.com/.

117. http://www.americasarmy.com/.

118. Morris, C. (2002, June 3). Your tax dollars at work. *CNNMoney*. Retrieved on May 14, 2008, from http://money.cnn.com/2002/05/31/commentary/game_over/column_gaming/.

119. Paragraph 3, *America's Army*. (n.d.) Letter from Leadership. Retrieved on May 14, 2008, from http://www.americasarmy.com/intel/makingof.php.

120. Quote 23, *Quotations and Sayings*. (n.d.) Quote for the day. Retrieved on May 15, 2008, from http://www.quotesandsayings.com/gdifference.htm.

CHAPTER 3

1. Chris Marlowe, "Verizon adds Nick content to cell phones," *Hollywood Reporter Online*, May 6, 2005.

2. Doreen Carvajal, "A Way to Calm a Fussy Baby: 'Sesame Street' by Cellphone," *New York Times*, April 18, 2005, sec. C, p. 10.

3. Ibid.

4. Donald F. Roberts et al., *Kids & Media @ the New Millennium* (Menlo Park, CA: The Henry J. Kaiser Family Foundation, 1999), 78.

5. Patricia Marks Greenfield, et al., "The Program-Length Commercial," in *Children and Television: Images in a Changing Sociocultural World*, Gordon Berry and Joy Keiko Asamen, eds. (Newbury Park: Sage Publications, 1993), 53–72.

6. I've always liked Bruno Bettelheim's *The Uses of Enchantment: The Meaning and Importance of Fairy Tales* (New York: Knopf, 1975), which takes a psychodynamic look at what fairy tales might mean to children and how they help children grapple with developmental challenges.

7. See Joseph Campbell's commentary on the history of fairy tales in *The Complete Grimm's Fairy Tales* (New York: Pantheon, 1972), 833–864.

8. Bruno Bettelheim, *The Uses of Enchantment* (New York: Knopf, 1976), 251.

9. Jacob and Wilhelm Grimm, *The Complete Grimm's Fairy Tales* (New York: Pantheon, 1972), 128.

10. Ibid., 258.

11. For an interesting discussion of the differences, see Bruno Bettelheim, *The Uses of Enchantment*, 250–267.

12. Personal communication with Clint Hayashi, manager of corporate communications, Disney Consumer Products, Disney, Inc., March 9, 2007.

13. Wendy Donahue, "Princesses Reign Supreme," *Buffalo News*, March 4, 2007, sec. G, p. 13.

14. The film *Mickey Mouse Monopoly: Disney, Childhood and Corporate Power* (Media Education Foundation, 2001), does a really good job of discussing racism and sexism in Disney films.

15. The others are Viacom, which owns Nickelodeon, and Time Warner, which owns the Cartoon Network.

16. "Kristie Kelly for Disney Fairytale Weddings," YouTube, www.youtube.com/watch?v=2M5WlQJCbyw. Accessed 10 July 07.

17. "Disney—Princess (2003)," Adland, http://commercial-archive.com/108397.php. Accessed July 17, 2007.

18. "MGA Entertainment Introduces the Girls With a Passion for Fashion, Bratz!" *Business Wire*, June 11, 2001. Accessed on Factiva July 11, 2007.

19. Brent Felgner, "Bringing up Bratz; MGA Entertainment's Isaac Larian Won't Settle for Second Best," *Playthings* 104 (6) (June 2006). Accessed on Factiva July 11, 2007.

20. For an interesting discussion, see Ariel Levy's *Female Chauvinist Pigs: Women and the Rise of Raunch Culture* (New York: Free Press, 2005), 9.

21. Despite product descriptions on the MGA site describing it as a "smoothie bar" (see "Bratz Formal Funk F.M. Limo," MGA Entertainment, www.mgae.com/products/new_fall_products_2003/_bratz/fmCruiserLimoBike.asp. Accessed July 11, 2007), Peter DeBenedittis points out that the glasses included distinctly resemble champagne flutes (see "Research: Alcohol Toys: Examples," Peter D. Media Literacy, http://medialiteracy.net/purchase/toys2.shtml. Accessed July 11, 2007).

22. Woolworth's Web site: www.woolworths.co.uk/ww_p2/product/index.jhtml?pid=50717538.

23. Michael Precker, "Animated Debate for Many Arab-Americans," *Dallas Morning News*, July 12, 1993, sec. C, p.1. Accessed on Factiva July 11, 2007.

24. See Heather May, "Study Finds Even Toddlers Know Gender Expectations," *Salt Lake Tribune*, June 14, 2007. Accessed on Factiva July 11, 2007. See also Kurt Kowalski, "The Emergence of Ethnic and Racial Attitudes in Preschool-Aged Children," *Journal of Social Psychology* 143 (6) (2003), 677–690.

25. "Disney First: Black Princess in Animated Film," MSNBC, http://www.msnbc.msn.com/id/17524865/. Accessed on July 10, 2007.

26. Jayne O'Donnell, "Marketers keep pace with 'tweens': Fashion-minded girls prove rich, but fast-moving target," *USA Today*, April 11, 2007, sec. B, p. 1.

27. Sharon Kennedy Wynne, "Site-Seeing with the Kids," *St. Petersburg Times*, June 29, 2007, sec E., p. 1; Katherine Snow Smith, "All Dolled Up," *St. Petersburg Times*, July 9, 2007, sec. E, p. 3.

28. Rheyne Rice, quoted in "Mattel Unveils Online Barbie Community," *Los Angeles Times*, April 19, 2007, sec. C, p. 3.

29. American Psychological Association, Task Force on the Sexualization of Girls, *Report of the APA Task Force on the Sexualization of Girls* (Washington, DC: American Psychological Association, 2007), 2. Available at www.apa.org/pi/wpo/sexualization.html. Accessed April 8, 2007.

30. Jayne O'Donnell, "Marketers Keep Pace with 'tweens'; Fashion-minded Girls Prove Rich, but Fast-moving Targets," *USA Today*, April 11, 2007, sec. B, p.1.

31. Centers for Disease Control, "Youth Risk Behavior Surveillance—United States 2005," June 9, 2006, table 44, p. 78. Available at www.cdc.gov/mmwr/PDF/SS/SS5505.pdf. Accessed on July 11, 2007.

32. See in particular *The Hurried Child*, 3rd ed. (Reading, MA: Addison-Wesley, 2001) and *All Grown Up and No Place to Go*, 2nd ed. (Reading, MA: Addison-Wesley, 1988).

33. See *The Disappearance of Childhood* (New York: Vintage, 1992).

34. Ellyn Spragins, "Out of the Classroom, Back in the House," *New York Times*, 3 August 2003, sec. C, p. 9. Accessed on Factiva July 12, 2007.

35. Kelli Kennedy, "College Grads Moving Back Home to Boomer Parents . . . and Staying," *Associated Press*, July 30, 2006. Accessed on Factiva July 11, 2007.

36. Kid Power 2007!, http://kidpowerx.com/cgibin/templates/document.html?topic=445&event=12748&document=92748#panel_can_kgoy_and_kysl_coexist. Accessed July 11, 2007.

37. Personal communication with researcher Sandra Hofferth, June 2, 2005.

CHAPTER 4

1. Euling S.Y., et al. "Examination of US Puberty Timing Data from 1940 to 1994 for Secular Trends: Panel Findings." *Pediatrics* 121 (2008), supplement 3: S172-96; Euling, S. Y. et al. "Environmental Factors and Puberty Timing: Summary of an Expert Panel Workshop." *The Toxicologist* 84 (2005): S-1.

2. Harlan, W. R., et al. "Secondary Sex Characteristics of Girls 12–17 Years of Age: the U.S. Health Examination Survey." *Journal of Pediatrics* 96 (1980): 1074–78; Herman-Giddens M. E., et al. "Secondary Sexual Characteristics and Menses in Young Girls Seen in Office Practice: A Study from the Pediatrics Research in Office Settings." *Pediatrics* 99 (1997): 505–12. See also Herman-Giddens, M. E., "The Decline in the Age of Menarche in the United States: Should We Be Concerned?" *Journal of Adolescent Health* 40 (2007): 201–3; Herman-Giddens, M. E., "The Decline in the Age of Menarche in the United States: Should We Be Concerned?" *Journal of Adolescent Health* 40 (2007): 201–3; Herman-Giddens, M. E., "Recent Data on Pubertal Milestones in United States Children: The Secular Trend Toward Earlier Development." *International Journal of Andrology* 29 (2006): 241–46; Kaplowitz, P., "Pubertal Development in Girls: Secular Trends." *Current Opinion in Obstetrics and Gynecology* 18 (2006): 487–91; Tanner, J. M., and Eveleth, P. B., "Variability between Populations in Growth and Development at Puberty" in S. R. Berenberg, ed., *Puberty, Biologic and Psychosocial Components* (Leiden, Netherlands: H.E. Stenfert Kroese, 1975), 256–73.

3. Herman-Giddens M. E., et al. "Secondary Sexual Characteristics and Menses in Young Girls Seen in Office Practice: A Study from the Pediatrics Research in Office Settings." *Pediatrics* 99 (1997): 505–12.

4. Kaplowitz, P., and Oberfield, S. E., "Reexamination of the Age Limit for Defining when Puberty is Precocious in Girls in the United States: Implications for Evaluation and Treatment." Drug and Therapeutics and Executive Committees of the Lawson Wilkins Pediatric Endocrine Society. *Pediatrics* 104 (1999): 936–41.

5. Zuckerman, D. "When Little Girls Become Women: Early Onset of Puberty in Girls." *The Ribbon* 6 (2001): 6–8.

6. Graber, J. A., et al. "Is Pubertal Timing Associated with Psychopathology in Young Adulthood?" *Journal of the American Academy of Child and Adolescent Psychiatry* 43 (2004): 718–27; Graber, J. A., et al., "Is Psychopathology Associated with

the Timing of Pubertal Development?" *Journal of the American Academy of Child and Adolescent Psychiatry* 36 (1997): 1768–76; Martin, K. A. *Puberty, Sexuality and the Self: Boys and Girls at Adolescence* (New York: Routledge, 1996); Zuckerman, D. "When Little Girls Become Women: Early Onset of Puberty in Girls." *The Ribbon* 6 (2001): 6–8.

7. Celio, M., et al. "Early Maturation as a Risk Factor for Aggression and Delinquency in Adolescent Girls: A Review." *International Journal of Clinical Practice* 60 (2006): 1254–62; Deardorff, J., et al. "Early Puberty and Adolescent Pregnancy: The Influence of Alcohol Use." *Pediatrics* 116 (2005): 1451–56; Golub, M. S., et al. "Public Health Implications of Altered Pubertal Timing." *Pediatrics* 121 (2008) suppl.3: S218–30; Graber, J. A., et al. "Is Pubertal Timing Associated with Psychopathology in Young Adulthood?" *Journal of the American Academy of Child and Adolescent Psychiatry* 43 (2004): 718–27; Graber, J. A., et al. "Is Psychopathology Associated with the Timing of Pubertal Development?" *Journal of the American Academy of Child and Adolescent Psychiatry* 36 (1997): 1768–76; Haynie, D. L., and Piquero, A. R., "Pubertal Development and Physical Victimization in Adolescence." *Journal of Research in Crime and Delinquency* 43 (2006): 3–35; Johansson, T., and Ritzen, E. M. "Very Long-Term Follow-Up of Girls with Early and Late Menarche." *Endocrinology and Development* 8 (2005): 126–36; Martin, K. A. *Puberty, Sexuality and the Self: Boys and Girls at Adolescence* (New York: Routledge, 1996).

8. Anderson, W. F., et al. "Estimating Age-Specific Breast Cancer Risks: A Descriptive Tool to Identify Age Interactions." *Cancer Causes and Control* 18 (2007): 439–47; Clavel-Chapelon, F., et al. "Differential Effects of Reproductive Factors on the Risk of Pre- and Postmenopausal Breast Cancer. Results from a Large Cohort of French Women." *British Journal of Cancer* 86 (2002): 723–27; Grumbach, M. M., and Styne, D. M. "Puberty: Ontogeny, Neuroendocrinology, Physiology, and Disorders" in P. R. Larsen et al., eds., *Williams' Textbook of Endocrinology*, 10th ed. (Philadelphia: Saunders, 2003), 1115–1286; Hsieh, C. C., et al. "Age at Menarche, Age at Menopause, Height, and Obesity as Risk Factors for Breast Cancer: Associations and Interactions in an International Case-Control Study." *International Journal of Cancer* 46 (1990): 796–800; Kelsey, J. F., et al., "Reproductive Factors and Breast Cancer." *Epidemiologic Review* 15 (1993): 36–47; Rosner, B., et al. "Reproductive Risk Factors in a Prospective Study of Breast Cancer: The Nurses' Health Study." *American Journal of Epidemiology* 139 (1994): 819–35.

9. Bellis M. A., et al. "Adults at 12? Trends in Puberty and Their Public Health Consequences." *Journal of Epidemiology and Community Health* 60 (2006): 910–11; Ellis, B. J., et al. "Quality of Early Family Relationships and Individual Differences in the Timing of Pubertal Maturation in Girls." *Journal of Personality and Social Psychology* 77 (1999): 387–401; Ellis, B. J., and Garber, J. "Psychosocial Antecedents of Variation in Girls' Pubertal Timing: Maternal Depression, Stepfather Presence, and Marital and Family Stress." *Child Development* 71 (2000): 485–501; Hulanicka, B., et al. "Effect of Familial Distress on Growth and Maturation of Girls: A Longitudinal Study." *American Journal of Human Biology* 13 (2001): 771–76; Kaplowitz, P., *Early Puberty in Girls: The Essential Guide to Coping with This Common Problem* (New York: Ballantine, 2004); Moffit, T. E., et al. "Childhood Experience and the Onset of Menarche: A Test of a Sociobiological Model." *Child Development* 63 (1992): 47–58; Romans, S. E., et al. "Age of Menarche: The Role of Some Psychosocial Factors." *Psychological Medicine* 33 (2003): 933–39; Tahirovic, H. F.

"Menarchal Age and the Stress of War: An Example from Bosnia." *European Journal of Pediatrics* 157 (1998): 978–80; Tremblay, L., and Frigon, J. Y. "Precocious Puberty in Adolescent Girls: A Biomarker of Later Psychosocial Adjustment Problems." *Child Psychiatry and Human Development* 36 (2005): 73–94; Zabin, L. S., et al. "Childhood Sexual Abuse and Early Menarche: The Direction of Their Relationship and its Implications." *Journal of Adolescent Health* 36 (2005): 393–400.

10. Anderson, S. E., et al. "Relative Weight and Race Influence Average Age and Menarche: Results from Two Nationally Representative Surveys of U.S. Girls Studied 25 Years Apart." *Pediatrics* 111 (2003): 844–50; Anderson, S. E., and Must, A. "Interpreting the Continued Decline in the Average Age at Menarche: Results from Two Nationally Representative Surveys of U.S. Girls Studied Ten Years Apart," *Journal of Pediatrics* 147 (2005): 753–60; Biro, F. M., et al "Pubertal Correlates in Black and White Girls," *Journal of Pediatrics* 148 (2006a): 234–40; Biro, F. M. "Puberty—Whither Goest?" *Journal of Pediatric and Adolescent Gynecology* 19 (2006b): 163–65; Biro, F. M. "Influence of Obesity on Timing of Puberty." *International Journal of Andrology* 29 (2006c): 272–77; Biro, F. M. "Stone-Age Genes, Space-Age Times," presentation at the Breast Cancer and Environmental Risk Factors scientific symposium, East Lansing, MI, November 2005; Biro, F. M. "Secular Trends in Menarche," *Journal of Pediatrics* 147 (2005a): 725–26; Foxhall, K. "Beginning to Begin: Reports from the Battle on Obesity," *American Journal of Public Health* 96 (2006): 2106–12; Kaplowitz, P. "Earlier Onset of Puberty in Girls: Relation to Increased Body Mass Index and Race." *Pediatrics* 108 (2001): 347–53; Kimbro, R. T., et al. "Racial and Ethnic Differentials in Children's Overweight and Obesity Among 3-Year-Olds." *American Journal of Public Health,* 28 December 2006 [epub ahead of print]; Ogden C. L., et al., "Prevalence and Trends in Overweight among U.S. Children and Adolescents, 1999–2000." *JAMA* 288 (2002): 1728–32.

11. Davison K. K., et al. "Percent Body Fat at Age 5 Predicts Earlier Pubertal Development Among Girls at Age 9." *Pediatrics* 111 (2003, 4 Pt 1): 816–21; Freedman, D. S., et al. "The Relation of Menarchal Age to Obesity in Childhood and Adulthood: The Bogalusa Heart Study." *BMC Pediatrics* 3 (2003): 3; Lee, J. M., et al. "Weight Status in Young Girls and the Onset of Puberty." *Pediatrics* 119 (2007): e624–30; Sloboda, D. M., et al. "Age at Menarche: Influences of Prenatal and Postnatal Growth." *Journal of Clinical Endocrinology and Metabolism* 92 (2007): 46–50.

12. De Muinck-Keizer, Schrama S., and Juul, A. "Role of Environmental Factors in Timing the Onset and Progression of Puberty." *International Journal of Andrology* 29 (2006): 286–90; Euling, S. Y., et al. "Role of Environmental Factors in the Timing of Puberty." *Pediatrics* 121 (2008) suppl. 3: S167–71; Juul, A., et al. "Pubertal Development in Danish Children: Comparison of Recent European and U.S. Data." *International Journal of Andrology* 29 (2006): 247–55; Slyper, A. H. "The Pubertal Timing Controversy in the USA, and a Review of Possible Causative Factors for the Advance in Timing of Onset of Puberty." *Clinical Endocrinology* 65 (2006): 1–8.

13. Linn, S. *Consuming Kids: Protecting Our Children from the Onslaught of Marketing and Advertising* (New York: Anchor Books, 2005).

14. Brown, J. D., et al. "Sexy Media Matter: Exposure to Sexual Content in Music, Movies, and Magazines Predicts Black and White Adolescents' Sexual Behavior." *Pediatrics* 117 (2006): 1018–27; Brown, J. D., et al. "Mass Media as a Sexual Super Peer for Early Maturing Girls." *Journal of Adolescent Health* 36 (2005): 420–27.

15. Levin, D. E. "So Sexy, So Soon: The Sexualization of Childhood." In S. Olfman, ed., *Childhood Lost: How American Culture is Failing Our Kids* (Westport, CT: Praeger Publishers, 2005), 137–54.

16. American Psychological Association. *Report of the APA Task Force on the Sexualization of Girls.* February 2007.

17. American Association of Pediatrics, Committee on Public Education, "Children, Adolescents, and Television," *Pediatrics* 107 (2001): 423–26; Christakis, D. A., et al. "Television, Video, and Computer Game Usage in Children under 11 Years of Age," *Journal of Pediatrics* 145 (2004): 652–56.

18. Certain, L. K., and Kahn, R. S. "Prevalence, Correlates, and Trajectory of Television Viewing among Infants and Toddlers." *Pediatrics* 109 (2002): 634–42; Cooper, T. V., et al. "An Assessment of Obese and Non-obese Girls' Metabolic Rate During Television Viewing, Reading, and Resting." *Eating Behaviors* 7 (2006): 105–14; Davison, K. K., et al. "Cross-sectional and Longitudinal Associations Between TV Viewing and Girls' Body Mass Index, Overweight Status, and Percentage of Body Fat." *Journal of Pediatrics* 149 (2006): 32–37; Dennison, B. A., et al. "Television Viewing and Television in Bedroom Associated with Overweight Risk Among Low-Income Preschool Children." *Pediatrics* 109 (2002): 1028–35; Gentile, D. A., et al. "Well-child Visits in the Video Age: Pediatricians and the American Academy of Pediatrics' Guidelines for Children's Media Use." *Pediatrics* 114 (2004): 1235–41. Dennison, B. A., et al. "Television Viewing and Television in Bedroom Associated with Overweight Risk among Low-Income Preschool Children." *Pediatrics* 109 (2002): 1028–35.

19. Centers for Disease Control. "Participation in High School Physical Education—United States, 1991–2003." *Morbidity and Mortality Weekly* 53 (2004): 844–47; Gordon-Larsen, P., et al. "Determinants of Adolescent Physical Activity and Inactivity Patterns." *Pediatrics* 105 (2000): e83; Kimm, S. Y., et al. "Decline in Physical Activity in Black Girls and White Girls During Adolescence." *New England Journal of Medicine* 347 (2002): 709–15; National Association for Sports and Physical Education. *2006 Shape of the Nation Report: Status of Physical Education in the USA;* Strauss, R. S., et al. "Psychosocial Correlates of Physical Activity in Healthy Children." *Archives of Pediatric & Adolescent Medicine* 155 (2001): 897–902.

20. Parent, A. S., et al. "The Timing of Normal Puberty and the Age Limits of Sexual Precocity: Variations around the World, Secular Trends, and Changes after Migration." *Endocrine Reviews* 24 (2003): 668–93.

21. Aksglaede, L., et al. "The Sensitivity of the Child to Sex Steroids: Possible Impact of Exogenous Estrogens." *Human Reproduction Update* 32 (2006): 341–49.

22. Blanck, H. M., et al. "Age at Menarche and Tanner Stage in Girls Exposed *in Utero* and Postnatally to Polybrominated Biphenyl." *Epidemiology* 11 (2000): 641–47.

23. Partsch, C. J., and Sippell, W. G. "Pathogenesis and Epidemiology of Precocious Puberty: Effects of Exogenous Oestrogens." *Human Reproductive Update* 7 (2001): 392–402.

24. Castellino, N., et al. "Puberty Onset in Northern Italy: A Random Sample of 3597 Italian Children," *Journal of Endocrinological Investigation* 28 (2005): 589–94; Fara, G. M., et al. "Epidemic of Breast Enlargement in an Italian School." *The Lancet* 2(8137) (1979): 295–97; Massart, F., et al. "How Do Environmental Estrogen

Disruptors Induce Precocious Puberty?" *Minerva Pediatrica* 58 (2006): 247–54; Massart, F., et al. "High Incidence of Central Precocious Puberty in a Bounded Geographic Area of Northwest Tuscany: An Estrogen Disruptor Epidemic?" *Gynecological Endocrinology* 20 (2005): 92–98; Parent, A. S., et al. "The Timing of Normal Puberty and the Age Limits of Sexual Precocity: Variations around the World, Secular Trends, and Changes after Migration." *Endocrine Reviews* 24 (2003): 668–93.

25. Aksglaede, L., et al. "The Sensitivity of the Child to Sex Steroids: Possible Impact of Exogenous Estrogens." *Human Reproduction Update* 32 (2006): 341–49; Donovan, M., et al. "Personal Care Products that Contain Estrogens or Xenoestrogens May Increase Breast Cancer Risk." *Medical Hypotheses* 68 (2007): 756–66; Massart, F., et al. "How Do Environmental Estrogen Disruptors Induce Precocious Puberty?" *Minerva Pediatrica* 58 (2006): 247–54; Tiwary, C. "Premature Sexual Development in Children Following Use of Estrogen- or Placenta-Containing Hair Products." *Clinical Pediatrics* 37 (1998): 733–40.

26. Wolff. M., et al. "Pilot Study of Urinary Biomarkers of Phytoestrogens, Phthalates, and Phenols in Girls." *Environmental Health Perspectives* 115 (2007): 116–21.

27. vom Saal, F. S. "Perinatal Programming of Obesity: Interaction of Nutrition and Environmental Exposures." Presentation to the American Association for the Advancement of Science annual meeting, San Francisco, Feb. 16, 2007.

28. Aksglaede, L., et al. "The Sensitivity of the Child to Sex Steroids: Possible Impact of Exogenous Estrogens." *Human Reproduction Update* 32 (2006): 341–49.

29. McLachlan, J. A., et al. "Endocrine Disrupters and Female Reproductive Health." *Best Practice & Research, Clinical Endocrinology & Metabolism* 20 (2006): 63–75.

30. Massart, F., et al. "How Do Environmental Estrogen Disruptors Induce Precocious Puberty?" *Minerva Pediatrica* 58 (2006): 247–54; Wang, R. Y., et al. "Effects of Environmental Agents on the Attainment of Puberty: Considerations when Assessing Exposure to Environmental Chemicals in the National Children's Study." *Environmental Health Perspectives* 113 (2005): 1100–07.

31. Durando, M., et al. "Prenatal Bisphenol A Exposure Induces Preneoplastic Lesions in the Mammary Gland in Wistar Rats." *Environmental Health Perspectives* 115 (2007): 80–86; Howdeshell, K., et al. "Plastic Bisphenol A Speeds Growth and Puberty," *Nature* 401 (1999): 762–64; Munoz-de-Toro, M., et al. "Perinatal Exposure to Bisphenol-A Alters Peripubertal Mammary Gland Development in Mice." *Endocrinology* 146 (2005): 4138–47; vom Saal, F. S., and Hughes, C. "An Extensive New Literature Concerning Low-Dose Effects of Bisphenol A Shows the Need for a New Risk Assessment." *Environmental Health Perspectives* 113 (2005): 926–33.

32. Andrade, A. J. M. "A Dose-Response Study Following In Utero and Lactational Exposure to di-(2-ethylhexyl)-phthalate (DEHP): Non-monotonic Dose-Response and Low Dose Effects on Rat Brain Aromatase Activity." *Toxicology* 227 (2006): 185–92.

33. Schettler, T. "Toward an Ecological View: Complex Systems, Health, and Disease." *San Francisco Medicine* (journal of the San Francisco Medical Society) 79 (2006): 12–15.

34. Hambrick-Dixon, P. J. "The Effects of Exposure to Physical Environmental Stressors on African-American Children: A Review and Research Agenda." *Journal of Children & Poverty* 8 (2002): 23–34.

35. Dewey, K. G. "Growth Characteristics of Breast-fed Compared to Formula-fed Infants." *Biology of the Neonate* 74 (1998): 94–105; Mayer-Davis, E. J., et al. "Breast-feeding and Risk for Childhood Obesity: Does Maternal Diabetes or Obesity Status Matter?" *Diabetes Care* 29 (2006): 2231–37; Schack-Nielsen, L., and Michaelsen, K. F. "Advances in Our Understanding of the Biology of Human Milk and its Effects on the Offspring." *Journal of Nutrition* 137 (2007): 503S–510S.

36. Chavarro, J. E., et al. "Effects of a School-Based Obesity-Prevention Intervention on Menarche (United States)." *Cancer Causes and Control* 16 (2005): 1245–52.

37. Ibid.

38. Foxhall, K., "Beginning to Begin: Reports from the Battle on Obesity." *American Journal of Public Health* 96 (2006): 2106–2112.

39. National Environmental Justice Advisory Council, Cumulative Risks/Impacts Work Group, "Ensuring Risk Reduction in Communities with Multiple Stressors: Environmental Justice and Cumulative Risks/Impacts." Report to the US EPA, December 2004.

CHAPTER 5

1. American Academy of Pediatrics, "Identifying and Treating Eating Disorders: Policy Statement, *Pediatrics* 111(1) (2003): 204–11; Society for Adolescent Medicine, "Eating Disorders in Adolescents: Position Paper of the Society for Adolescent Medicine," *Journal of Adolescent Health* 33 (2003): 496–503.

2. Croll, J., Neumark-Sztainer, D., Story, M., and Ireland, M., "Prevalence and Risk and Protective Factors Related to Disordered Eating," *Journal of Adolescent Health* 31(2) (2002): 166–75.

3. Gordon, R. A., "Eating Disorders East and West: A Culture-bound Syndrome Unbound," in M. Nasser, M. A. Katzman, and R. A. Gordon (eds.), *Eating Disorders and Cultures in Transition*, 1–23 (New York: Taylor and Francis, 2001).

4. World Health Organization, *Women's Mental Health: An Evidence-based Review.* (Geneva, Switzerland: Mental Health Determinants and Populations, Department of Mental Health and Substance Dependence, World Health Organization, 2000).

5. Striegel-Moore, R. H., and Bulik, C. M., "Risk Factors for Eating Disorders," *American Psychologist* 62(3) (2007): 181–98.

6. Treasure, J., "The Trauma of Self-Starvation: Eating Disorders and Body Image," in M. Nasser, K. Baistow, and J. Treasure (eds.), *The Female Body in Mind: The Interface Between the Female Body and Mental Health*, 57–71 (London: Routledge, 2007).

7. American Psychiatric Association, *Diagnostic and Statistical Manual of Mental Disorders*, 4th ed. (Washington, DC: American Psychiatric Association, 1994); Sullivan, P., "Course and Outcome of Anorexia Nervosa and Bulimia Nervosa," in Fairburn, C. G., and Brownell, K. D. (eds.), *Eating Disorders and Obesity*, 2nd ed., 226–32 (New York: Guilford Press, 2002).

8. Sullivan. P. F., "Mortality in Anorexia Nervosa," *American Journal of Psychiatry* 152 (1995): 1073–74.

9. Patrick, L., "Eating Disorders: A Review of the Literature with Emphasis on Medical Complications and Clinical Nutrition," *Alternative Medicine Review* 7(3) (2002): 184–202.

10. Maine, M., and Kelly, J., *The Body Myth: Adult Women and the Pressure to Be Perfect* (Hoboken: Wiley, 2005).

11. Croll, Neumark-Sztainer, Story, and Ireland, "Disordered Eating."

12. Centers for Disease Control and Prevention, Youth Risk Behavior Surveillance (YRBSS), *Morbidity and Mortality Report (MMWR)* 51 (SS-4), 2002.

13. Chavez, M., and Insel, T. R., "Eating Disorders: National Institute of Mental Health's Perspective," *American Psychologist* 62(3) (2007): 159–66.

14. Becker, A. E., and Burwell, R. A., "Acculturation and Disordered Eating in Fiji," presented at the 152nd Annual Meeting of the American Psychiatric Association, 1999. Bordo, S., *Unbearable Weight: Feminism, Western Culture, and the Body* (Berkeley: University of California Press, 1993).

15. Levine, M. P., and Smolak, L., *The Prevention of Eating Problems and Eating Disorders: Theory, Research and Practice* (Mahwah, NJ: Lawrence Erlbaum Associates, 2006).

16. The National Center on Addiction and Substance Abuse at Columbia University (CASA), *Food for Thought: Substance Abuse and Eating Disorders* (New York: CASA, 2003); Then, D., "Women's Magazines: Messages They Convey about Looks, Men, and Careers," paper presented at American Psychological Association, Washington DC, 1992.

17. Plous, S., and Neptune, D., "Racial and Gender Biases in Magazine Advertisements: A Content Analytic Study," *Psychology of Women's Quarterly* 21 (1997): 627–44.

18. American Psychological Association, *Report of the APA Task Force on the Sexualization of Girls* (Washington DC: American Psychological Association, 2007).

19. Maine, M., *Body Wars: Making Peace with Women's Bodies* (Carlsbad, CA: Gurze Books, 2000).

20. Roberts, D., Foehr, U., and Rideout, V., *Generation M: Media in the Lives of 8–18 Year Olds* (Menlo Park, CA: Kaiser Family Foundation, 2005).

21. Lampmann, C., Rolfe-Maloney, B., David, E. J., Yan, M., McCermott, N., Winters, S., et al., "Messages about Sex in the Workplace: A Content Analysis of Prime-Time Television," *Sexuality & Culture* 6 (2002): 3–21.

22. Montemurro, B., "Not a Laughing Matter: Sexual Harassment as 'Material' on Workplace-based Situation Comedies," *Sex Roles* 48 (2003): 433–45.

23. Smith, S. L., *Bare Naked Ladies: A Content Analysis of the Hypersexualization of Males and Females in G, PG, & PG-13 Rated Films,* unpublished manuscript, 2006.

24. Linn, S., *Consuming Kids: The Hostile Takeover of Childhood* (New York: The New Press, 2004).

25. Dines, G., "Yale Sex Week Glosses Over Porn's Dark Side," *Hartford Courant,* February 11, 2008, A9.

26. National Organization for Women, "Where Are the Women? Feminists Pick the Champs and Chumps of the Super Bowl Commercials," 2008, http://www.nowfoundation.org/issues/communications/tv/ads/superbowl-2008-report.html.

27. Frederickson, B. L., and Roberts, T. A., "Objectification Theory: Toward Understanding Women's Lived Experiences and Mental Health Risks," *Psychology of Women Quarterly* 21 (1997): 173–206.

28. Levine and Smolak, *Prevention of Eating Problems.*

29. Bandura, A., "Self-Regulation Through Anticipatory and Self-reactive Mechanisms," in R. A. Dienstbier (ed.), *Nebraska Symposium on Motivation*, Vol. 38: *Perspectives on Motivation*, 69–164 (Lincoln: University of Nebraska Press, 1991).

30. Bordo, S., *Unbearable Weight: Feminism, Western Culture, and the Body* (Berkeley: University of California Press, 1993).

31. Tiggemann, M., and Slater, A., "A Test of Objectification Theory in Former Dancers and Non-Dancers," *Psychology of Women Quarterly* 2 (2001): 57–64.

32. Piran, N., and Cormier, H. C., "The Socialconstruction of Women and Disordered Eating Patterns," *Journal of Counseling Psychology* 52 (2005): 549–58.

33. Stice, E., "Risk and Maintenance Factors for Eating Pathology: A Meta-analytic Review," *Psychological Bulletin* 128 (2002): 825–48; Thompson, K. and Stice, E., "Internalization of the Thin-Ideal: Mounting Evidence for a New Risk Factor for Body Image Disturbance and Eating Pathology," *Current Directions in Psychological Science* 10 (2001): 181–83.

34. Kilbourne, J., "Still Killing Us Softly: Advertising and the Obsession with Thinness," in P. Fallon, M. A. Katzman, and S. C. Wooley (eds.), *Feminist Perspectives on Eating Disorders*, 395–418 (New York: Guilford Press, 1994); Girls, Women, Media Project: What Are You Looking At? "What's the Problem? Facts about Girls, Women + Media," September 2, 2002, www.mediaandwomen.org.

35. Segall, R., "The New Product Placement," *The Nation*, February 24, 2003, 30–33.

36. Bronfenbrenner, U., "Toward an Experimental Ecology of Human Development," *American Psychologist* 32 (1979): 513–31.

37. Levine and Smolak, *Prevention of Eating Problems*.

38. Pipher, M., *Reviving Ophelia: Saving the Selves of Adolescent Girls* (New York: Ballantine Books, 1994).

39. Murnen, S. K., Smolak, L., Mills, J. A., and Good, L., "Thin, Sexy Women and Strong, Muscular Men: Grade-School Children's Responses to Objectified Images of Women and Men," *Sex Roles* 43 (2003): 1–17.

40. Grabe, S., Shibley-Hyde, J., and Lindberg, S. M., "Body Objectification and Depression in Adolescents: The Role of Gender, Shame, and Rumination," *Psychology of Women Quarterly* 31 (2007): 164–75.

41. Stice, E., Hayward, C., Cameron, R. P., Killen, J. D., and Taylor, C. B., "Body-Image and Eating Disturbances Predict Onset of Depression among Female Adolescents: A Longitudinal Study," *Journal of Abnormal Psychology* 109 (2000): 438–44.

42. Kaplowitz, P., "Earlier Onset of Puberty in Girls: Relation to Increased Body Mass Index and Race," *Pediatrics* 108 (2) (2001): 347–53.

43. Centers for Disease Control and Prevention, Youth Risk Behavior Surveillance System (YRBSS), *Percentage of Students Who Had Sexual Intercourse: 2001, U.S., Grouped by Grade*, 2001, http://apps.nccd.cdc.gov/YRBSS/GraphV.asp; Field, A. E., Camargo, C. A., Taylor, C. B., Berkey, C., Frazier, A. L., Gillman, M. W., and Colditz, G. A., "Overweight, Weight Concerns and Bulimic Behaviors Among Girls and Boys," *Journal of the Academy for Child and Adolescent Psychiatry* 38 (1999): 754–60.

44. Brumberg, J. J., *The Body Project: An Intimate History of American Girls* (New York: Random House, 1997).

45. Murnen, S. K., and Smolak, L., "The Experience of Sexual Harassment among Grade-School Students: Early Socialization of Female Subordination?" *Sex Roles* 43 (2000): 1–17.

46. Smolak, L., and Murnen, S. K., "A Feminist Approach to Eating Disorders," in J. K. Thompson (ed.), *Handbook of Eating Disorders and Obesity,* 590–605 (Hoboken, NJ: Wiley, 2004).

47. Murnen, and Smolak, "Sexual Harassment."

48. Kimmel, M. S., and Mosmiller, T. E., eds., *Against the Tide: Pro-feminist Men in the United States, 1776–1990: A Documentary History* (Boston: Beacon Press, 1992).

CHAPTER 6

1. Denizet-Lewis, Benoit, "Friends, Friends with Benefits and the Benefits of the Local Mall," *New York Times Magazine,* May 30, 2004, pp. 30–35, 54, 56, 58.

2. Ibid., p. 33.

3. Ibid., p. 32.

4. Ibid., p. 33.

5. Lehigh, Scot, "The Casual Emptiness of Teenage Sex," *Boston Globe,* June 2, 2004, p. A11.

6. For instance, see Thornburgh, Dick, and Lin, Herbert (eds.), *Youth, Pornography and the Internet* (Washington, DC: National Academy Press, 2002). It was sponsored by the Computer Science and Telecommunications Board of the National Research Council. "The Cyberporn Generation," *People Magazine,* April 26, 2004. Whether this legislation will become a vehicle for limiting children's access to the Internet is now in the courts. On June 30, 2004, the Supreme Court upheld a Philadelphia District Court order that blocked the implementation of COPA on First Amendment grounds.

7. Silverman, Jay, Raj, Anita, and Clements, Karen, "Dating Violence and Associated Sexual Risk and Pregnancy among Adolescent Girls in the United States," *Pediatrics* 114(2), August 2004, pp. e220–e225.

8. American Academy of Pediatrics, "Policy Statement: Identifying and Treating Eating Disorders," *Pediatrics* 111(1), January 2003, pp. 204–11.

9. For a more complete discussion of these issues, see: Levin, Diane E., and Kilbourne, Jean, *So Sexy So Soon: The New Sexualized Childhood and What Parents Can Do to Protect Their Kids* (New York: Ballantine Books, in press).

10. Researchers who study violence and children have concluded from a much larger body of research that patterns of aggression at age 8 are highly correlated with adult aggressive behavior. For instance, see Eron, Leonard, Gentry, Jacquelyn, and Schlegel, Peggy (eds.), *Reason to Hope: A Psychosocial Perspective on Violence and Youth* (Washington, DC: American Psychological Association, 1994). The authors conclude that to reduce adult aggression, it is vital to work with children when they are young. Although we do not have a similar body of research on the relationship of early sexual development to later sexual behavior to draw the same definitive conclusions, child development experts generally accept the importance of the first eight years in laying the foundations for later behavior.

11. See Donnerstein, Ed, and Smith, Stacy, "Sex in the Media: Theory, Influences, and Solutions" in *The Handbook of Children and the Media,* Singer, Dorothy G., and Singer, Jerome L. (eds.) (Thousand Oaks, CA: Sage, 2001), 289–307. Also see Lamb, Sharon, and Brown, Lynn M., *Packaging Girlhood: Rescuing Our Daughters from Marketers' Schemes* (New York: Norton, 2006).

12. Rideout, Victoria, Vandewater, Elizabeth, and Wartella, Ellen, *Zero to Six: Electronic Media in the Lives of Infants, Toddlers and Preschoolers*, The Kaiser Family Foundation, Fall 2003, p. 12.

13. *Sex on TV: Executive Summary*, A Biennial Report of the Kaiser Family Foundation, 2001, p. 2.

14. *Sex, Kids and the Family Hour: A Three-Part Study of Sexual Content on Television*. Report from Children Now and the Kaiser Family Foundation, 1996.

15. Donnerstein, Ed, and Smith, Stacy, op. cit.

16. Greenhouse, L. "Court Blocks Law Regulating Internet Access to Pornography." *New York Times*, June 30, 2004.

17. The action figure is "Sable Bomb" Series 2 from World Wrestling Federation made by Jakks Pacific, Inc., 1998. Its age recommendation is "for ages four and up."

18. For more detailed explanations of the connections among sexualization, consuming, and corporate interests, see the following books: Levin, Diane E., and Kilbourne, Jean, *So Sexy So Soon*, op cit.; Linn, Susan, *Consuming Kids: Protecting Our Children from the Onslaught of Marketing and Advertising* (New York: Anchor, 2005); Schor, Juliet, *Born to Buy: The Commercialized Child and the New Consumer Culture* (New York: Scribner, 2005); and Kilbourne, Jean, *Deadly Persuasion: Why Women and Girls Must Fight the Addictive Power of Advertising* (New York: Free Press, 1999).

19. Meltz, Barbara, "Super Sexy Fashion Dolls Are Asking for Trouble." *The Boston Globe*, December 11, 2003, pp. H1 and H4.

20. MGA Entertainment Press Release: "Bratz Becomes No. 1 Fashion Themed Dolls and Accessories in the USA. February 5, 2009. Retrieved April 10, 2007 from www.mgae.com/downloads/pressreleases/Bratz%20Press%20Release.pdf.

21. Stories like these prompted the *Boston Globe* column by Barbara Meltz "Dodging the Britney Spears Bandwagon," August 17, 2000, pp. F1 and F3, and *Good Morning America* to do a feature called "Too Sexy Too Soon" in April 2001 about the influence of such singers on children.

22. Rideout, V., *Parents, Children & Media*. A Kaiser Family Foundation Survey, 2007, www.kff.org.

23. *Sex, Kids and the Family Hour: A Three-Part Study of Sexual Content on Television*. A Special Report from Children Now and the Kaiser Family Foundation, 1996, www.kff.org.

24. American Psychological Association, *Report of the APA Task Force on the Sexualization of Girls*, 2007.

25. For a more detailed account of how children's ideas about gender are shaped by the information and images that surround them, see Carlsson-Paige, Nancy, and Levin, Diane, "Whatever Happened to Annie Oakley: Girls, Sexism, and War Play," op. cit.; Pipher, Mary, *Reviving Ophelia: Saving the Selves of Adolescent Girls* (New York: Ballantine Books, 2001); and Pollack, William, *Real Boys: Rescuing Our Sons from the Myths of Boyhood* (New York: Random House, 1998).

26. These characteristics of young children's thinking outlined here are adapted from what Jean Piaget called the "preoperational stage of development." See Piaget, Jean, *The Language and Thought of the Child* (New York: Routledge & Kegan Paul, 1926).

27. For instance, see Linn, Susan, *Consuming Kids: The Hostile Takeover of Childhood* (New York: The New Press, 2004), and Pipher, Mary, *Reviving Ophelia*, op. cit.

28. Stepp, Laura Sessions, "Unsettling New Fad Alarms Parents: Middle School Oral Sex," *Washington Post*, July 8, 1999, p. A1.

29. Farkas, Steve, Johnson, Jean, and Duffett, Ann, *A Lot Easier Said Than Done: Parents Talk about Raising Children in Today's America*, New York: Public Agenda, October 2002.

30. For instance, see Hewlett, Sylvia A., and West, Cornel, *The War on Parents: What We Can Do for America's Beleaguered Moms and Dads* (New York: Houghton Mifflin, 1998).

31. The book So *Sexy So Soon*, op. cit., provides much more detailed help on how to work with children on issues related to the sexualization of childhood.

32. For concrete help doing this, see Levin, Diane E., *Remote Control Childhood? Combating the Hazards of Media Culture*, op. cit.

33. For help shaping responses to the age, needs, and questions of specific children, see Chrisman, Kent, and Couchenour, Conna, *Healthy Sexual Development: A Guide for Early Childhood Educators and Families*, op. cit.

34. There are a growing number of organizations working to accomplish this. Many of them can be found on the Web site of the Campaign for a Commercial-Free Childhood, www.commercialfreechildhood.org.

CHAPTER 7

1. Jones, K., "Are rap videos more violent? Style differences and the prevalence of sex and violence in the age of MTV," *Howard Journal of Communication* 8 (1997): 343–56; Pough, G. D., *Check It while I Wreck It: Black Womanhood, Hip Hop Culture, and the Public Sphere* (Boston: Northeastern University Press, 2004).

2. American Psychological Association, Task Force on the Sexualization of Girls, *Report of the APA Task Force on the Sexualization of Girls* (Washington, DC: American Psychological Association, 2007), retrieved on February 11, 2008 from www.apa.org/pi/wpo/sexualization.html.

3. Stephens, D. P., and Phillips, L. D., "Integrating Black feminist thought into conceptual frameworks of African American adolescent women's sexual scripting processes," *Sexualities, Evolution, and Gender* 7 (2005): 37–55.

4. Squires, C. R., Kohn-Wood, L. P., Chavous, T., and Carter, P. L., "Evaluating agency and responsibility in gendered violence: African American youth talk about violence and hip hop," *Sex Roles* 55 (2006): 725–37; Johnson, J. D., Adams, M. S., Ashburn, L., and Reed, W., "Differential gender effects of exposure of rape music on African American adolescents' acceptance of teen dating violence," *Sex Roles* 33 (1995): 597–605; Stephens, D. P., and Few, A. L., "The effects of images of African American women in Hip Hop on early adolescents' attitudes toward physical attractiveness and interpersonal relationships," *Sex Roles* 56 (2007): 251–64.

5. Wingood, G. M., DiClemente, R. J., Rernhardt, J. M., Harrington, K., Davies, S. L., Robillard, A., and Hook, E. W., "A prospective study of exposure to rap music videos and African American female adolescents' health," *American Journal of Public Health* 93 (2003): 437–39.

6. Collins, P. H., *Black Sexual Politics: African Americans, Gender, and New Racism* (New York: Routledge, 2004).

7. Ibid.

8. Collins, P. H., "New commodities, new consumers: Selling blackness in a global marketplace," *Ethnicities* 6 (2006): 297–317.

9. Sharpley-Whiting, T. D., *Pimps Up, Ho's Down: Hip Hop's Hold on Young Black Women* (New York: New York University Press, 2007).

10. Cole, J. B., and Guy-Sheftall, B., *Gender Talk: The Struggle for Women's Equality in African American Communities* (New York: Ballantine Publishing Group, 2003); Sharpley-Whiting, T. D., Congressional Testimony: Subcommittee on Commerce, Trade and Consumer Protection of the Committee on Energy and Commerce, "From Imus to Industry: The Business of Stereotypes and Degrading Images," 2007, retrieved on May 22, 2008, from http://energycommerce.house.gov/cmte_mtgs/110-ctcp-hrg.092507.Imus.to.Industry.shtml.

11. Stephens, D. P., and Phillips, L. D., "Freaks, Gold Diggers, Divas, and Dykes: The sociohistorical development of adolescent African American women's sexual scripts," *Sexuality & Culture* 7 (2003): 3–47; Stephens, D. P., and Few, A. L., "The effects of images of African American women in Hip Hop on early adolescents' attitudes toward physical attractiveness and interpersonal relationships," *Sex Roles* 56 (2007): 251–64.

12. Stephens and Phillips, "Freaks, Gold Diggers, Divas, and Dykes."

13. Ibid.

14. Ibid.

15. Ibid.

16. Ibid.

17. Ibid.

18. Stokes, C. E., "Representin' in cyberspace: Sexual scripts, self-definition and hip hop culture in Black American adolescent girls' home pages," *Culture, Health, & Sexuality* 9 (2007): 169–84.

19. Stephens and Phillips, "Freaks, Gold Diggers, Divas, and Dykes."

20. Stokes, "Representin' in cyberspace," 176.

21. Ibid., 173.

22. Ibid., 178.

23. Ibid., 179.

24. Stephens and Phillips, "Black feminist thought."

25. Ibid.

26. Martyn, K. K., and Hutchinson, S. A., "Low-income African American adolescents who avoid pregnancy: Tough girls who rewrite negative scripts," *Qualitative Health Research* 11 (2001): 238–56.

27. Perry, I., "Who(se) am I? The identity and image of women in Hip-Hop," in G. Dines and J. M. Humez (eds.), *Gender, Race, and Class in Media: A Text Reader*, 136–48 (Thousand Oaks, CA: Sage, 2003); Sharpley-Whiting, *Pimps Up, Ho's Down*.

28. Sharpley-Whiting, *Pimps Up, Ho's Down*.

29. West, C. M., "Mammy, Jezebel, Sapphire, and their Homegirls: Developing an 'oppositional gaze' toward the images of Black women," in J. C. Chrisler, C. Golden, and P. D. Rozee (eds.), *Lectures on the Psychology of Women*, 287–99 (New York: McGraw-Hill, 2008).

30. Stephens, D. P., and Few, A. L., "The effects of images of African American women in Hip Hop on early adolescents' attitudes toward physical attractiveness and interpersonal relationships," *Sex Roles* 56 (2007): 251–64.

31. Carroll, R., *Sugar in the Raw: Voices of Young Black Girls in America*, 131–32 (New York: Crown, 1998).

32. Edwards, J. M., Iritani, B. J., and Hallfors, D. D., "Prevalence and correlates of exchanging sex for drugs or money among adolescents in the United States," *Sexually Transmitted Infections* 82 (2006): 354–58.

33. Boxill, N. A., and Richardson, D. J., "Ending sex trafficking of children in Atlanta," *Affilia* 22 (2007): 138–49; Dunlap, E., Golub, A., and Johnson, B. D., "Girls' sexual development in the inner city: From compelled childhood sexual contact to sex-for-things exchanges," *Journal of Child Sexual Abuse* 12 (2003): 73–96.

34. Motivational Educational Entertainment (MEE) Productions, *This Is My Reality: The Price of Sex: An Inside Look at Black Urban Youth Sexuality and the Role of the Media* (Philadelphia: MEE, 2005).

35. Ward, L. M., Hansbrough, E., and Walker, E., "Contributions of music video exposure to Black adolescents' gender and sexual schemas," *Journal of Adolescent Research* 20 (2005): 143–66.

36. Stephens, D. P., and Few, A. L., "Hip hop honey or video ho: African American preadolescents' understanding of female sexual scripts in Hip Hop culture," *Sexuality and Culture* 11 (2007): 48–69.

37. Squires, Kohn-Wood, Chavous, and Carter, "Evaluating agency and responsibility."

38. Stephens and Phillips, "Freaks, Gold Diggers, Divas, and Dykes."

39. Townsend, T. G., "Protecting our daughters: Intersections of race, class, and gender in African American mothers' socialization of their daughters' heterosexuality," *Sex Roles* (in press).

40. Motivational Educational Entertainment Productions, *This Is My Reality.*

41. Bryant, Y., "Relationships between exposure to rap music videos and attitudes toward relationships among African American youth," *Journal of Black Psychology* (in press).

42. Squires, Kohn-Wood, Chavous, and Carter, "Evaluating agency and responsibility."

43. Motivational Educational Entertainment Productions, *This Is My Reality.*

44. Bryant, "Relationships."

45. Wade, B., and Thomas-Gunnar, C., "Explicit rap music lyrics and attitudes toward rape: The perceived effects on African American college students' attitudes," *Challenges: A Journal of Research on African American Men* 58 (1993): 51–60.

46. Ward, Hansbrough, and Walker, "Music video exposure," 161.

47. For examples, see Adams, T. M., and Fuller, D. B., "The words have changed but the ideology remains the same: Misogynistic lyrics in rap music," *Journal of Black Studies* 36 (2006): 938–57; Armstrong, E. G., "Gangsta misogyny: A content analysis of the portrayals of violence against women in rap music, 1987–1993," *Journal of Criminal Justice and Popular Culture* 8 (2001): 96–126.

48. Adams and Fuller, "Misogynistic lyrics in rap music."

49. Wade, B., and Thomas-Gunnar, C., "Explicit rap music lyrics."

50. Like, T. Z., and Miller, J., "Race, inequality, and gender violence: A contextual examination," in R. D. Peterson, L. J. Krivo, and J. Hagan (eds.), *The Many*

Colors of Crime: Inequalities of Race, Ethnicity, and Crime in America, 137–76 (New York: New York University Press, 2006).

51. Motivational Educational Entertainment Productions, *This Is My Reality*; West, C. M., "'A thin line between love and hate?': Black men as victims and perpetrators of dating violence," *Journal of Aggression, Maltreatment, & Trauma* (in press).

52. Johnson, Adams, Ashburn, and Reed, "Differential gender effects."

53. Squires, Kohn-Wood, Chavous, and Carter, "Evaluating agency and responsibility."

54. For reviews see West, C. M., ed., *Violence in the Lives of Black Women: Battered, Black, and Blue* (Binghamton, NY: The Haworth Press, 2002); West, C. M., *Sexual Violence in the Lives of African American Women: Risk, Response, and Resilience* (Harrisburg, PA: VAWnet, 2006), a project of the National Resource Center on Domestic Violence/Pennsylvania Coalition Against Domestic Violence. Retrieved from http://www.vawnet.org.

55. Cecil, H., and Matson, S. C., "Differences in psychological health and family dysfunction by sexual victimization type in a clinical sample of African American adolescent women," *Journal of Sex Research* 42 (2005): 203–14; West, C. M., and Rose, S., "Dating aggression among low income African American youth: An examination of gender differences and antagonistic beliefs," *Violence Against Women*, 6 (2000): 470–94.

56. Neville, H. A. Heppner, M. J., Oh, E., Spanierman, L. B., and Clark, M., "General and culturally specific factors influencing Black and White rape survivors' self-esteem," *Psychology of Women Quarterly* 28 (2004): 83–94.

57. Adams and Fuller, "Misogynistic lyrics in rap music"; Jones, "Are rap videos more violent?"; Pough, G. D., *Check It while I Wreck It: Black Womanhood, Hip Hop Culture, and the Public Sphere* (Boston: Northeastern University Press, 2004); Sharpley-Whiting, *Pimps Up, Ho's Down*.

58. Wingood, DiClemente, Rernhardt, Harrington, Davies, Robillard, and Hook, "Exposure to rap music videos."

59. Peterson, S. H., Wingood, G. M., DiClemente, R. J., Harrington, K., and Davies, S., "Images of sexual stereotypes in rap videos and the health of African American female adolescents," *Journal of Women's Health* 16 (2007): 1157–64.

60. Centers for Disease Control and Prevention, *HIV/AIDS Surveillance Report* 13 (2003): 1–44.

61. Squires, Kohn-Wood, Chavous, and Carter, "Evaluating agency and responsibility."

62. Martyn and Hutchinson, "Tough girls who rewrite negative scripts."

63. Tyson, E. H., "Rap-music attitude and perception scale: A validation study," *Research on Social Work Practice* 16 (2006): 211–23.

64. Richardson, E., "'She was workin like foreal': Critical literacy and discourse practices of African American females in the age of hip hop," *Discourse & Society* 18 (2007): 789–809.

65. Bryant, "Relationships."

66. Richardson, E., "African American females in the age of hip hop."

67. Ward, L. M., "Understanding the role of entertainment media in the sexual socialization of American youth: A review of empirical research," *Developmental Review* 23 (2003): 347–88.

68. Holsendolph, E., "'Taking back the music': Spelman students combat hip-hop's negative portrayal of Black women," *Black Issues in Higher Education* 22 (March 24, 2005): 8–9.

69. Sharpley-Whiting, "From Imus to industry."

70. American Psychological Association, *Sexualization of Girls*; Motivational Educational Entertainment Productions, *This Is My Reality.*

71. Wingood, DiClemente, Rernhardt, Harrington, Davies, Robillard, and Hook, "Exposure to rap music videos."

72. Brown, J. D., L'Engle, K. L., Pardun, C. J., Guo, G., Kenneavy, K., and Jackson, C., "Sexy media matter: Exposure to sexual content in music, movies, television, and magazines predicts Black and White adolescents' sexual behavior," *Pediatrics* 117 (2006): 1018–27.

73. Elligan, D., *Rap therapy: A practical guide for communicating with youth and young adults* (New York: Kensignton Books, 2004).

74. Motivational Educational Entertainment Productions, *This Is My Reality.*

75. Collins, *Black Sexual Politics.*

76. Squires, Kohn-Wood, Chavous, and Carter, "Evaluating agency and responsibility," 734.

77. Stokes, "Representin' in cyberspace."

CHAPTER 8

1. S. Cooper, "A Brief History of Child Sexual Exploitation," in *Medical, Legal and Social Science Aspects of Child Sexual Exploitation,* ed. S. Cooper, R. Estes, A. Giardino, N. Kellogg, and V. Vieth (St Louis: GW Medical Publishing, 2005).

2. Trifiletti C., "Investigating Internet Child Exploitation Cases," in *Medical, Legal and Social Science Aspects of Child Sexual Exploitation,* ed. S. Cooper, R. Estes, A. Giardino, N. Kellogg, and V. Vieth (St Louis: GW Medical Publishing, 2005).

3. E. Quayle and M. Taylor, "Child Pornography and the Internet: Perpetuating a Cycle of Abuse," *Deviant Behavior* 23(4) (2002): 331–362.

4. Sher J., "Buried in a Landslide," in *Caught in the Net: Inside the Police Hunt to Rescue Children from Online Predators* (New York: Carroll & Graf Publishers, 2007).

5. Leth I., "Child Sexual Exploitation from a Global Perspective," in *Medical, Legal and Social Science Aspects of Child Sexual Exploitation,* ed. S. Cooper, R. Estes, A. Giardino, N. Kellogg, and V. Vieth (St Louis: GW Medical Publishing, 2005); Muir, D., *Violence against Children in Cyberspace: A Contribution to the United Nations Study on Violence against Children* (sponsored by ECPAT International, 2005).

6. Ryan, J., "Mueller, 'We're Losing' the Child Porn War,'" ABC News, April 23, 2008, available at http://abcnews.go.com/TheLaw/FedCrimes/Story?id=4712725&page=1.

7. L. Jones and D. Finkelhor, "The Decline in Child Sexual Abuse Cases," *Juvenile Justice Bulletin* January 2001.

8. M. Collins, personal communication as Director of the Child Victims of Internet Pornography, National Center for Missing and Exploited Children, 2008.

9. J. Wolak, K. Mitchell, and D. Finkelhor, "Internet Sex Crimes Against Minors: The Response Of Law Enforcement," National Center for Missing and Exploited Children, 2003.

10. *Children and Young Persons with Abusive and Violent Experiences Connected to Cyberspace: Challenges for Research, Rehabilitation, Prevention and Protection*, report from an Expert Meeting sponsored by the Swedish Children's Welfare Foundation and the Working Group for Cooperation of Children at Risk under Council of the Baltic Sea States, 2006.

11. R. F. Hanson, H. S. Resnick, B. E. Sanders, D. G. Kilpatrick, and C. Best, "Factors Related to the Reporting of Childhood Rape," *Child Abuse & Neglect* 23 (1999): 559–69.

12. T. Palmer, *Just a Click* (UK: Barnardo's Children' Charity, 2004).

13. *Abusive and Violent Experiences Connected to Cyberspace.*

14. Collins, personal communication.

15. J. A. Adams, K. Harper, S. Knudson, and J. Revilla, "Examination Findings in Legally Confirmed Child Sexual Abuse: It's Normal to be Normal," *Pediatrics* 97(1) (1994): 148–50.

16. J. Wolak, D. Finkelhor, and K. Mitchell, "Internet-Initiated Sex Crimes against Minors: Implications for Prevention Based on Findings from a National Study," *Journal of Adolescent Health* 35 (2004): 424.e11–424.e20.

17. K. Eichenwald, "Through His Webcam, a Boy Joins a Sordid Online World," *New Your Times*, December 19, 2005; testimony of Justin Berry before the House Committee on Energy and Commerce of the United States Congress, April 4, 2006.

18. Wolak, Finkelhor, and Mitchell, "Internet-Initiated Sex Crimes against Minors."

19. Alicia Kozakiewicz, testimony before the Judiciary Committee of the United States Congress, October 17, 2007.

20. *Frontline*, "Growing up Online: Just How Radically Is the Internet Transforming the Experience of Childhood?" January 22, 2008, available at http://www.pbs.org/wgbh/pages/frontline/kidsonline.

21. Palmer, *Just A Click.*

22. K. Subrahmanyam and P. Greenfield, "Online Communication and Adolescent Relationships," *The Future of Children*, 18 (1) (spring 2008): 119–46.

23. Wolak, Finkelhor, and Mitchell, "Internet-Initiated Sex Crimes against Minors."

24. S. S. Sun, C. M. Schubert, W. C. Chumlea, A. F. Roche, H. E. Kulin, P. A. Lee, J. H. Himes, and A. S. Ryan, "National Estimates of the Timing of Sexual Maturation and Racial Differences among US Children," *Pediatrics* 110 (2002): 911–19.

25. M. Leary, "Self-Produced Child Pornography: The Appropriate Societal Response to Juvenile Self-Exploitation," *Virginia Journal of Social Policy & the Law* 15 (1) (fall 2007).

26. Muir, *Violence against Children in Cyberspace.*

27. R. B. Flowers, "Teen Prostitutes, Arrest and the Criminal Justice System," in *Runaway Kids and Teenage Prostitution America's Lost, Abandoned, and Sexually Exploited Children* (Westport, CT: Greenwood Press, 2001); Lloyd, R., "Acceptable Victims? Sexually Exploited Youth in the U.S.," *Encounter* 18 (3, 6–18) (Autumn 2005).

28. S. Friedman, *Who Is There to Help Us? How the System Fails Sexually Exploited Girls in the United States Examples from Four American Cities* (ECPAT-USA, 2005).

29. R. J. Estes and N. A. Weiner, "The Commercial Sexual Exploitation of Children in the US, Canada, And Mexico," September 2001, available at

http://caster.ssw.upenn.edu/~restes/CSEC.htm (accessed April 20, 2008); Azaola, E., *Stolen Childhood: Girl and Boy Victims of Sexual Exploitation in Mexico* (Mexico City: United Nations Children's Fund, 2001).

30. M. Farley, A. Cotton, J. Lynne, S. Zumbeck, F. Spiwak, M. Reyes, D. Alvarez, and U. Sezgin, "Prostitution and Trafficking in Nine Countries: An Update on Violence and Posttraumatic Stress Disorder," in *Prostitution, Trafficking, and Traumatic Stress*, ed. Farley, M. (New York: Haworth Maltreatment & Trauma Press, 2003).

31. D. Sheridan and D. Van Pelt, "Intimate Partner Violence in the Lives of Prostituted Adolescents," in *Medical, Legal and Social Science Aspects of Child Sexual Exploitation*, ed. S. Cooper, R. Estes, A. Giardino, N. Kellogg, and V. Vieth (St Louis: GW Medical Publishing, 2005).

32. Farley, Cotton, Lynne, Zumbeck, Spiwak, Reyes, Alvarez, and Sezgin. "Prostitution and Trafficking in Nine Countries."

33. C. Lapierre, A. Schwehler, and B. Labauve, "Posttraumatic Stress and Depression Symptoms in Soldiers Returning from Combat Operations in Iraq and Afghanistan," *Journal of Trauma Stress* 20(6) (December 2007): 933–43.

CHAPTER 9

1. For a more extensive analysis, see Jhally (1990).

2. See chapter 6, "So Sexy, So Soon," in this volume; also see Bishop (2007).

3. This is the term developed by Pamela Paul (2005) to describe a culture in which pornography has become part of mainstream pop culture.

4. "Give me Gape" *Adult Video News*, September 2004, p. 58. Quoted in Jensen (2007).

5. For a more complete discussion on the various genres within Internet pornography, see Jensen (2007).

6. There are also gay porn sites with childified men. For the purpose of this discussion, I am going to focus only on heterosexual pornography because gay pornography has its own distinct visual codes and conventions.

7. I am using the term pseudo-child pornography (PCP) to refer to those sites in which the adult woman is made to look like a child. Because the performer is 18 or over, the pornography is legal, but the imagery nonetheless resembles illegal child pornography.

8. Although the female performers are 18 and over, I am using the term "girls" to refer to them because they are represented that way by the pornographers.

9. The PCP discussed in this article is only that which uses live human beings, rather than computer-generated images.

10. I refer to the user in masculine terms because the majority of porn consumers are men. Although it is impossible to give an accurate breakdown of male and female consumers, Mark Kernes, senior editor of the pornography trade magazine *Adult Video News*, stated, "Our statistics show that 78 percent of the people that go into adult stores are men. They may have women with them, but it's men, and 22 percent, conversely, is women or women with other women or women alone." Interview at the Adult Entertainment Expo in Las Vegas, January 7, 2005.

11. http://www.ultrateenlist.com.

12. http://internet-filter-review.toptenreviews.com/internet-pornography-statistics.html.

13. http://www.cbp.gov/hot-new/pressrel/2001/0516-00.htm.

14. See especially Russell (2006) and Quayle and Taylor (2002).

15. "A Typology of Online Child Pornography Offending." Australian Institute of Criminology http://www.crime-research.org/articles/1236/2.

16. The COPINE (Combating Paedophile Information Networks in Europe) project was founded in 1997 and is based in the Department of Applied Psychology, University College, Cork, Ireland. For more information, go to http://www.copine.ie/background.php.

17. I have not found any PCP sites that include bestiality through the main porn portals, which is not surprising because this is still a taboo in mainstream Internet pornography.

18. Cokal (2007).

19. http://forum.adultdvdtalk.com/forum/topic.dlt/topic_id=108072/forum_id=1/cat_id=1/108072.htm.

20. http://soloteengirls.net/index9.php?.

21. http://soloteengirls.net/?agent_name=webmaster&account=5586&referer%5B%5D=http%3A%2F%2Fpretty-pussies.com%2FSait1%2Fmain.htm&agent_id=5586&agent_account=5586&idproduct=11.

22. Feature porn movies make some attempt at a story line and dialogue, but ultimately the focus is on explicit sex.

23. http://www.defloration.tv/eng/hymen.htm.

24. Kenneth Lanning (2001). "Child Molesters: A Behavioral Analysis." http://www.missingkids.com/en_US/publications/NC70.pdf.

25. Quayle and Taylor (2002), p. 340.

26. Ibid.

27. These types of pornography represent the hard-core end of the market and are the best-selling and most profitable type of pornography today. The movies consist of sex scene after sex scene with no attempt at a story line or plot structure.

28. For a more complete description of hard-core Gonzo pornography, see Jensen (2007).

29. For an in-depth account of the violence women suffer in pornography, see Stark and Whisnant (2005).

30. http://www.teendirtbags.com/t2/index.html?site=TDB&pid=1&revid=0&tour=2&popup=1&join=0&lang=en&ref_url=http%3A%2F%2Fwww.google.com%2Fsearch%3Fq%3Dteen%2Bdirt%2Bbags%26ie%3Dutf-8%26oe%3Dutf-8%26aq%3Dt%26rls%3Dorg.mozilla%3Aen-US%3Aofficial%26client%3Dfirefox-a&opt=&track=&a=&prog_id=1.

31. http://tryteens.com/main.php?ref=567&stream=.

32. http://assplundering.com/tr/index.php/?nats=beano33:psu30:ap,0,0,0,0.

33. http://www.teensforcash.com/s1/index.html?page=3&screen=tour&revid=13265&nopop=1.

34. http://youngdaughter.com/.

35. http://incestpaysites.info/.

36. http://www.ftwdaddy.com/?advId=4960.

37. http://www.daddyswhores.com/tour-2.php?.

38. Herman (1993).

39. Ibid., p. 401.

40. http://www.usemydaughter.com/t1/pps2=whaleven/tour1.htm.

41. http://incestpaysites.org/.

42. For a discussion of the possible role that Internet communities play in reinforcing illegal sexual behavior, see Durkin, Craig, and Quinn (2006).

43. http://www.animatedincest.com/?advId=4775.

44. Quayle and Taylor (2002).

45. Pamela Paul, ibid.

46. The Child Porn Pipeline. http://www.buffalonews.com/home/story/185614.html.

47. Russell (2006).

48. Quayle (2002).

49. Cited on the Web site of the Center for Missing and Exploited Children, http://www.missingkids.com/missingkids/servlet/PageServlet?LanguageCountry=en_US&PageId=1504.

50. A 2007 government study of convicted child pornography offenders found that 85 percent of men convicted of downloading child pornography had committed acts of sexual abuse against minors, from inappropriate touching to rape. An article detailing the findings was submitted to the *Journal of Family Violence* and then pulled by the Federal Bureau of Prisons. According to an article in the *New York Times*, many experts in the field are angry that the findings have been suppressed. For a more complete account of the findings and the controversy surrounding publication, see http://www.nytimes.com/2007/07/19/us/19sex.html.

51. For a discussion of the findings of over 30 years of studies on how media shapes the social construction of reality, see Gerbner (1998).

CHAPTER 10

1. Leidholdt, D. (1984). *Some Notes on Objectification: From Objectification to Violence.* New York: Women Against Pornography. Flyer distributed by Women Against Pornography in author's possession.

2. Bartky, S. (1990). "Femininity and Domination." New York: Routledge. Cited in Wesely, J.K. (2002), Growing up sexualized: Issues of power and violence in the lives of female exotic dancers. *Violence Against Women* 8(10): 1182–1207.

3. Levy, A. (2005). *Female Chauvinist Pigs: Women and the Rise of Raunch Culture.* New York: Free Press.

4. Dworkin, A. (1997). "Prostitution and Male Supremacy." In *Life and Death.* New York: Free Press. Also available at http://www.prostitutionresearch.com/how_prostitution_works/000011.html.

5. American Psychological Association. (2007). *Report of the APA Task Force on the Sexualization of Girls.* Retrieved March 20, 2007, from http://www.apa.org/pi/wpo/sexualization.html.

6. Cynthia Peters (2002). "G-Strings for Seven-Year-Olds! What's a Parent to Do?" *Z-Net Commentary.* November 2, 2002. Retrieved April 5, 2008, from http://www.zmag.org/Sustainers/Content/2002-11/02peters.cfm.

7. Ibid.

8. Kanner, A. (2005). Globalization and the commercialization of childhood. *Tikkun* 20(5): 49–51.

9. Susan Villani. (2001). Impact of media on children and adolescents: A 10-year review of the research. *Journal of the American Academy of Child and Adolescent Psychiatry* 40(4): 392–401.

10. Ibid.

11. Bushman, Brad J., and Craig A. Anderson. (2001). Media violence and the American public: Scientific facts versus media misinformation. *American Psychologist* 56(6/7): 477–89.

12. Ibid.

13. Kilbourne, J. (2000). "Killing Us Softly: Advertising's Image of Women." Retrieved March 22, 2008, from http://www.mediaed.org/videos/Media GenderAndDiversity/KillingUsSoftly3.

14. Smith, L. W., M. E. Herman-Giddens, and V. D. Everette. (2005). "Commercial Sexual Exploitation of Children in Advertising." In Sharon W. Cooper, Richard J. Estes, Angelo P. Giardino, Nancy D. Kellogg, and Victor I. Vieth (eds.), *Medical, Legal, and Social Science Aspects of Child Sexual Exploitation: A Comprehensive Review of Pornography, Prostitution, and Internet Crimes.* Volumes 1 & 2, pp. 25–57. St. Louis: GW Medical Publishing.

15. Ibid.

16. Dworkin, A. (1981). *Pornography: Men Possessing Women.* New York: Putnam; Dworkin, A. (1997). *Prostitution and Male Supremacy, in Life and Death.* New York: Free Press; Dworkin, A. (1997). "Suffering and Speech." In Catharine A. MacKinnon and Andrea Dworkin (eds.), *In Harm's Way: The Pornography Civil Rights Hearings.* Cambridge: Harvard University Press; MacKinnon, C. A. (2006). *Are Women Human? And Other International Dialogues.* Cambridge: Harvard University Press; MacKinnon, C. A. (2000). Points against postmodernism. *Chicago-Kent Law Review* 75: 687–712; MacKinnon, C. A. (1993). Prostitution and civil rights. *Michigan Journal of Gender and Law* 1: 13–31; MacKinnon, C. A. (2001). *Sex Equality.* New York: Foundation Press.

17. Herbert, Bob. (2006). "Why Aren't We Shocked?" *New York Times*, October 16, 2006. Retrieved February 2, 2007, from http://select.nytimes.com/2006/10/16/opinion/16herbert.html?hp.

18. Ibid.

19. Criddle, Linda. (2008). Personal communication, Seattle, WA, April 26, 2008.

20. Wolak, J., K. Mitchell, and D. Finkelhor. "Online Victimization of Youth: Five Years Later." National Center for Missing and Exploited Children. Report #07-06-025. Alexandria, VA.

21. Familysafemedia.com. (2008). Retrieved April 26, 2008.

22. Criddle, L. (2008). Human trafficking and the Internet. www.look-both-ways.com. Retrieved April 2008.

23. Barry, K. (1995). *The Prostitution of Sexuality.* New York: New York University Press.

24. Labi, N. (2001) Britney Brigade. *Time Magazine.* Retrieved March 27, 2001, from http://www.time.com/time/magazine/printout/0,8816,97065,00.html. See also Jeffreys, S. (2005). *Beauty and Misogyny: Harmful Cultural Practices in the West.* Oxford: Routledge.

25. Sohm, A. (2005). Dirty minds: Pamela Paul argues that a surge in pornography is hurting families. *New York Times Book Review.* September 11, 2005, p. 24.

26. Junod, T. (2001). "The Devil Greg in Dark." *Esquire*, February 2001. Retrieved April 9, 2008, from http://www.esquire.com/ESQ0201-FEB_Greg_Dark_rev.

27. Grigoriadis, V. (2008). "The Tragedy of Britney Spears." *Rolling Stone*, February 1, 2008, pp. 47–56.

28. Merskin, D. (2004). Reviving Lolita? A media literacy examination of sexual portrayals of girls in Fashion advertising. *American Behavioral Scientist* 48(1): 119–29.

29. Bell, R. (2004). "Subvert the Dominant Pimpiarchy The F-word: Contemporary UK Feminism." Retrieved April 25 2008, from http://www.thefword.org.uk/features/2004/11/subvert_the_dominant_pimpiarchy.

30. Criddle, L. (2008). Personal communication, Seattle, WA, April 26, 2008.

31. Smith, L. W., M. E. Herman-Giddens, and V. D. Everette. (2005). Commercial Sexual Exploitation of Children in Advertising. In Sharon W. Cooper, Richard J. Estes, Angelo P. Giardino, Nancy D. Kellogg, and Victor I. Vieth (eds.) *Medical, Legal, and Social Science Aspects of Child Sexual Exploitation: A Comprehensive Review of Pornography, Prostitution, and Internet Crimes.* Volumes 1 & 2, pp. 25–57. St. Louis: GW Medical Publishing.

32. Barnes, B. (2008). "Revealing Photo Threatens a Major Disney Franchise." *New York Times* April 28, 2008. Retrieved April 28, 2008, from http://www.nytimes.com/2008/04/28/business/media/28hannah.html?scp=1&sq=topless+photo+disney+franchise&st=nyt.

33. Hudepohl, D. (2002). "87 Sex Tips from the Pros." *Marie Claire*, May 2002.

34. Blume, J. (2005). "Prostitution Gives Me Power." *Marie Claire*, July 2005, pp. 108–11.

35. Paul, P. (2005). *Pornified; How Pornography is Transforming Our Lives, Our Relationships, and our Families.* New York: Times Books.

36. Cosmogirl (2007). Retrieved April 19, 2008, from http://www.cosmogirl.com/lifeadvice/sex-questions/talk-about-sex-oct07.

37. MacKinnon, C. A. (2006). Pornography as Trafficking. In *Are Women Human? And Other International Dialogues*, pp. 247–58. Cambridge: Harvard University Press.

38. See Ariel Levy (2005), *Female Chauvinist Pigs*. New York: Free Press, pages 7–17, for an extended description of a Joe Francis shoot. See also Associated Press (2008), "Florida: 'Wild' Girls Founder Is Set Free." *New York Times*, March 13, 2008. Retrieved March 27, 2008, from http://www.nytimes.com/2008/03/13/us/13brfs-8216WILD8217_BRF.html?scp=13&sq=&st=nyt. See also CNN.com (2008) Spitzer escort's 'Girls Gone Wild' videos surface Via Associated Press. Retrieved April 4, 2008, from http://www.cnn.com/2008/US/03/18/dupree.girls.gone.wild.ap/index.html. See also TMZ.com (2008), Ashley Dupre Gone "Wild"—Legal or Jailbait? Retrieved April 4, 2008, from http://www.tmz.com/2008/03/19/ashley-dupre-gone-wild-legal-or-jailbait/ Posted Mar 19th 2008 1:50 p.m. by TMZ Staff.

39. Levy, Ariel. (2005). *Female Chauvinist Pigs: Women and the Rise of Raunch Culture.* New York: Free Press. See also Gold, G.K. (2007), What is liberation? Feminism

past, present and future. Retrieved January 1, 2007, from http://sisyphe.org/article.php3?id_article=2551.

40. Yamine, E. (2007). "Girls Gaining Fitness or Losing Innocence? *Daily Telegraph*, Australia. October 8, 2007. Retrieved February 24, 2008 from http://www.news.com.au/story/0,23599,22545912-2,00.html.

41. Allexperts.com. (2005). "Teen Dating Issues." Retrieved April 25, 2008, from http://en.allexperts.com/q/Teen-Dating-Issues-849/lap-dance.htm.

42. Goodale, G. (2000). "Erotica Runs Rampant." *Christian Science Monitor*, February 1, 2002. Retrieved March 5, 2002, from http://www.csmonitor.com/2002/0201/p13s01-altv.html.

43. Paul, P. (2005). *Pornofied: How Pornography Is Transforming Our Lives, Our Relationships, and our Families*. New York: Times Books.

44. Fox News. (2007). "Wal-Mart Yanks Pink 'Credit Card' Panties Off Racks." Retrieved December 12, 2007, from http://www.foxnews.com/story/0,2933,316580,00.html.

45. Hoffman, C. (2006). "Joe Francis' Baby Give Me a Kiss." *Los Angeles Times*. Retrieved August 7, 2006 from http://www.latimes.com/features/magazine/west/la-tm-gonewild32aug06,0,2664370.story?coll=la-home-headlines. See also Carrie Denny (2008), "Trend: Pretty Babies." *Philadelphia Magazine*, April 2008. Retrieved May 3, 2008, from http://www.phillymag.com/articles/pretty_babies/page1.

46. American Psychological Association. *Task Force on the Sexualization of Girls*, pp. 14–6.

47. Femail (2006). "Over-sexed and Over hee: The 'Tarty' Bratz Doll." *UK Daily Mail*, October 20, 2006. Retrieved November 30, 2006, from http://www.dailymail.co.uk/pages/live/femail/article.html?in_article_id=411266&in_page_id=1879.

48. Brooks, R. (2006). No Escaping Sexualization of Young Girls: With JonBenet Back in the Headlines, It's Hard for a Parent to Avoid Paranoia. *Los Angeles Times*, August 25, 2006. Retrieved June 28, 2007, from http://www.commondreams.org/views06/0825-33.htm. Prostitution is advertised at X-rated clubs where young women perform pole dances, mattress dances, and sing "If You've Got It, Flaunt It," mirroring the words used to sell Bratz infant dolls.

49. Television Council. (2008). "The Rap on Rap: A Content Analysis of BET and MTV's Daytime Music Video Programming." April 2008. Available at http://www.parentstv.org/PTC/publications/release/2008/0410.asp.

50. Ryan, Kim (2005). "Bump, Grind Your Way to Riches, Students Told." *San Francisco Chronicle*, January 14, 2005. Retrieved January 14, 2005 from http://www.fradical.com/Pimping_at_school_career_day.htm.

51. Smith, L. W., M. E. Herman-Giddens and V. D. Everette. (2005). "Commercial Sexual Exploitation of Children in Advertising." In Sharon W. Cooper, Richard J. Estes, Angelo P. Giardino, Nancy D. Kellogg, and Victor I. Vieth (eds.). *Medical, Legal, and Social Science Aspects of Child Sexual Exploitation: A Comprehensive Review of Pornography, Prostitution, and Internet Crimes, Volumes 1 & 2*, p. 25–57. St. Louis: GW Medical Publishing.

52. Ho, J. (2003). "From Spice Girls to Enjo-Kosai: Formations of Teenage Girls' Sexualities in Taiwan." Center for the Study of Sexualities, National Central

University, Chungli, Taiwan. Retrieved April 15, 2008, from http://sex.ncu. edu.tw/members/Ho/tokyo/lecture03.htm.

53. Paul, P. (2005). *Pornified: How Pornography Is Transforming Our Lives, Our Relationships, and Our Families.* New York: Times Books.

54. Kopkowski, C. (2008, March). "The Sexualization of Girls: Lolita in the Classroom." *NEA Today.* Retrieved April 8, 2008, from http://www.nea.org/ neatoday/0803/sexualization.html.

55. http://www.amazon.co.uk/Re-Creation-Group-Plc-Peekaboo/dp/ B000EW3PJ2/ref=pd_sim_k_h_b_ cs_img_6.

56. Fernandez, C. (2006). "Tesco Condemned for Selling Pole Dancing Toy." *UK Daily Mail,* October 24, 2006. Retrieved November 25, 2006, from http:// www.dailymail.co.uk/pages/live/articles/news/news.html?in_article_id=412195 &in_page_id=17.

57. Yamine, E. (2007). Fury over Pole-Dancing Kids. *Daily Telegraph,* Australia. October 8, 2007. Retrieved January 9, 2008, from http://www.news. com.au/ dailytelegraph/story/0,22049,22546875-5001021,00.html.

58. Martino, S. C., R. C. Collins, M. N. Elliott, A. Strachman, D. E. Kanouse, and S. H. Berry, S.H. (2006). Exposure to degrading versus nondegrading music lyrics and sexual behavior among youth. *Pediatrics* 118(2): 430–41. Available at http://pediatrics.aappublications.org/cgi/content/full/118/2/e430.

59. American Psychological Association. (2007). *Report of the APA Task Force on the Sexualization of Girls.* Washington, DC: American Psychological Association.

60. Armstrong, E. G. (2001). Gangsta misogyny: A content analysis of the portrayals of violence against women in rap music 1987–1993. *Journal of Criminal Justice and Popular Culture* 8(2): 96–126.

61. Davis, T. (2004). "New Study on Hip-Hop Sexuality Finds Anti-Woman Strain Even among Young Women." *Village Voice,* March 17, 2004. Retrieved May 22, 2005, from http://www.villagevoice.com/issues/0411/davis.php.

62. Crenshaw, K. (1993). "Beyond Racism and Misogyny: Black Feminism and 2 Live Crew." In Mari J. Matsuda, Charles R. Lawrence, and Richard Delgado (eds.), *Words that Wound.* Boulder, CO: Westview Press, pp. 111–32. A remarkable DVD was released in 2006, critiquing the misogyny and homophobia in hip-hop, which was directed by Byron Hurt: *Hip Hop: Beyond Beats and Rhymes.*

63. http://www.flakmag.com/web/lilpimp.html.

64. Smith, L. W., M. E. Herman-Giddens, and V. D. Everette. (2005). "Commercial Sexual Exploitation of Children in Advertising." In Sharon W. Cooper, Richard J. Estes, Angelo P. Giardino, Nancy D. Kellogg, and Victor I. Vieth (eds.). *Medical, Legal, and Social Science Aspects of Child Sexual Exploitation: A Comprehensive Review of Pornography, Prostitution, and Internet Crimes.* Volumes 1 & 2, pp. 25–57. St. Louis: GW Medical Publishing.

65. http://www.cafepress.com/worldsfair/3421693.

66. Steffans, K. (2005). *Confessions of a Video Vixen.* New York: Amistad.

67. Goldberg, M. (2000). "The Hip-Hop Pornographer." Salon.com, July 18, 2000. Retrieved September 6, 2001, from http://www.salon.com/ent/music/ feature/2000/07/18/kim/index.html.

68. http://www.lyricstime.com/lil-kim-don-t-mess-with-me-lyrics.html.

69. For a discussion of Hurt's documentary and the violent consequences for women of the cultural environment that mainstreams violence against women who

are defined as 'ho's, bitches, and strippers, see Jackson Katz (2006), *The Macho Paradox: Why Some Men Hurt Women and How All Men Can Help.* Naperville, IL: Sourcebooks.

70. Crockett, S. A. (2002). "For Young Fans, the Name of the Video Game is Gore." *Washington Post.* August 24, 2002. Retrieved April 19, 2008 from http://www.washingtonpost.com/ac2/wp-dyn/A55183-2002Aug23?language= printer.

71. Rockstar Games. (2008). See http://www.gamespot.com/xbox360/action/grandtheftauto4/index.html or http://www.rockstargames.com/IV/.

72. Brathwaite, B. (2007). Interview with Steve Meretzky quoted in B. Brathwaite. (2007). *Sex in Video Games.* Boston: Charles River Media, p. 206.

73. Brathwaite, B. (2007). *Sex in Video Games.* Boston: Charles River Media, p 205.

74. Brathwaite, B. (2007). *Sex in Video Games.* Boston: Charles River Media.

75. Anonymous. (2005). "Sexism in Video Games." Retrieved April 18, 2008, from http://spooky.ms11.net/pages/p2.html.

76. Brathwaite, B. (2007). Sex in Video Games, p. 398–400.

77. Brathwaite, B. (2007). Sex in Video Games, p. 200.

78. Brathwaite, B. (2007). Sex in Video Games, p. 201.

79. Criddle, L. (2008). "Human Trafficking and the Internet." Retrieved April 2008 from www.look-both-ways.com.

80. Ibid.

81. Stone, B. (2007) "Using Web Cams but Few Inhibitions, the Young Turn to Risky Social Sites." *New York Times.* January 2, 2007. Retrieved from http://www.nytimes.com/2007/01/02/technology/02net.html?_r=1&ref=business&oref=slogin.

82. Criddle, L. (2008). "Human Trafficking and the Internet." Retrieved April 2008 from www.look-both-ways.com.

83. Ibid.

84. Klien, G. (2008). "MySpace Predator Pimps 16 year-old." *Marin Independent Journal*, April 15, 2008. Retrieved April 15, 2008, from http://www.marinij.com/sanrafael/ci_8939903.

85. Farley, M. (2006). Prostitution, trafficking, and cultural amnesia: What we must *not* know in order to keep the business of sexual exploitation running smoothly. *Yale Journal of Law and Feminism* 18: 109–44.

86. Branson, S. (2006). "Online Child Prostitution, An Alarming Trend." Sacramento Channel 31, a CBS affiliate. Retrieved September 16, 2007, from http://cbs13.com/local/child.prostitution.online.2.472452.html.

87. Diedrich, J. (2008). "Craigslist Child Sex Ads Lead to Arrests: Investigators Follow Rising Use of Web Site in Prostitution." *Milwaukee Journal-Sentinel*, April 8, 2008. Retrieved April 8, 2008, from http://www.jsonline.com/story/index. aspx?id=737115.

88. Snell, R., and M. Hicks. (2008). "Federal Probe Breaks Up Two Child Prostitution Sex Rings." *The Detroit News*, March 21, 2008. Retrieved March 22, 2008, from http://www.detnews.com/apps/pbcs.dll/article?AID=/20080321/ METRO/803210383/1409/METRO.

89. Robertson, G. D. (2007). "MySpace.com Finds 29,000 Sex Offenders, More than 4 Times Previous Total, Officials Say." Associated Press release posted at ABCNews.com. Retrieved January 4, 2008, from http://www.abcnews.go.com/print?id=3409947.

90. Shreve, J. (2006). "MySpace Faces a Perp Problem." *Wired*, April 18, 2006. Retrieved November 22, 2007, from http://www.wired.com/culture/lifestyle/news/2006/04/70675.

91. Account of a young woman to whom this occurred. Confidential interview, 2005.

92. A prostitution researcher in Las Vegas commented that she didn't plan to study prostitution when she moved to Las Vegas 7 years ago. But after she was propositioned three times in 9 months, that changed. "I decided I had to either study it," she said, "or move." Josh Bohling (2004). "Sex and the State." *The Shorthorn Online*, University of Texas at Arlington. Retrieved July 8, 2006, from http://www.theshorthorn.com/archive/2004/spring/04-apr-01/n040104-05.html.

93. Farley, M. (2007). *Prostitution and Trafficking in Nevada: Making the Connections*. San Francisco: Prostitution Research & Education.

94. American Psychological Association. (2007). *Report of the APA Task Force on the Sexualization of Girls*, page 34. Retrieved March 20, 2007, from http://www.apa.org/pi/wpo/sexualization.html.

95. Kurt Eichenwald. (2005). Through His Webcam, a Boy Joins a Sordid Online World. *New York Times*, December 19, 2005. Retrieved December 29, 2005, from http://www.nytimes.com/2005/12/19/national/19kids.ready.html?ei=5070&en=6915868c2227c0f9&ex=1181707200&adxnnl=1&adxnnlx=1181587446-EQqaCtbzIeK55+2a3EqssA.

96. Boyer, D., L. Chapman, and B. K. Marshall. (1993). *Survival Sex in King County: Helping Women Out*. Report submitted to King County Women's Advisory Board. Seattle: Northwest Resource Associates.

97. Nadon, S. M., C. Koverola, and E. H. Schludermann. (1998). Antecedents to prostitution: Childhood victimization. *Journal of Interpersonal Violence* 13: 206–21.

98. Silbert, M. H., and A. M. Pines. (1981). Sexual child abuse as an antecedent to prostitution. *Child Abuse & Neglect* 5: 407–11; Silbert, M. H., and A. M. Pines. (1982). Entrance into prostitution *Youth & Society* 13: 471–500.

99. McIntyre, S. (1995). "The Youngest Profession: The Oldest Oppression." Doctoral dissertation. Department of Law, University of Sheffield. Assistant Deputy Ministers' Committee on Prostitution and the Sexual Exploitation of Youth. (2000). *Sexual Exploitation of Youth in British Columbia*. Vancouver: Ministry of the Attorney General.

100. Phoenix, J. (2003). Rethinking youth prostitution: National provision at the margins of child protection and youth justice. Youth Justice 3: 152–68. For a narrative description of how our failure to protect children is directly connected to their sexual abuse by families, by neighbors, in foster homes, and eventually by pimps and johns, see Jessica Lustig's (2007) description of one girl's life in "The 13-Year-Old-Prostitute," *New York Magazine*. Retrieved December 19, 2007, from http://nymag.com/news/features/30018/.

101. Widom, C. S. (1995). Victims of childhood sexual abuse—Later criminal connections. *National Institute of Justice Research in Brief*. March 1995. Retrieved July 8, 2007, from http://72.14.253.104/search?q=cache:8RnjY_C-9lgJ:www.ncjrs.gov/pdffiles/abuse.pdf+site:www.ncjrs.gov+Victims+of+Childhood+Sexual+Abuse+%E2%80%93+Later+Criminal+Connections.+National+Institute+of+Justice+Research+in+Brief.&hl=en&ct=clnk&cd=1&gl=us. Thank you, Sharon Cooper, for reminding me of the importance of Widom's research on the connections between childhood sexual assault and subsequent prostitution.

102. Farley, M., J. Lynne, and A. Cotton. (2005). Prostitution in Vancouver: Violence and the colonization of First Nations women. *Transcultural Psychiatry* 42: 242–71.

103. Silbert, M. H., and A. M. Pines. (1983). Early sexual exploitation as an influence in prostitution. *Social Work* 28: 285–89.

104. Dworkin, A. (1997). "Prostitution and Male Supremacy." In *Life and Death*. New York: Free Press.

105. Spitzer complaint. (2008). From a federal wiretap of Emperor's Club VIP. Retrieved March 11, 2008, from http://72.14.253.104/search?q=cache: VdbX1DVu5QwJ:graphics8.nytimes.com/packages/pdf/nyregion/20080310spit zer complaint.pdf+spitzer%2Bcomplaint%2Bpdf&hl=en&ct=clnk&cd=1&gl=us.

106. Silbert, M. H., and A. M. Pines. (1982). Entrance into prostitution. *Youth & Society* 13: 471–500.

107. Lords, T. (2003). *Underneath It All*. New York: Harper, p. 92.

108. Siegel, J. A., and L. M. Williams. (2003). Risk factors for sexual victimization of women: Results from a prospective study. *Violence Against Women* 9: 902–30.

109. West, C. M., L. M. Williams, and J. M. Siegal. (2000). Adult sexual revictimization among black women sexually abused in childhood: A prospective examination of serious consequences of abuse. *Child Maltreatment* 5 (1): 49–57.

110. Lacey, M. (2008). "Abuse Trails Central American Girls Into Gangs." *New York Times*, April 11, 2008. Retrieved April 12, 2008, from http://www.nytimes. com/2008/04/11/world/americas/11guatemala.html?_r=1&scp=1&sq=abuse+ trails+central+american+girls&st=nyt&oref=slogin]].

111. Levy, A. (2005). *Female Chauvinist Pigs: Women and the Rise of Raunch Culture*. New York: Free Press, p. 150.

112. *PBS Frontline*. (2000). "Sypillis Outbreak in a Small Town, Conyers, Georgia." February 8, 2000. 1999 PBS Online and WGBH/FRONTLINE.

113. DearCupid.Org Relationship Advice. (July 2007). Responses to "Why Are So Many Children Having Sex?" Retrieved February 9, 2008, from http://www. dearcupid.org/question/why-are-so-many-children-having-sex.html.

114. Kaiser Family Foundation. (2001). *Generation Rx.com: How Young People Use the Internet for Health Information*. Menlo Park: Henry J. Kaiser Foundation.

115. Crabbe, M. (2007). "Young People Duped by Culture of Degrading Sexual Attitudes." In *The Age*. Retrieved November 15, 2007, from http://www. theage.com.au/news/opinion/young-people-duped-by-culture-of-degrading-sexual-attitudes/2007/11/07/1194329315416.html.

116. DearCupid.Org Relationship Advice. (July 2007). Responses to "Why Are So Many Children Having Sex?" Retrieved February 9, 2008, from http:// www.dearcupid.org/question/why-are-so-many-children-having-sex.html.

117. Scobie. C. (2007). Wild Things. *The Bulletin*, Australia. June 2, 2007.

118. Brady, S. S., and Halpern-Fisher, B. L. (2007). Adolescents' Reported Consequences of Having Oral Sex Versus Vaginal Sex. *Pediatrics* 19(2): 229–236.

119. Criddle L. (2006). *Look Both Ways: Help Protect your family on the Internet*. Microsoft Press.

120. Levin, D. (2008). So Sexy So Soon: The Sexualization of Childhood. Speech at *Consuming Kids: The Sexualization of Children and Other Commercial Calamities*. Campaign for a Commerical-Free Childhood 6th Summit. Boston, April 3–5, 2008.

121. Galician, M. and Merskin, D. L. (2007). *Critical Thinking about Sex, Love, and Romance in the Mass Media*. Mahwah, N.J.: Lawrence Erlbaum.

122. Media Awareness Network. (2008). Retrieved April 13, 2008 from http://www.media-awareness.ca/english/tools/main_search/search_ results.cfm.

123. See examples of MediaWatch resource materials at http://www.media-awareness.ca/english/teachers/lesson_search_results.cfm.

Index

About the Editor and Contributors

EDITOR

Sharna Olfman is a professor of clinical and developmental psychology at Point Park University, and the editor of the *Childhood In America Book* series for Praeger Publishers. Her books include *Bipolar Children* (2007), *Child Honoring: How to Turn This World Around* (with Raffi Cavoukian, 2006), *No Child Left Different* (2006), *Childhood Lost* (2005), and *All Work and No Play* (2003). Dr. Olfman has given numerous invited addresses both in the United States and internationally. She is a member of the Council of Human Development and a partner in the Alliance for Childhood.

CONTRIBUTORS

Sharon W. Cooper is an internationally acclaimed expert and author on the sexual exploitation of children through Internet crimes and prostitution. Dr. Cooper holds faculty positions at the University of North Carolina—Chapel Hill School of Medicine and the Uniformed Services University of Health Sciences in Bethesda, Maryland.

Gail Dines is a professor of sociology and women's studies at Wheelock College in Boston, the co-author of *Pornography: The Production and Consumption of Inequality*, and co-editor of the best-selling textbook *Gender, Race and Class in Media*. A leading expert on the impact of pornography on women's lives, she is alarmed by the increasing use of children as pornographic models and the growing number of men who seek out child pornography.

Matthew B. Ezzell is an antiviolence activist and a PhD candidate in the Department of Sociology at the University of North Carolina at Chapel Hill. An award-winning teacher, he has been facilitating discussions, nationally and internationally, about men's violence against women and the harmful consequences of pornography for over a decade.

Melissa Farley, a clinical psychologist, has conducted groundbreaking research on trafficking and prostitution in nine countries. She has written two critically acclaimed books: *Prostitution, Trafficking, and Traumatic Stress* and *Trafficking in Nevada: Making the Connections*. In her research, Dr. Farley has addressed children in the United States and other countries who are trafficked for prostitution. She is the director of *Prostitution Research and Education*, a nonprofit organization that has begun a multicountry study of johns.

Diane E. Levin is a professor of education at Wheelock College in Boston and an internationally recognized expert on the impact of violence and media on children's development. Her eighth book, *So Sexy So Soon* (co-authored with Jean Kilbourne), was published in 2008. Dr. Levin is the co-founder of the Campaign for a Commercial Free Childhood (CCFC) and Teachers Resisting Unhealthy Children's Entertainment (TRUCE).

Susan Linn is a psychologist at Judge Baker Children's Center and Harvard Medical School. She is the author of the recently published *The Case for Make Believe: Saving Play in a Commercialized World* and *Consuming Kids: The Hostile Takeover of Childhood*, which has been praised in publications as diverse as the *Wall Street Journal* and *Mother Jones*. Dr Linn is the director and co-founder of the Campaign for a Commercial Free Childhood (CCFC).

Margo Maine is a clinical psychologist who has specialized in the treatment of eating disorders for over 25 years. Her books include *The Body Myth: The Pressure on Adult Women to Be Perfect* (co-authored with Joe Kelly), *Body Wars: Making Peace with Women's Bodies*, and *Father Hunger: Fathers, Daughters and the Pursuit of Thinness*. Maine is a senior editor of *Eating Disorders: The Journal of Treatment and Prevention*, a founding member and fellow of the Academy for Eating Disorders and assistant clinical professor at the University of Connecticut Department of Psychiatry.

Sandra Steingraber is an internationally recognized expert on the environmental links to cancer and reproductive health. In 2007 she was commissioned to write a report on the falling age of puberty in U.S. girls for the Breast Cancer Fund. Dr. Steingraber is the author of the critically acclaimed books *Living Downstream: An Ecologist Looks at Cancer and the Environment* and *Having Faith: An Ecologist's Journey to Motherhood.*

Carolyn M. West is an associate professor of psychology and the Bartley Dobb Professor for the Study and Prevention of Violence in the Interdisciplinary Arts and Sciences Program at the University of Washington. Dr. West writes, trains, consults, and lectures internationally on interpersonal violence and sexual assault, with a special focus on violence in the lives of African American women. She is an award-winning scholar and author of *Violence in the Lives of Black Women: Battered, Black, and Blue.*